Portraits of Places

HENRY JAMES

Portraits of Places

With an Essay on James as a Traveller
By GEORGE ALVIN FINCH

LEAR PUBLISHERS   NEW YORK

CONTENTS

Portraits of Places

James as a Traveller

though it was not until the eighteen-seventies that Henry James began to make himself known as a writer of travel sketches, his experience as a traveler began in the days of his boyhood before the Civil War. His father, of course, was responsible for the early exposure of his most impressionable child in Europe. Out of the uniquely unorthodox store of ideas that made Henry James, Sr., one of the most interesting fathers of his generation came the desire to give his sons a "sensuous education." And his one believed world to be a better proving ground for the senses than America. For his children he wanted nothing more than that their developing intelligence should be given free range; that their ideas, their tastes should expand within a widening cultural framework, the same one that stimulated his roving and restless mind.

For the younger Jameses the trips to Europe meant a succession of cities, London, Paris, Geneva; among foreign life in hotels and pensions—a strange sequence of boarding schools and tutors. Always changing diversion, new sights, fresh undertakings; a curious course of education in which reading, conversation, sight-seeing, the constant intrusion of new people filled up the days. Removed from regular courses of study, from the compilation of credits, from any occasion to prepare for some distant goal, Henry and William James were educated to know books and people; and within the family circle the spirited exchanges on youthful accessions of experience and idea provoked the critical play of mind (already present in its presiding genius) that was to stamp thereafter the intellectual lives of the two sons.

As Henry James told in later life the story of the early episodes in Europe, the oddity of the experience as "education" becomes a veritable delight to him and he hovers fondly over the paradox of a course of learning in which conventional school values were unthought of. To his father, "Pedantics were anathema.

THOUGH it was not until the eighteen-seventies that
Henry James began to make himself known as a
writer of travel sketches, his experience as a traveler
began in the days of his boyhood before the Civil War.
His father, of course, was responsible for the early
exposure of his most impressionable child in Europe.
Out of the uniquely unorthodox store of ideas that
made Henry James, Sr., one of the most interesting
fathers of his generation came the desire to give his
sons a "sensuous education." And Europe he believed
would be a better proving ground for the senses than
America. For his children he wanted nothing more
than that their developing intelligence should be given
free range; that their ideas, their tastes should expand
within a widening cultural framework, the same one
that stimulated his roving and restless mind.

For the younger Jameses the trips to Europe meant
a succession of cities, London, Paris, Geneva among
them; life in hotels and pensions — a strange sequence of boarding schools and tutors. Always change,
diversion, new sights, fresh undertakings; a curious
course of education in which reading, conversation,
sight-seeing, the constant intrusion of new people
filled up the days. Removed from regular courses of
study, from the compilation of credits, from any
occasion to prepare for some distant goal, Henry and
William James were educated to know books and
people; and within the family circle the spirited
exchanges on youthful accessions of experience and
idea provoked the critical play of mind (already
present in its presiding genius) that was to stamp
thereafter the intellectual lives of the two sons.

As Henry James told in later life the story of the
early episodes in Europe, the oddity of the experience
as "education" becomes a veritable delight to him
and he hovers fondly over the paradox of a course of
learning in which conventional school values were
unthought of. To his father, 'Pedantics were anathema.

. . . Method certainly never raged among us." There
was nothing in his father's scheme that did not prove
congenial to Henry James, for if the test of the worth
of his boyhood experience "is of the injection of more
things into the consciousness," how he asks "could
his have done with more?" An irony may appear to
us in the fact that from a father who wished to bring
up his children above all without a directed emphasis
on a special activity — insisting that they be not any
one thing — should come a design that would most
happily provide the nurture for a novelist. In after
years William James was never able to share his
brother's beguiled amusement with the inspired ir-
regularity of these odd school years, but it is quite
clear that the outward satisfactions drawn from them
by Henry provided an inward sustenance for him they
never held for William.

Even at this time — and his memories of Europe
reach back to his twelfth year — the pleasures of
Henry James were mainly passive. Enlarged and
elaborated as they are, seen through the years, the
ample recall is of strolling through streets, gazing by
turn into windows or across city squares; watching
the others, occasionally to drop some small witty remark. It is wonderful indeed that so many of the
things he quietly enjoyed as a man seem reflected, as
in a time mirror, by his childhood. Of course the
experiences are fully composed in his reminiscences:
just the right details fall into place to show that his
young mind seemed ever to turn towards the fascinating business of getting and gathering impressions.
His delighted walks as a small boy along Fourteenth
Street he makes us believe are but a prefiguring of the
pleasures he will take "in the streets of great towns."
With no touch of melancholy, he tells us: "What I
look back to as my infant license can only have had
for its ground some timely conviction that the only
form of riot or revel ever known to me would be that

16

of the visiting mind." Whether or not his elders had the conviction and acceded to it so comprehendingly, James assures us that as a boy — "The very pattern and measure of all he was to demand was just to *be* somewhere . . . and somehow receive an impression or an accession, feel a relation or a vibration. He was to go without many things, ever so many . . . but everywhere, in the years that came soon after, and that in fact continued long . . . in New York . . . and then for a while in London, in Paris, in Geneva, wherever it might be, he was to enjoy more than anything the so far from showy practice of wondering and dawdling and gaping; he was really, I think, much to profit by it."

It is with this habit of mind that his youthful experience of traveling in Europe becomes inseparably linked. As for the "profit of it," that certainly begins to appear in his earliest promptings towards the writing of fiction, for they were even then, though dimly, the issue of his fondness for gathering impressions. Actually a way of life begins to form out of the pattern of traveling: even an itinerary is beginning to evolve — Liverpool or London, Paris and little tours through France; then on to Italy, Milan, Florence, at last Rome. There can be no doubt that the easy accommodation James made as a boy to hotel life, to the tourist's manner of existence, prepared him to welcome the resumption of this life as a confident young writer. But the main thing was that a formative association had been established between his vivid youthful sensations of the places where he had stayed in Europe and the enticements of his imagination. In his childhood he seems to have achieved a rare balance between the outward investigations of his senses and the inward delight in fantasticating experience.

At the age of twenty-six — the year was 1869 — Henry James went abroad once more. Twelve years had passed since the family's return to the States. He

17

had seen his two younger brothers enlist in the Union army; he had, to complete the inconsequential history of his formal schooling, attended Harvard Law School. He had also suffered an injury to his back that was to prostrate him intermittently for years but at the time it seemed to confirm and justify for him his strong tendencies towards passive experience. This was also the decade in which his hopes as a writer were first fulfilled by publication. In 1864 his first book review appeared — starting him on a routine of regular production for American magazines which did not relax until 1881. As a workaday writer, a young man who came to rely upon reviewing, correspondence, and a miscellany of articles as a fairly steady source of income, James is not well known; but by far the greater volume of his writing before 1880 is of this journalistic sort. And among this work his travel sketches should be counted, although in fastidiousness of style and careful elaboration of his observations they are akin to his fiction.

As soon as James found lodgings in London, he began to send letters home. In what is probably the first of these letters (addressed from 7 Half Moon St., W. and dated March 10, 1869), he wrote to his sister Alice, "I really feel as if I had lived — I don't say a lifetime — but a year in this murky metropolis. I actually believe that this feeling is owing to the singular permanence of the impressions of childhood, to which any present experience joins itself on, without a broken link in the chain of sensation." So often taken as an indication of the easy transition he made to living again abroad, these sentences are followed by a heavy "nevertheless" . . . and we learn that James was a dazed young man, affected by "an indefinable flatness of mind," who found himself paralyzed "for any appreciation of details." Oppressed by the "mere magnitude" of the city, he had to overcome the shock of its strangeness and, far from gliding into a world of fresh sensation inviting inquiry, he was thrown back on himself, as he admits two weeks later, "on his prejudices and national passions."

There was much to write about aside from his own state of mind. Through excellent family connections he saw in a short space of time Leslie Stephen and Ruskin and spent a day at the home of William Morris. He confided to his mother, however, that he did not feel "in working order"; and then one day he took a little sail up the Thames. "It was a grey, raw English day, and the banks of the river, as far as I went, hideous. Nevertheless I enjoyed it." From this he dates a return of confidence, this little note marking his first independent excursion abroad. With this venture he begins to recover his ability to get his impressions, to assert his judgments. One feels that he is on his way.

In the following months James went on to Italy where the wonders of each successive city yielded at last the overpowering interest of Rome. Visiting the great places of Rome, the irresistible magnet for the art-hungry American, he began to sense fully what was demanded of him. Each letter he sent home shows how much he wanted to be judged by his responses to Italian art and to every evidence of the "picturesque." (To the James family what was "picturesque" in Europe was not so designated only by virtue of pictorial quality, design and form — but also by the historical impact of the object, the stamp it bore of the weight of an older civilization and all that implied for the culture of the New World.)

To distinguish himself as a traveler, and to validate the claim his high ambitions in art had made upon him meant that he should have a comprehensive response at one of the great proving grounds of taste. He wished to prove to himself no less than to his family that he could have an original impression of a Michelangelo or a Tintoretto and that he could com-

19

municate the impression. The letters sent home from
Italy are but a foretaste of the travel sketches he was
to write several years later; as preparation the experience was essential, yet James later regretted that
he had not written his travel pieces when the glow of
morning was diffused through his first impressions.

When he returned to England in March 1870 for a
short stay before sailing home, the mantle of the
traveler had fallen gracefully about his shoulders.
Now he could write without stint or check of the things
he had been seeing. The English countryside attracted
him more than ever. A letter to his father at this time
shows the rapid progress he had been making in
clothing his notations with a style adaptable to, indeed quite worthy of full-length travel pieces.

*"As I neared the good old town I saw the
great Cathedral tower, high and square, rise far
into the cloud-dappled blue. And as I came
nearer still I stopped on the bridge and viewed
the great ecclesiastical pile cast downward into
the yellow Severn. And going further yet I entered the town and lounged about the close and
gazed my fill at that most soul-sustaining sight
—the waning afternoon, far aloft on the broad
perpendicular field of the Cathedral spire —
tasted too, as deeply, of the peculiar stillness
and repose of the close — saw a ruddy English
lad come out and lock the door of the old foundation school which marries its heavy gothic
walls to the basement of the church, and carry
the vast big key into one of the still canonical
houses — and stood wondering as to the effect
on a man's mind of having in one's boyhood
haunted the Cathedral shade as a King's scholar
and yet kept ruddy with much cricket in misty
meadows by the Severn."*

20

Already William James had told him — "Your
letters from Italy are beyond praise. It is a great
pity that they should be born to blush unseen by the
general public and that just the matter they contain,
in a little less rambling style, should not appear in
the columns of the *Nation*." In the offices of the
Nation there were those who saw the matter in the
same light, for in the summer of 1870 after his return
from Europe he visited Saratoga and Newport and
went on to Niagara and Quebec for the purpose of
writing his impressions of these famous spots for the
magazine. In these articles, later used to round out
*Portraits of Places,** James showed himself to be an
acute observer of the trivia of American resort life.
At Saratoga he was filled with a sense of "the absence
of serious associations" and "the nearness, indeed, of
the vulgar and trivial associations of the least complete of all the cities of pleasure." Watching in detachment the social life of America's small leisure
class, he could only sigh and reflect, no doubt with
Italy in mind, "that a society that does nothing is
decidedly more pictorial . . . than a society which
is hard at work." Underneath the surfaces on which
his tourist eye dwelt, he knew that things were stirring
in American life which he felt unprepared to face and
examine. Even in re-visiting Newport, with all its
fond associations from late youth, he realized that he
could make more for fiction out of travel experience
in Europe. The two stories he was working on at
the time, *Travelling Companions* and *The Passionate
Pilgrim*, both important forerunners of the coming

---

* In the present edition the American travel sketches have not
been included, because they were originally added to fill out
the volume, and also because they have been reprinted in *The
American Scene*, published by Scribner's in 1946. Two other
articles, *From Normandy to the Pyrenees* and *An English
Winter Watering Place*, have been omitted in the present
collection.

21

international story, were to show as concrete proof of the progress he had made in fiction since 1869.

His ability as a writer of travel sketches securely established, he was commissioned by the *Nation* to do a series on his next trip to Europe, in the summer of 1872. So the course of his travels may be followed in the "Transatlantic Sketches" he sent back to America. Starting out in England he browsed around the cathedral towns, wandering over the precincts of old churches for his "field work." Then he spent some time in Switzerland; and in the fall of 1872 he settled in Paris for a while. Thereafter came six months in Italy and finally the trip north through Germany, Holland, and Belgium. Though he was learning how to combine careful annotation of detail in the sketches of this trip with the toning quality of reflection and opinion, his tourist status comes through quite plainly. His letters home speak frankly of his dismay and resentment at being constantly the outsider. He bewails his barren social life; in France he knows only waiters, in Italy he adds washerwomen to the company of the waiters. Impressions — he has a superfluity of them, but what he yearns for is the right company — "a régal of intelligent and suggestive society, especially male."

In spite of such disappointments, James' deepest conviction was that he had not yet given Europe a sufficient trial. And in 1875, when he begins a year in Paris, with a fresh assignment to write correspondence from the French capital for the *New York Tribune*, he has girded up all his energies this time to strike his roots firmly. The years 1875-1876 saw a great expansion in his interests. He began to shake off gradually his American diffidence. Judging from his *Tribune* letters, Parisian life often offended his sensibilities, but only to draw him more closely to matters in life, art, and even politics, whose relevance to his impressions he had only had hints of before.

Though his native prejudices at times seemed to be fortified by the ever questionable "morality" of the French nation, they were also sensibly modified by an acquired urbanity of outlook: his need for cosmopolitan tastes and standards as an active principle in his adjustment to living abroad made him privately more tolerant. As a daily rover of the boulevards he enjoyed a new-found sophistication although he continued to recommend the conventional view of "*l'article de Paris*" to his readers. In Paris James felt the ground under his feet; realism began to take on some of its French literary connotation for him, and the words *pretty* and *picturesque* appear less frequently in his reportings. In his last letter from Paris to the *Tribune* there is a sentence which seems to compress much of what he had learned there:

"To write a good book one must hang one's ideal on a peg where one can reach it."

In the spring of 1876 James left Paris on a tour of French towns and noted places he had not yet covered. His first stop was Chartres, and the article he wrote on the famous cathedral town became the first of the later series of articles he gathered together in *Portraits of Places*. By the end of the year he was established at last in England; London was to be his residence in the old world; literary and social success was hovering on the doorstep of 3 Bolton St. W. He had determined to saturate himself in English life; he looked freshly at the city of London, went into the country, discovered at first hand what some of her famous institutions and seasonal events were like. For over a year he continued to sketch his impressions of England and the English people. A trip to Italy in the winter of 1877 gave him a new article on Italy which he called "Italy Revisited" and a stay in Venice in 1881 called forth a final article. By that time he had all he needed for a volume; in 1883 *Portraits of Places* was published.

Looking over the titles of these sketches, the question is likely to form in our minds whether James' readers in 1883 were not as much attracted by the places he visited as by the name of the author. Today the interest of the reader is bound to be James — not Chartres, Venice, London, Warwickshire. Perhaps his readers then felt a little cheated. But he warned them at the bottom of the first page, apropos of Venice: "I write these lines with the full consciousness of having no information whatever to offer." Though only a badly confused person could have mistaken a copy of James for a copy of Murray — which James himself often consulted in traveling — there may be justice now in the fact that these sketches will be read principally for what they tell us of James' experience, his tastes and opinions.

In these pages James composed a personal record through which the reader may traverse a middle ground lying between his letters and his fiction. For the most part his attitudes towards places and peoples are those of his letters, but they are never expressed with the spontaneity and sharpness one finds in the comments strewn through his letters. Actually the style is something that James evolved for this branch of his writing; though related to the style of his letters and his fiction, it has its own special stamp. Casualness, ease, grace are the qualities he strived for, a style that above all would suggest cosmopolitan urbanity and the reference of ample comparison. At its best it is marvelously fluent and tactfully personal; at its worst it exposes its own artifice, especially when he cloaks a commonplace thing in unnaturally elegant expression. Avoidance of the colloquial word and the literal note often produces a sense of over-writing that is mostly absent from his concurrent stories.

James' fiction of the seventies, the "international" stories in particular, come from the same reservoir of experience that made it possible for him to do travel

24

articles. Furthermore, to ask the question, what kind of a person James was during the seventies, demands a knowledge that *Portraits of Places*, with its record of mainly pleasurable experience, can supply as well as any writing of his at this time. One qualifying fact must be borne in mind: these were formative years for James. The limitations we discover, in depth of understanding and range of appreciation, are not fixed. Yet we may be grateful that James was not overcautious in displaying his preferences. If in his role as a "sentimental tourist," he sometimes suspends in an absurd way his power to undertake rational inquiry, we are rewarded, when he becomes the "analytic tourist," with honest cogitations that do full justice to the family tradition of spirited inquiry into the culture and national traits of European peoples.

It is well to reflect, too, that although James had a keen appreciation of the travel sketch as a form of literary engagement, he always kept this work in subordinate relation to his fiction. Gathering impressions was the way in which he had pledged himself to live, but by the middle of the seventies he knew that he must make them count for something more than pleasure. Italy, for example, the very source of the "picturesque," never failed to supply him with golden moments, yet he knew that there was a limit to the degree in which his fiction could profit from its everlasting charm on the senses. For another thing we may be sure that James preferred to be offstage as a writer; he found it more "attaching" to decipher the *other* point of view than to voice directly his own. Writing these articles was neither an ungrateful nor an uncongenial business, but his mind was always on the main issue — which was *not* the interest he had taken in all he had seen and felt along the tourist highways of Europe but what particular things could rightly be transmuted into his kind of fiction.

As for the point of connection between *Portraits*

of Places and his international fiction of the late seventies, it may be said that the sketches fill in backgrounds for us and supply generalizations on the international scene; the stories are the particulars, the special cases that James invariably became attached to. Sometimes the connection is very close, and the sketch seems to play somewhat the same part for his writing of fiction that the notebooks did later. (It is worth observing that the end of the steady production of travel sketches coincides with the regular adoption of notebook keeping.) For example, "Occasional Paris" ends with James' account of a performance he saw of Dumas *fils* ' *Le Demi-Monde* at the Theátre Francaise. His interest in that play comes back to us later in *The Siege of London* in terms of that earlier situation and the theme of his comment then. Likewise, his sketching of the French working-man in the same piece provides the clue to some of the documentation that went into *The Princess Casamassima*. In his fiction oftentimes the feeling for places annotated in the *Portraits* volume appears in much more exciting and affecting accents — We may recall the Florentine setting that warms the impulses of Isabel Archer and partially clouds her vision and the Roman vignettes in *Daisy Miller*. Reading James on Italy gives us a much better understanding of his handling of the impact, on certain sensitive young Americans, of Italy. And the mention of *Daisy Miller* brings Winterbourne to mind — that fastidious, aesthetic, cautious young American who was famed more for the enjoyment of his impressions than the enjoyment of love. Many more points appear at which some moment, some reflection noted in James' *Portraits* enmeshes or overlap the materials of his international fiction.

The best way certainly of understanding the personal side of James in his travel writing is to observe how his approach to his subjects changes. As he tells us, he started out in 1870 at Saratoga as a

26

"sentimental tourist;" the first thing he learned was that he had to part with the images of places formed beforehand in his mind. Immediately they began to give way before the facts; unreluctantly he found that "accidents and details . . . give more to the imagination than they receive from it." Indeed, the close study of details was instructive to his imagination; the main interest became the composition of all details into a pleasing pictorial account of a place. And in America illusions were readily tempered by facts which suggested an incompleteness in our social life, an idea influenced by the implied contrast of his feelings about Europe. To define the place of imagination as he does, however, points to a correspondence with a growing tendency in his fiction towards realism.

Twelve years later he launches his article on Venice, as I have mentioned before, by telling the reader not to expect "information" from him, for he adds, "I hold any writer sufficiently justified who is himself in love with his topic." Over this span of years James *had* studied Europe; the kindling of imagination, the spontaneity of fresh appraisals had yielded to the accumulative effect of sensory experience. In place of the test of the qualifying impression, there was now a background of personal living on which reflection, debate, and re-examination had registered their influence. His sense of the difference between modern Italy and the Italy that was ruled by the "historical picturesque" gives the point to "Italy Revisited." Yet even in that essay, in spite of his training as an "analytic tourist," he put forward, as the main purpose of traveling, a relaxed enjoyment in one's impressions: the sobering effect of historical change and the presence of today's problems did not act as a full counterweight to the principle of pleasure.

More and more the bias of personal preference bestows a definable mark on the details that pass through his vision. In truth the degree of affection

27

that James felt for a particular place or an object is in direct proportion to its power to satisfy some particular requirement of his own. The circumstances that shaped his decision to move to England are reflected in his sketches of France, and the swift accommodation he made to English life is echoed repeatedly in the subsequent articles on England. That he felt himself an outsider in France one might not suspect at once from his pieces on France, but reading on, following him into England, one receives a vivid sense of contrast. The difference, of course, is explained by the exchange of his acceptance into British society for the social rejection he had felt in Paris.

Not that James is not as skillful a reporter at the Rheims cathedral as he was at the unnamed Norman abbey he visits and writes about in "Abbeys and Castles." But observe that his imagination is acted upon in England by a potent organization of associations — "You feast upon the pictorial, you inhale the historic." At Rheims he is sufficiently disenchanted as to brood aggressively over the question whether his imagination should be "bribed" by beauty away from the "revelation of an anti-Catholic passion." "How far," he asks, "should a lover of old cathedrals let his hands be tied by the sanctity of their traditions?" An interesting question, but its like never comes to him in his tour of English abbeys and castles.

Comparison, he tells us in "Occasional Paris," is the natural element of the cosmopolitan; it is instructive, enlightening, and of course its greatest value is to temper prejudice. But as one reads on in the essay one actually gets a lesson in the way in which a sense of alienation in France checked his enthusiasm for her people, accentuated his slanting, and at times left him with nothing but a bare prejudice. He seems to be attracted by the Paris *ouvrier*. Of him he says quite astonishingly, "In some cases he looks depraved and perverted, but at his worst he looks refined." Now "refined" for James was a token of approval — and giving the working-man that distinction is certainly curious, particularly when James proceeds at once to remark that this judgment strikes him as courageous after reading *L'Assomoir*. To add to the ambiguity, he informs the reader that Zola's affliction is a "horrible uncleanness of imagination." Yet in the next breath "sociability" is called "the classic quality of the French nature," and he adds a very acute insight to the effect that in France sociability operates "as it never does in England, from below upward." But even if James does not reconcile his premises for the reader, he never argues them; the relaxed manner of his writing did not press consistency upon him.

Even if the French working class by fairly superficial standards comes off better for him then their English brothers, one of James' most inveterate preferences comes to light when he says that the men of the Parisian population "do not look like gentlemen as so many Englishmen do." His bias in favor of the English gentleman was as flagrant as his anthropology was fantastic. The young English gentlemen "present to view very much fewer occidental noses and inexpressive mouths, fewer sloping shoulders and ill-planted heads of hair, than their American kinsmen."

This kind of unlimited approbation of the English people, taken merely on the grounds of physiognomy, is of the same piece as his general delight in the surfaces of English life. Reveling in his new-found sense of participation in amenities of British society of the wealthy classes, James discovers for the first time in his stay abroad a sense of really being involved in the social life of the old world. It was a precious feeling, and he had no difficulty in believing that for him it was a natural, inevitable development. In his English sketches the feeling is communicated through a recognition of historical and national influences, infrequently mentioned heretofore, and the way in which he warmly embraces English traditions and institutions. What he calls the system of English "comfort" he chooses to believe a unique contribution of a people that best understands the use of leisure. At last James discards the manners of the tourist. Now he is more than the dutiful notetaker giving a brilliant report of the usual sights and scenes but with the convenional coverage of details and emphasis. All the emotion felt for a country where one has established a long wanted identification influences his point of view. Viewing everything English with sympathy and concern, his sketches are rounded out with observations on the matters of daily concern to the English people. Full of timely references, the travel sketch becomes for him a kind of journal in which the seasons and the changing political scene and even the effects of the depression in trade, bitterly felt in 1879, give new interest to his reporting.

Of course, the tones in the picture are not all bright and cheering. The faces of the poor disturb him; the situation of the "masses" is something he attempts to look at squarely, but he only succeeds in defending the reasons the comfortable classes offer for withdrawing into their privacy. The destiny of England was a topic that James brooded over again and again, but a romantic view of her greatness veiled the future in a hazy cloud. Forebodings of despair were somehow reconciled with his prevailing view that whatever happened to England would be a "spectacle" which would, for him, top any other.

As a history of James' responses to living abroad at the time when he was rapidly coming into full possession of the art of fiction, *Portraits of Places* is an interesting predecessor of the unqualified personal records of later years. The most valuable portrait in the book is the one which he sketched of himself. For in spite of the charm that lingers around a view of the serenity and ease of a vanished day of American

Portraits of Places

Venice

IT is a great pleasure to write the word; but I am not sure there is not a certain impudence in pretending to add anything to it. Venice has been painted and described many thousands of times, and of all the cities of the world it is the easiest to visit without going there. Open the first book and you will find a rhapsody about it; step into the first picture-dealer's and you will find three or four high-coloured "views" of it. There is nothing more to be said about it. Every one has been there, and every one has brought back a collection of photographs. There is as little mystery about the Grand Canal as about our local thoroughfare; and the name of St. Mark is as familiar as the postman's ring. It is not forbidden, however, to speak of familiar things, and I believe that, for the true Venice-lover, Venice is always in order. There is nothing new to be said about it certainly, but the old is better than any novelty. It would be a sad day, indeed, when there should be something new to say. I write these lines with the full consciousness of having no information whatever to offer. I do not pretend to enlighten the reader; I pretend only to give a fillip to his memory; and I hold any writer sufficiently justified who is himself in love with his topic.

I.

Mr. Ruskin has given it up, that is very true; but it is only after extracting half a life-time of pleasure and an immeasurable quantity of fame from it. We all may do the same, after it has served our turn, which it probably will not cease to do for many a year to come. Meantime, it is Mr. Ruskin who, beyond any one, helps us to enjoy. He has, indeed, lately produced several aids to depression in the shape of certain little humorous— ill-humorous — pamphlets (the series of *St. Mark's Rest*), which embody his latest reflections on the subject of Venice and describe the latest atrocities that have been perpetrated there. These latter are numerous and deeply to be deplored; but to admit that they have spoiled Venice would be to admit that Venice may be spoiled — an admission pregnant, as it seems to us, with disloyalty. Fortunately, one reacts against the Ruskinian contagion, and one hour of the lagoon is worth a hundred pages of demoralised prose. This queer, late-coming prose of Mr. Ruskin (including the revised and condensed issue of the *Stones of Venice*, only one little volume of which has appeared or, perhaps, will ever appear) is all to be read, though much of it seems to be addressed to children of tender age. It is pitched in the nursery-key, and might be supposed

38

to emanate from an angry governess. It is, however, all suggestive, and much of it is delightfully
just. There is an inconceivable want of form in
it, though the author has spent his life in laying
down the principles of form, and scolding people
for departing from them; but it throbs and flashes
with the love of his subject—a love disconcerted
and abjured, but which has still some of the force
of inspiration. Among the many strange things that
have befallen Venice, she has had the good fortune
to become the object of a passion to a man of
splendid genius, who has made her his own, and,
in doing so, has made her the world's. There is no
better reading at Venice, therefore, as I say, than
Ruskin, for every true Venice-lover can separate
the wheat from the chaff. The narrow theological
spirit, the moralism à tout propos, the queer pro-
vincialities and pruderies, are mere wild weeds in
a mountain of flowers. One may doubtless be very
happy in Venice without reading at all—without
criticising or analysing or thinking a strenuous
thought. It is a city in which, I suspect, there is
very little strenuous thinking, and yet it is a city
in which there must be almost as much happiness
as misery. The misery of Venice stands there for
all the world to see; it is part of the spectacle—
a thorough-going devotee of local colour might
consistently say it is part of the pleasure. The
Venetian people have little to call their own—little
more than the bare privilege of leading their lives
in the most beautiful of towns. Their habitations
are decayed; their taxes heavy; their pockets light;
their opportunities few. One receives an impres-

sion, however, that life presents itself to them with attractions not accounted for in this meagre train of advantages, and that they are on better terms with it than many people who have made a better bargain. They lie in the sunshine; they dabble in the sea; they wear bright rags; they fall into attitudes and harmonies; they assist at an eternal *conversazione*. It is not easy to say that one would have them other than they are, and it certainly would make an immense difference should they be better fed. The number of persons in Venice who evidently never have enough to eat is painfully large; but it would be more painful if we did not equally perceive that the rich Venetian temperament may bloom upon a dog's allowance. Nature has been kind to it, and sunshine and leisure and conversation and beautiful views form the greater part of its sustenance. It takes a great deal to make a successful American; but to make a happy Venetian takes only a handful of quick sensibility. The Italian people have, at once, the good and evil fortune to be conscious of few wants; so that if the civilisation of a society is measured by the number of its needs, as seems to be the common opinion to-day, it is to be feared that the children of the lagoon would make but a poor figure in a set of comparative tables. Not their misery, doubtless, but the way they elude their misery, is what pleases the sentimental tourist, who is gratified by the sight of a beautiful race that lives by the aid of its imagination. The way to enjoy Venice is to follow the example of these people and make the most of simple pleasures. Almost all the pleasures of the place are simple; this may be maintained even under the imputation of ingenious paradox. There is no simpler pleasure than looking at a fine Titian —unless it be looking at a fine Tintoret, or strolling into St. Mark's—it is abominable, the way one falls into the habit—and resting one's light-wearied eyes upon the windowless gloom; or than floating in a gondola, or hanging over a balcony, or taking one's coffee at Florian's. It is of these superficial pastimes that a Venetian day is composed, and the pleasure of the matter is in the emotions to which they minister. These, fortunately, are of the finest; otherwise, Venice would be insufferably dull. Reading Ruskin is good; reading the old records is, perhaps, better; but the best thing of all is simply staying on. The only way to care for Venice as she deserves it, is to give her a chance to touch you often—to linger and remain and return.

II.

The danger is that you will not linger enough— a danger of which the author of these lines had known something. It is possible to dislike Venice, and to entertain the sentiment in a responsible and intelligent manner. There are travellers who think the place odious, and those who are not of this opinion often find themselves wishing that the others were only more numerous. The sentimental tourist's only quarrel with his Venice is that he has too many competitors there. He likes to be alone; to be original; to have (to himself, at least) the air of making discoveries. The Venice of to-day is a vast museum where the little wicket that admits you is perpetually turning and creaking, and you march through the institution with a herd of fellow-gazers. There is nothing left to discover or describe, and originality of attitude is completely impossible. This is often very annoying; you can only turn your back on your impertinent playfellow and curse his want of delicacy. But this is not the fault of Venice; it is the fault of the rest of the world. The fault of Venice is that, though it is easy to admire it, it is not so easy to live in it. After you have been there a week, and the bloom of novelty has rubbed off, you wonder whether you can accommodate yourself to the peculiar conditions. Your old habits become impracticable, and you find yourself obliged to form new ones of an undesirable and unprofitable character. You are tired of your gondola (or you think you are), and you have seen all the principal pictures and heard the names of the palaces announced a dozen times by your gondolier, who brings them out almost as impressively as if he were an English butler bawling titles into a drawing-room. You have walked several hundred times round the Piazza, and bought several bushels of photographs. You have visited the antiquity-mongers whose horrible sign-boards dishonour some of the grandest vistas in the Grand Canal; you have tried the opera and found it very bad; you have bathed at the Lido and found the water flat. You have begun to have a shipboard-feeling—to regard the Piazza as an enormous saloon and the Riva degli Schiavoni as a promenade-deck. You are obstructed and encaged; your desire for space is unsatisfied; you miss your usual exercise. You try to take a walk, and you fail, and meantime, as I say, you have come to regard your gondola as a sort of magnified baby's cradle. You have no desire to be rocked to sleep, though you are sufficiently kept awake by the irritation produced, as you gaze across the shallow lagoon, by the attitude of the perpetual gondolier, with his turned-out toes, his protruded chin, his absurdly unscientific stroke. The canals have a horrible smell, and the everlasting Piazza, where you have looked repeatedly at every article in every shop-window and found them all rubbish, where the young Venetians who sell bead-bracelets and "panoramas" are perpetually thrusting their wares at you, where the same tightly-buttoned officers are for ever sucking the same black weeds, at the same empty tables, in front of the same caffès—the Piazza, as I say, has resolved itself into a sort of magnificent tread-mill. This is the state of mind of those shallow inquirers who find Venice all very well for a week; and if in such a state of mind you take your departure, you act with fatal rashness. The loss is your own, moreover; it is not—with all deference to your personal attractions —that of your companions who remain behind; for though there are some disagreeable things in Venice, there is nothing so disagreeable as the visitors. The conditions are peculiar, but your intolerance of them evaporates before it has had time to become a prejudice. When you have called for the bill to go, pay it and remain, and you will find on the morrow that you are deeply attached to Venice. It is by living there from day to day that you feel the fulness of its charm; that you invite its exquisite influence to sink into your spirit. The place is as changeable as a nervous woman, and you know it only when you know all the aspects of its beauty. It has high spirits or low, it is pale or red, gray or pink, cold or warm, fresh or wan, according to the weather or the hour. It is always interesting and almost always sad; but it has a thousand occasional graces and is always liable to happy accidents. You become extraordinarily fond of these things; you count upon them; they make part of your life. Tenderly fond you become; there is something indefinable in those depths of personal acquaintance that gradually establish themselves. The place seems to personify itself, to become human and sentient, and conscious of your affection. You desire to embrace it, to caress it, to possess it; and finally, a soft sense of possession grows up, and your visit becomes a perpetual love-affair. It is very true that if you go there, like the author of these lines, about the middle of March, a certain amount of disappointment is possible. He had not been there for several years, and in the interval the beautiful and helpless city had suffered an increase of injury. The barbarians are in full possession, and you tremble for what they may do. You are reminded, from the moment of your arrival, that Venice scarcely exists any more as a city at all; that it exists only as a battered peep-show and bazaar. There was a horde of savage Germans encamped in the Piazza, and they filled the Ducal Palace and the Academy with their uproar. The English and Americans came a little later. They came in good time, with a great many French,

44

who were discreet enough to make very long repasts
at the Caffè Quadri, during which they were out of
the way. The months of April and May of the
year 1881 were not, as a general thing, a favour-
able season for visiting the Ducal Palace and the
Academy. The valet-de-place had marked them for
his own, and held triumphant possession of them.
He celebrates his triumphs in a terrible brassy
voice, which resounds all over the place, and has,
whatever language he be speaking, the accent of
some other idiom. During all the spring months in
Venice these gentry abound in the great resorts, and
they lead their helpless captives through churches
and galleries in dense irresponsible groups. They
infest the Piazza; they pursue you along the Riva;
they hang about the bridges and the doors of the
caffès. In saying just now that I was disappointed
at first, I had chiefly in mind the impression that
assails me to-day in the whole precinct of St.
Mark's. The condition of this ancient sanctuary
is surely a great scandal. The pedlars and com-
missioners ply their trade—often a very unclean
one—at the very door of the temple; they follow
you across the threshold, into the sacred dusk, and
pull your sleeve, and hiss into your ear, scuffling
with each other for customers. There is a great
deal of dishonour about St. Mark's altogether, and
if Venice, as I say, has become a great bazaar, this
exquisite edifice is now the biggest booth.

III.

It is treated as a booth in all ways, and if it had not, somehow, a great spirit of solemnity within it, the traveller would soon have little warrant for regarding it as a religious affair. The restoration of the outer walls, which has lately been so much attacked and defended, is certainly a great shock. Of the necessity of the work only an expert is, I suppose, in a position to judge; but there is no doubt that, if a necessity it be, it is one that is deeply to be regretted. To no more distressing necessity have people of taste lately had to resign themselves. Wherever the hand of the restorer has been laid all semblance of beauty has vanished; which is a sad fact, considering that the external loveliness of St. Mark's has been for ages less impressive only than that of the still comparatively uninjured interior. I know not what is the measure of necessity in such a case, and it appears indeed to be a very delicate question. To-day, at any rate, that admirable harmony of faded mosaic and marble, which, to the eye of the traveller emerging from the narrow streets that lead to the Piazza, filled all the farther end of it with a sort of dazzling, silvery presence—to-day this lovely vision is in a way to be completely reformed and, indeed, well-nigh abolished. The old softness and mellowness of colour—the work of the quiet centuries and of the breath of the salt sea—is giving way to large crude patches of new material, which have the effect of a monstrous malady rather than of a restoration to health.

46

They look like blotches of red and white paint
and dishonourable smears of chalk on the cheeks of
a noble matron. The face toward the Piazzetta is
in especial the newest-looking thing conceivable—
as new as a new pair of boots, or as the morning's
paper. We do not profess, however, to undertake
a scientific quarrel with these changes; we admit
that our complaint is a purely sentimental one.
The march of industry in united Italy must doubtless be looked at as a whole, and one must endeavour
to believe that it is through innumerable lapses of
taste that this deeply interesting country is groping
her way to her place among the nations. For the
present, it is not to be denied, certain odd phases
of the process are more visible than the result, to
arrive at which it seems necessary that, as she was
of old a passionate votary of the beautiful, she should
to-day burn everything that she has adored. It
is, doubtless, too soon to judge her, and there are
moments when one is willing to forgive her even
the restoration of St. Mark's. Inside, as well, there
has been a considerable attempt to make the place
more tidy; but the general effect, as yet, has not
seriously suffered. What I chiefly remember is the
straightening out of that dark and rugged old pavement—those deep undulations of primitive mosaic,
in which the wondering tourist was thought to perceive an intended resemblance to the waves of the
ocean. Whether intended or not, the analogy was
an image the more in a treasure-house of images;
but from a considerable portion of the church it
has now disappeared. Throughout the greater part,
indeed, the pavement remains as recent generations

have known it—dark, rich, cracked, uneven, spotted
with porphyry and time-blackened malachite, and
polished by the knees of innumerable worshippers;
but in other large sections the idea imitated by the
restorers is that of the ocean in a dead calm, and the
model they have taken, the floor of a London club-
house or of a New York hotel. I think no Venetian
and scarcely any Italian cares much for such differences; and when, a year ago, people in England
were writing to the *Times* about the whole business,
and holding meetings to protest against it, the dear
children of the lagoon (so far as they heard, or
heeded, the rumour) thought them partly busy-
bodies and partly asses. Busy-bodies they doubtless were, but they took a good deal of disinterested
trouble. It never occurs to the Venetian mind of
to-day that such trouble may be worth taking; the
Venetian mind vainly endeavours to conceive a
state of existence in which personal questions are
so insipid that people have to look for grievances
in the wrongs of brick and marble. I must not,
however, speak of St. Mark's as if I had the pretension of giving a description of it, or as if the reader
desired one. The reader has been too well served
already. It is surely the best-described building
in the world. Open the *Stones of Venice*, open
Théophile Gautier's *Italia*, and you will see. These
writers take it very seriously, and it is only because
there is another way of taking it that I venture
to speak of it; the way that offers itself after you
have been in Venice a couple of months, and the
light is hot in the great Square, and you pass in
under the pictured porticoes with a feeling of habit

48

and friendliness, and a desire for something cool
and dark. There are moments, after all, when the
church is comparatively quiet and empty, when
you may sit there with an easy consciousness of its
beauty. From the moment, of course, that you go
into any Italian church for any purpose but to say
your prayers or look at the ladies, you rank yourself among the trooping barbarians I just spoke of ;
you treat the place like an orifice in the peep-show.
Still, it is almost a spiritual function—or, at the
worst, an amorous one—to feed one's eyes on the
moulten colour that drops from the hollow vaults and
thickens the air with its richness. It is all so quiet
and sad and faded ; and yet it is all so brilliant and
living. The strange figures in the mosaic pictures,
bending with the curve of niche and vault, stare
down through the glowing dimness ; and the bur-
nished gold that stands behind them catches the
light on its little uneven cubes. St. Mark's owes
nothing of its character to the beauty of proportion
or perspective ; there is nothing grandly balanced
or far-arching ; there are no long lines nor triumphs
of the perpendicular. The church arches indeed ;
but it arches like a dusky cavern. Beauty of surface, of tone, of detail, of things near enough to touch
and kneel upon and lean against—it is from this
the effect proceeds. In this sort of beauty the place
is incredibly rich, and you may go there every day
and find afresh some lurking pictorial nook. It is
a treasury of bits, as the painters say ; and there
are usually three or four painters, with their easels
set up in uncertain equilibrium on the undulating
floor. It is not easy to catch the real complexion

of St. Mark's, and these laudable attempts at portraiture are apt to look either lurid or livid. But, if you cannot paint the old loose-looking marble slabs, the great panels of basalt and jasper, the crucifixes, of which the lonely anguish looks deeper in the vertical light, the tabernacles whose open doors disclose a dark Byzantine image, spotted with dull, crooked gems—if you cannot paint these things, you can at least grow fond of them. You grow fond even of the old benches of red marble, partly worn away by the breeches of many generations, and attached to the base of those wide pilasters, of which the precious plating, delightful in its faded brownness, with a faint gray bloom upon it, bulges and yawns a little with honourable age.

IV.

Even at first, when the vexatious sense of the city of the Doges having been reduced to earning its living as a curiosity-shop was in its keenness, there was a great deal of entertainment to be got from lodging on the Riva degli Schiavoni and looking out at the far-shimmering lagoon. There was entertainment indeed in simply getting into the place and observing the queer incidents of a Venetian installation. A great many persons contribute indirectly to this undertaking, and it is surprising how they spring out at you during your novitiate to remind you that they are bound up in some mysterious manner with the constitution of your little establishment. It was an interesting problem, for instance, to trace the subtle connection existing

between the niece of the landlady and the occu-
pancy of the fourth floor. Superficially, it was not
easily visible, as the young lady in question was a
dancer at the Fenice theatre—or, when that was
closed, at the Rossini—and might have been supposed to be absorbed by her professional duties.
It proved to be necessary, however, that she should
hover about the premises in a velvet jacket and
a pair of black kid gloves, with one little white
button ; as also, that she should apply a thick
coating of powder to her face, which had a charming oval and a sweet, weak expression, like that of
most of the Venetian maidens, who, as a general
thing (it was not a peculiarity of the landlady's
niece), are fond of besmearing themselves with flour.
It soon became plain that it is not only the many-
twinkling lagoon that you behold from a habitation
on the Riva ; you see a little of everything Venetian.
Straight across, before my windows, rose the great
pink mass of San Giorgio Maggiore, which, for an
ugly Palladian church, has a success beyond all
reason.   It is a success of position, of colour, of
the immense detached Campanile, tipped with a
tall gold angel.   I know not whether it is because
San Giorgio is so grandly conspicuous, and because
it has a great deal of worn, faded-looking brickwork ;
but for many persons the whole place has a kind
of suffusion of rosiness.   If we were asked what is
the leading colour at Venice we should say pink,
and yet, after all, we cannot remember that this
elegant tint occurs very often.   It is a faint, shimmering, airy, watery pink ; the bright sea-light seems
to flush with it, and the pale whitish-green of

51

lagoon and canal to drink it in. There is, indeed, in Venice a great deal of very evident brickwork, which is never fresh or loud in colour, but always burnt out, as it were, always exquisitely mild. There are certain little mental pictures that rise before the sentimental tourist at the simple mention, written or spoken, of the places he has loved. When I hear, when I see, the magical name I have written above these pages, it is not of the great Square that I think, with its strange basilica and its high arcades, nor of the wide mouth of the Grand Canal, with the stately steps and the well-poised dome of the Salute; it is not of the low lagoon, nor the sweet Piazzetta, nor the dark chambers of St. Mark's. I simply see a narrow canal in the heart of the city—a patch of green water and a surface of pink wall. The gondola moves slowly; it gives a great, smooth swerve, passes under a bridge, and the gondolier's cry, carried over the quiet water, makes a kind of splash in the stillness. A girl is passing over the little bridge, which has an arch like a camel's back, with an old shawl on her head, which makes her look charming; you see her against the sky as you float beneath. The pink of the old wall seems to fill the whole place; it sinks even into the opaque water. Behind the wall is a garden, out of which the long arm of a white June rose—the roses of Venice are splendid—has flung itself by way of spontaneous ornament. On the other side of this small water-way is a great shabby façade of Gothic windows and balconies—balconies on which dirty clothes are hung and under which a cavernous-looking doorway opens from a low flight of slimy water-steps. It is very hot and still, the canal has a queer smell, and the whole place is enchanting. It is poor work, however, talking about the colour of things in Venice. The sentimental tourist is perpetually looking at it from his window, when he is not floating about with that delightful sense of being for the moment a part of it, which any gentleman in a gondola is free to entertain. Venetian windows and balconies are a dreadful lure, and while you rest your elbows on these cushioned ledges the precious hours fly away. But, in truth. Venice is not, in fair weather, a place for concentration of mind. The effort required for sitting down to a writing-table is heroic, and the brightest page of MS. looks dull beside the brilliancy of your *milieu.* All nature beckons you forth, and murmurs to you sophistically that such hours should be devoted to collecting impressions. Afterward, in ugly places, at unprivileged times, you can convert your impressions into prose. Fortunately for the present proser, the weather was not always fine; the first month was wet and windy, and it was better to look at the lagoon from an open casement than to respond to the advances of persuasive gondoliers. Even then, however, there was a constant entertainment in the view. It was all cold colour, and the steel-gray floor of the lagoon was stroked the wrong way by the wind. Then there were charming cool intervals, when the churches, the houses, the anchored fishing-boats, the whole gently-curving line of the Riva, seemed to be washed with a pearly white. Later it all turned warm—warm to the eye as well as to other senses. After the middle of May the whole place was in a glow. The sea took on a thousand shades, but they were only infinite variations of blue, and those rosy walls I just spoke of began to flush in the thick sunshine. Every patch of colour, every yard of weather-stained stucco, every glimpse of nestling garden or daub of sky above a *calle*, began to shine and sparkle—began, as the painters say, to " compose." The lagoon was streaked with odd currents, which played across it like huge, smooth finger-marks. The gondolas multiplied and spotted it all over ; every gondola and every gondolier looking, at a distance, precisely like every other. There is something strange and fascinating in this mysterious impersonality of the gondola. It has an identity when you are in it, but, thanks to their all being of the same size, shape, and colour, and of the same deportment and gait, it has none, or as little as possible, as you see it pass before you. From my windows on the Riva there was always the same silhouette— the long, black, slender skiff, lifting its head and throwing it back a little, moving yet seeming not to move, with the grotesquely-graceful figure on the poop. This figure inclines, as may be, more to the graceful or to the grotesque—standing in the " second position" of the dancing-master, but indulging, from the waist upward, in a freedom of movement which that functionary would deprecate. One may say, as a general thing, that there is something rather awkward in the movement of even the most graceful gondolier, and something graceful in the movement of the most awkward. In the graceful men of course the grace predominates, and nothing can be finer than the large firm way in which, from their point of vantage, they throw themselves over their tremendous oar. It has the boldness of a plunging bird, and the regularity of a pendulum. Sometimes, as you see this movement in profile, in a gondola that passes you—see, as you recline on your own low cushions, the arching body of the gondolier lifted up against the sky—it has a kind of nobleness which suggests an image on a Greek frieze. The gondolier at Venice is your very good friend— if you choose him happily—and on the quality of the personage depends a good deal that of your impressions. He is a part of your daily life, your double, your shadow, your complement. Most people, I think, either like their gondolier or hate him ; and if they like him, like him very much. In this case they take an interest in him after his departure ; wish him to be sure of employment, speak of him as the gem of gondoliers, and tell their friends to be certain to "secure" him. There is usually no difficulty in securing him ; there is nothing elusive or reluctant about a gondolier. They are, for the most part, excellent fellows, and the sentimental tourist must always have a kindness for them. More than the rest of the population, of course, they are the children of Venice ; they are associated with its idiosyncrasy, with its essence, with its silence, with its melancholy. When I say they are associated with its silence, I should immediately add that they are associated also with its sound. Among themselves they are an extraordinarily talkative company. They chatter at the *traghetti,* where they always have some sharp point under discussion; they bawl across the canals; they bespeak your commands as you approach; they defy each other from afar. If you happen to have a *traghetto* under your window, you are well aware that they are a vocal race. I should go even farther than I went just now, and say that the voice of the gondolier is, in fact, the sound of Venice. There is scarcely any other, and that, indeed, is part of the interest of the place. There is no noise there save distinctly human noise; no rumbling, no vague uproar, nor rattle of wheels and hoofs. It is all articulate, personal sound. One may say, indeed, that Venice is, emphatically, the city of conversation; people talk all over the place, because there is nothing to interfere with their being heard. Among the populace it is a kind of family party. The still water carries the voice, and good Venetians exchange confidences at a distance of half a mile. It saves a world of trouble, and they don't like trouble. Their delightful garrulous language helps them to make Venetian life a long *conversazione*. This language, with its soft elisions, its odd transpositions, its kindly contempt for consonants and other disagreeables, has in it something peculiarly human and accommodating. If your gondolier had no other merit, he would have the merit that he speaks Venetian. This may rank as a merit, even —some people perhaps would say especially—when you don't understand what he says. But he adds to it other graces which make him an agreeable feature in your life. The price he sets on his services is touchingly small, and he has a happy art of being obsequious, without being, or at least, without seeming, abject. For occasional liberalities he evinces an almost lyrical gratitude. In short, he has delightfully good manners, a merit which he shares, for the most part, with Venetians at large. One grows very fond of these people, and the reason of one's fondness is the frankness and sweetness of their address. That of the Italian people, in general, has much to recommend it; but in the Venetian manner there is something peculiarly ingratiating. One feels that the race is old, that it has a long and rich civilisation in its blood, and that if it has not been blessed by fortune, it has at least been polished by time. It has not a genius for morality, and indeed makes few pretensions in that direction. It scruples not to represent the false as the true, and is liable to confusion in-the attribution of pro-perty. It is peculiarly susceptible to the tender sentiment, which it cultivates with a graceful dis-regard of the more rigid formalities. I am not sure that it is very brave, and was not struck with its being very industrious. But it has an unfailing sense of the amenities of life; the poorest Venetian is a natural man of the world. He is better com-pany than persons of his class are apt to be among the nations of industry and virtue—where people are also, sometimes, perceived to lie and steal. He has a great desire to please and to be pleased.

V.

In this latter point the cold-blooded stranger begins at last to imitate him; he begins to lead a life that is, before all things, good-humoured: unless,

indeed, he allow himself, like Mr. Ruskin, to be put
out of his good-humour by Titian and Tiepolo.
The hours he spends among the pictures are his
best hours in Venice, and I am ashamed of myself
to have written so much of common things when
I might have been making festoons of the names
of the masters. But, when we have covered our
page with such festoons, what more is left to say?
When one has said Carpaccio and Bellini, the
Tintoret and the Veronese, one has struck a note
that must be left to resound at will. Everything
has been said about the mighty painters, and it is
of little importance to record that one traveller the
more has found them to his taste. "Went this
morning to the Academy; was very much pleased
with Titian's 'Assumption.'" That honest phrase
has doubtless been written in many a traveller's
diary, and was not indiscreet on the part of its
author. But it appeals little to the general reader,
and we must, moreover, not expose our deepest
feelings. Since I have mentioned Titian's "Assumption," I must say that there are some people
who have been less pleased with it than the gentleman we have just imagined. It is one of the possible disappointments of Venice, and you may, if
you like, take advantage of your privilege of not
caring for it. It imparts a look of great richness
to the side of the beautiful room of the Academy
on which it hangs; but the same room contains
two or three works less known to fame which are
equally capable of inspiring a - passion. "The
'Annunciation' struck me as coarse and superficial": that was once written in a simple-minded

traveller's note-book. At Venice, strange to say, Titian is altogether a disappointment; the city of his adoption is far from containing the best of him. Madrid, Paris, London, Florence, Dresden, Munich —these are the homes of his greatness. There are other painters who have but a single home, and the greatest of these is the Tintoret. Close beside him sit Carpaccio and Bellini, who make with him the dazzling Venetian trio. The Veronese may be seen and measured in other places; he is most splendid in Venice, but he shines in Paris and in Dresden. You may walk out of the noon-day dusk of Trafalgar Square in November, and in one of the chambers of the National Gallery see the family of Darius rustling and pleading and weeping at the feet of Alexander. Alexander is a beautiful young Venetian in crimson pantaloons, and the picture sends a glow into the cold London twilight. You may sit before it for an hour, and dream you are floating to the water-gate of the Ducal Palace, where a certain old beggar, with one of the handsomest heads in the world—he has sat to a hundred painters for Doges, and for personages more sacred—has a prescriptive right to pretend to pull your gondola to the steps and to hold out a greasy, immemorial cap. But you must go to Venice, in fact, to see the other masters, who form part of your life while you are there, and illuminate your view of the universe. It is difficult to express one's relation to them; for the whole Venetian art-world is so near, so familiar, so much an extension and adjunct of the actual world, that it seems almost invidious to say one owes more to one of them than to another

Nowhere (not even in Holland, where the corre
spondence between the real aspects and the little
polished canvases is so constant and so exquisite)
do art and life seem so interfused and, as it were,
so consanguineous. All the splendour of light and
colour, all the Venetian air and the Venetian history,
are on the walls and ceilings of the palaces; and all
the genius of the masters, all the images and visions
they have left upon canvas, seem to tremble in the
sunbeams and dance upon the waves. That is the
perpetual interest of the place—that you live in a
certain sort of knowledge as in a rosy cloud. You
don't go into the churches and galleries by way of
a change from the streets; you go into them because
they offer you an exquisite reproduction of the
things that surround you. All Venice was both
model and painter, and life was so pictorial that art
could not help becoming so. With all diminutions
life is pictorial still, and this fact gives an extraordinary freshness to one's perception of the great
Venetian works. You judge of them not as a con-
noisseur, but as a man of the world, and you enjoy
them because they are so social and so actual.
Perhaps, of all works of art that are equally great,
they demand least reflection on the part of the
spectator—they make least of a mystery of being
enjoyed. Reflection only confirms your admiration
but it is almost ashamed to show its head. These
things speak so frankly and benignantly to the sense
that we feel there is reason as well in such an
address. But it is hard, as I say, to express all
this, and it is painful as well to attempt it—painful,
because in the memory of vanished hours so filled

with beauty the sense of present loss is overwhelming. Exquisite hours, enveloped in light and
silence, to have known them once is to have always
a terrible standard of enjoyment. Certain lovely
mornings of May and June come back with an ineffaceable fairness. Venice is not smothered in
flowers at this season, in the manner of Florence
and Rome; but the sea and sky themselves seem
to blossom and rustle. The gondola waits at the
wave-washed steps, and if you are wise you will take
your place beside a discriminating companion. Such
a companion, in Venice, should, of course, be of the
sex that discriminates most finely. An intelligent
woman who knows her Venice seems doubly intelligent, and it makes no woman's perceptions less keen
to be aware that she cannot help looking graceful
as she glides over the waves. The handsome Pas-
quale, with uplifted oar, awaits your command,
knowing, in a general way, from observation of your
habits, that your intention is to go to see a picture
or two. It perhaps does not immensely matter what
picture you choose: the whole affair is so charming.
It is charming to wander through the light and
shade of intricate canals, with perpetual architecture
above you and perpetual fluidity beneath. It is
charming to disembark at the polished steps of a
little empty *campo*—a sunny, shabby square, with
an old well in the middle, an old church on one side,
and tall Venetian windows looking down. Sometimes the windows are tenantless; sometimes a
lady in a faded dressing-gown is leaning vaguely
on the sill. There is always an old man holding
out his hat for coppers; there are always three or

61

four small boys dodging possible umbrella-pokes while
they precede you, in the manner of custodians, to the
door of the church.

VI.

The churches of Venice are rich in pictures, and
many a masterpiece lurks in the unaccommodating
gloom of side-chapels and sacristies. Many a noble
work is perched behind the dusty candles and muslin
roses of a scantily-visited altar; some of them, indeed, are hidden behind the altar, in a darkness
that can never be explored. The facilities offered
you for approaching the picture, in such cases, are
a kind of mockery of your irritated desire. You
stand on tip-toe on a three-legged stool, you climb
a rickety ladder, you almost mount upon the
shoulders of the *custode*. You do everything but
see the picture You see just enough to perceive
that it is beautiful. You catch a glimpse of a
divine head, of a fig-tree against a mellow sky; but
the rest is impenetrable mystery. You renounce
all hope, for instance, of approaching the magnificent
Cima da Conegliano in San Giovanni in Bragora;
and bethinking yourself of the immaculate purity
that dwells in the works of this master, you renounce it with chagrin and pain. Behind the high
altar, in that church, there hangs a Baptism of Christ,
by Cima, which, I believe, has been more or less
repainted. You can make the thing out in spots;
you can see that it has a fulness of perfection. But
you turn away from it with a stiff neck, and promise yourself consolation in the Academy and at
the Madonna dell' Orto, where two noble pictures,

by the same hand—pictures as clear as a summer
twilight — present themselves in better circumstances. It may be said, as a general thing, that
you never see the Tintoret. You admire him, you
adore him, you think him the greatest of painters,
but, in the great majority of cases, you don't see
him. This is partly his own fault; so many of his
works have turned to blackness and are positively
rotting in their frames. At the Scuola di San
Rocco, where there are acres of the Tintoret, there is
scarcely anything at all adequately visible save the
immense " Crucifixion " in the upper story. It is
true that in looking at this huge composition you
look at many pictures; it has not only a multitude
of figures, but a wealth of episodes; and you pass
from one of these to the other as if you were " doing "
a gallery. Surely, no single picture in the world
contains more of human life; there is everything
in it, including the most exquisite beauty. It is
one of the greatest things of art; it is always
interesting. There are pictures by the Tintoret
which contain touches more exquisite, revelations of
beauty more radiant, but there is no other vision of
so intense a reality and an execution so splendid. The
interest, the impressiveness, of that whole corner
of Venice, however melancholy the effect of its
gorgeous and ill-lighted chambers, gives a strange
importance to a visit to the Scuola. Nothing that
all travellers go to see appears to suffer less from
the incursions of travellers. It is one of the lone-
liest booths of the bazaar, and the author of these
lines has always had the good fortune, which he
wishes to every other traveller, of having it to him-

self. I think most visitors find the place rather alarming and wicked-looking. They walk about a while among the fitful figures that gleam here and there out of the great tapestry (as it were) with which the painter has hung all the walls, and then, depressed and bewildered by the portentous solemnity of these objects, by strange glimpses of unnatural scenes, by the echo of their lonely footsteps on the vast stone floors, they take a hasty departure, and find themselves again, with a sense of release from danger, and of the *genius loci* having been a sort of mad white-washer, who worked with a bad mixture, in the bright light of the *campo*, among the beggars, the orange-vendors, and the passing gondolas. Solemn, indeed, is the place, solemn and strangely suggestive, for the simple reason that we shall scarcely find four walls elsewhere that inclose within a like area an equal quantity of genius. The air is thick with it, and dense and difficult to breathe; for it was genius that was not happy, inasmuch as it lacked the art to fix itself for ever. It is not immortality that we breathe at the Scuola di San Rocco, but conscious, reluctant mortality. Fortunately, however, we have the Ducal Palace, where everything is so brilliant and splendid that the poor dusky Tintoret is lifted in spite of himself into the concert. This deeply original building is, of course, the loveliest thing in Venice, and a morning's stroll there is a wonderful illumination. Cunningly select your hour — half the enjoyment of Venice is a question of dodging—and go at about one o'clock, when the tourists have gone to lunch and the echoes of the charming chambers have

gone to sleep among the sunbeams. There is no
brighter place in Venice ; by which I mean that, on
the whole, there is none half so bright. The reflected
sunshine plays up through the great windows from
the glittering lagoon, and shimmers and twinkles
over gilded walls and ceilings. All the history of
Venice, all its splendid, stately past, glows around
you in a strong sea-light. Every one here is
magnificent, but the great Veronese is the most
magnificent of all. He swims before you in a silver
cloud ; he thrones in an eternal morning. The
deep blue sky burns behind him, streaked across
with milky bars ; the white colonnades sustain the
richest canopies, under which the first gentlemen
and ladies in the world both render homage and
receive it. Their glorious garments rustle in the air
of the sea, and their sun-lighted faces are the very
complexion of Venice. The mixture of pride and
piety, of politics and religion, of art and patriotism,
gives a magnificent dignity to every scene. Never
was a painter more nobly joyous, never did an artist
take a greater delight in life, seeing it all as a kind
of breezy festival and feeling it through the medium
of perpetual success. He revels in the gold-framed
ovals of the ceilings, with the fluttering movement
of an embroidered banner that tosses itself into the
blue. He was the happiest of painters, and he
produced the happiest picture in the world. The
" Rape of Europa " surely deserves this title ; it is
impossible to look at it without aching with envy.
Nowhere else in art is such a temperament revealed ;
never did inclination and opportunity combine to
express such enjoyment. The mixture of flowers

and gems and brocade, of blooming flesh and shining
sea and waving groves, of youth, health, movement,
desire—all this is the brightest vision that ever
descended upon the soul of a painter. Happy the
artist who could entertain such a vision; happy the
artist who could paint it as the "Rape of Europa"
is painted. The Tintoret's visions were not so
bright as that; but he had several that were radiant
enough. In the room that contains the "Rape of
Europa" are several smaller canvases by the greatly
more complex genius of the Scuola di San Rocco,
which are almost simple in their loveliness, almost
happy in their simplicity. They have kept their
brightness through the centuries, and they shine
with their neighbours in those golden rooms. There
is a piece of painting in one of them which is one of
the sweetest things in Venice, and which reminds
one afresh of those wild flowers of execution that
bloom so profusely and so unheeded in the dark
corners of all of the Tintoret's work. "Pallas chas-
ing away Mars" is, I believe, the name that is given
to the picture; and it represents in fact a young
woman of noble appearance administering a gentle
push to a fine young man in armour, as if to tell
him to keep his distance. It is of the gentleness
of this push that I speak, the charming way in
which she puts out her arm, with a single bracelet
on it, and rests her young hand, with its rosy fingers
parted, upon his dark breastplate. She bends her
enchanting head with the effort—a head which has
all the strange fairness that the Tintoret always sees
in women—and the soft, living, flesh-like glow of all
these members, over which the brush has scarcely

66

paused in its course, is as pretty an example of
genius as all Venice can show. But why speak of
the Tintoret when I can say nothing of the great
" Paradise," which unfolds its somewhat smoky
splendour, and the wonder of its multitudinous
circles, in one of the other chambers ? If it were
not one of the first pictures in the world, it would
be about the biggest, and it must be confessed that
at first the spectator gets from it chiefly an impression of quantity. Then he sees that this quantity
is really wealth ; that the dim confusion of faces is
a magnificent composition, and that some of the
details of this composition are supremely beautiful.
It is impossible, however, in a retrospect of Venice,
to specify one's happiest hours, though, as one looks
backward, certain ineffaceable moments start here
and there into vividness. How is it possible to
forget one's visits to the sacristy of the Frari, however frequent they may have been, and the great
work of John Bellini which forms the treasure of
that apartment ?

VII.

Nothing in Venice is more perfect than this, and
we know of no work of art more complete. The
picture is in three compartments : the Virgin sits
in the central division with her child ; two venerable saints, standing close together, occupy each of
the others. It is impossible to imagine anything
more finished or more ripe. It is one of those
things that sum up the genius of a painter, the experience of a life, the teaching of a school. It
seems painted with molten gems, which have only

been clarified by time, and it is as solemn as it is gorgeous, and as simple as it is deep. John Bellini is, more or less, everywhere in Venice, and wherever he is, he is almost certain to be first—first, I mean, in his own line; he paints little else than the Madonna and the saints; he has not Carpaccio's care for human life at large, nor the Tintoret's, nor that of the Veronese. Some of his greater pictures, however, where several figures are clustered together, have a richness of sanctity that is almost profane. There is one of them on the dark side of the room at the Academy, containing Titian's " Assumption," which, if we could only see it—its position is an inconceivable scandal—would evidently be one of the mightiest of so-called sacred pictures. So, too, is the Madonna of San Zaccaria, hung in a cold, dim, dreary place, ever so much too high, but so mild and serene, and so grandly disposed and accompanied, that the proper attitude for even the most critical amateur, as he looks at it, seems to be the bended knee. There is another noble John Bellini, one of the very few in which there is no Virgin, at San Giovanni Crisostomo—a St. Jerome, in a red dress, sitting aloft upon the rocks, with a landscape of extraordinary purity behind him. The absence of the peculiarly erect Madonna makes it an interesting surprise among the works of the painter, and gives it a somewhat less strenuous air. But it has brilliant beauty, and the St. Jerome is a delightful old personage. The same church contains another great picture, for which he must find a shrine apart in his memory; one of the most interesting things he will have seen, if not the most brilliant. Nothing appeals

more to him than three figures of Venetian ladies
which occupy the foreground of a smallish canvas of
Sebastian del Piombo, placed above the high altar
of San Giovanni Crisostomo. Sebastian was a Venetian by birth, but few of his productions are to be
seen in his native place; few, indeed, are to be seen
anywhere. The picture represents the patron-saint
of the church, accompanied by other saints, and
by the worldly votaries I have mentioned. These
ladies stand together on the left, holding in their
hands little white caskets; two of them are in profile, but the foremost turns her face to the spectator.
This face and figure are almost unique among the
beautiful things of Venice, and they leave the susceptible observer with the impression of having
made, or rather having missed, a strange, a danger-
ous, but a most valuable, acquaintance. The lady,
who is superbly handsome, is the typical Venetian
of the sixteenth century, and she remains in the
mind as the perfect flower of that society. Never
was there a greater air of breeding, a deeper expression of tranquil superiority. She walks like a
goddess—as if she trod, without sinking, the waves
of the Adriatic. It is impossible to conceive a
more perfect expression of the aristocratic spirit,
either in its pride or in its benignity. This magnificent creature is so strong and secure that she
is gentle, and so quiet that, in comparison, all minor
assumptions of calmness suggest only a vulgar alarm.
But for all this, there are depths of possible disorder in her light-coloured eye. I had meant, however, to say nothing about her, for it is not right to
speak of Sebastian when one has not found room

for Carpaccio. These visions come to one, and one can neither hold them nor brush them aside. Memories of Carpaccio, the magnificent, the delightful—it is not for want of such visitations, but only for want of space, that I have not said of him what I would. There is little enough need of it for Carpaccio's sake, his fame being brighter to-day—thanks to the generous lamp Mr. Ruskin has held up to it—than it has ever been. Yet there is something ridiculous in talking of Venice without making him, almost, the refrain. He and the Tintoret are the two great realists, and it is hard to say which is the more human, the more various. The Tintoret had the mightier temperament, but Carpaccio, who had the advantage of more newness and more responsibility, sailed nearer to perfection. Here and there he quite touches it, as in the enchanting picture, at the Academy, of St. Ursula asleep in her little white bed, in her high, clean room, where the angel visits her at dawn; or in the noble St. Jerome in his study, at S. Giorgio degli Schiavoni. This latter work is a pearl of sentiment, and I may add, without being fantastic, a ruby of colour. It unites the most masterly finish with a kind of universal largeness of feeling, and he who has it well in his memory will never hear the name of Carpaccio without a throb of almost personal affection. This, indeed, is the feeling that descends upon you in that wonderful little chapel of St. George of the Slaves, where this most personal and sociable of artists has expressed all the sweetness of his imagination. The place is small and incommodious, the pictures are out of sight and ill-lighted, the custodian is rapacious, the visitors are mutually intolerable, but the shabby little chapel is a palace of art. Mr. Ruskin has written a pamphlet about it which is a real aid to enjoyment, though I cannot but think the generous artist, with his keen senses and his just feeling, would have suffered at hearing his eulogist declare that one of his other productions—in the Museo Civico in Palazzo Correr, a delightful portrait of two Venetian ladies, with pet animals—is the " finest picture in the world." It has no need of that to be thought admirable; and what more can a painter desire?

VIII.

May in Venice is better than April, but June is best of all. Then the days are hot, but not too hot, and the nights are more beautiful than the days. Then Venice is rosier than ever in the morning, and more golden than ever as the day descends. It seems to expand and evaporate, to multiply all its reflections and iridescences. Then the life of its people and the strangeness of its constitution become a perpetual comedy, or, at least, a perpetual drama. Then the gondola is your sole habitation, and you spend days between sea and sky. You go to the Lido, though the Lido has been spoiled. When I was first in Venice, in 1869, it was a very natural place, and there was only a rough lane across the little island from the landing-place to the beach. There was a bathing-place in those days, and a restaurant, which was very bad, but where, in the warm evenings, your dinner did not much matter as you sat letting it cool upon

71

the wooden terrace that stretched out into the sea. To-day the Lido is a part of united Italy, and has been made the victim of villainous improvements. A little cockney village has sprung up on its rural bosom, and a third-rate boulevard leads from Santa Elisabetta to the Adriatic. There are bitumen walls and gas-lamps, lodging-houses, shops, and a *teatro diurno*. The bathing-establishment is bigger than before, and the restaurant as well; but it is a compensation, perhaps, that the cuisine is no better. Such as it is, however, you will not scorn occasionally to partake of it on the breezy platform under which bathers dart and splash, and which looks out to where the fishing-boats, with sails of orange and crimson, wander along the darkening horizon. The beach at the Lido is still lonely and beautiful, and you can easily walk away from the cockney village. The return to Venice in the sunset is classical and indispensable, and those who, at that glowing hour, have floated toward the towers that rise out of the lagoon, will not easily part with the impression. But you indulge in larger excursions—you go to Burano and Torcello, to Malamocco and Chioggia. Torcello, like the Lido, has been improved; the deeply interesting little cathedral of the eighth century, which stood there on the edge of the sea, as touching in its ruin, with its grassy threshold and its primitive mosaics, as the bleached bones of a human skeleton washed ashore by the tide, has now been restored and made cheerful, and the charm of the place, its strange and suggestive desolation, has well-nigh departed. It will still serve you as a pretext, however, for a day

72

on the lagoon, especially as you will disembark at
Burano and admire the wonderful fisher-folk, whose
good looks—and bad manners, I am sorry to say—
can scarcely be exaggerated. Burano is celebrated
for the beauty of its women and the rapacity of its
children, and it is a fact that though some of the
ladies are rather bold about it, every one of them
shows you a handsome face. The children assail
you for coppers, and, in their desire to be satisfied,
pursue your gondola into the sea. Chioggia is a
larger Burano, and you carry away from either place
a half-sad, half-cynical, but altogether pictorial impression; the impression of bright-coloured hovels,
of bathing in stagnant canals, of young girls with
faces of a delicate shape and a susceptible expression, with splendid heads of hair and complexions
smeared with powder, faded yellow shawls that hang
like old Greek draperies, and little wooden shoes
that click as they go up and down the steps of the
convex bridges; of brown-cheeked matrons with
lustrous tresses and high tempers, massive throats
encased with gold beads, and eyes that meet your
own with a certain traditional defiance. The men
throughout the islands of Venice are almost as handsome as the women; I have never seen so many
good-looking fellows. At Burano and Chioggia
they sit mending their nets, or lounge at the street
corners, where conversation is always high-pitched,
or clamour to you to take a boat; and everywhere
they decorate the scene with their splendid colour—
cheeks and throats as richly brown as the sails of
their fishing-smacks—their sea-faded tatters which
are always a "costume"—their soft Venetian jargon,

and the gallantry with which they wear their hats
—an article that nowhere sits so well as on a mass
of dense Venetian curls. If you are happy, you will
find yourself, after a June day in Venice (about ten
o'clock), on a balcony that overhangs the Grand
Canal, with your elbows on the broad ledge, a cigar-
ette in your teeth, and a little good company beside
you. The gondolas pass beneath, the watery surface
gleams here and there from their lamps, some of
which are coloured lanterns that move mysteriously
in the darkness. There are some evenings in June
when there are too many gondolas, too many lanterns, too many serenades in front of the hotels.
The serenading (in particular) is overdone; but on
such a balcony as I speak of you needn't suffer from
it, for in the apartment behind you — an accessible
refuge—there is more good company, there are more
cigarettes. If you are wise you will step back there
presently.

Italy Revisited

I WAITED in Paris until after the elections for the new Chamber (they took place on the 14th of October); for only after one had learned that the celebrated attempt of Marshal MacMahon and his ministers to drive the French nation to the polls like a flock of huddling sheep, each with the white ticket of an official candidate round his neck, had not achieved the success which the energy of the process might have promised — only then was it possible to draw a long breath and deprive the republican party of such support as might have been conveyed in one's sympathetic presence. Seriously speaking, too, the weather had been enchanting, and there were Italian sensations to be encountered without leaving the banks of the Seine. Day after day the air was filled with golden light, and even those chalkish vistas of the Parisian *beaux quartiers* assumed the iridescent tints of autumn. Autumn-weather in Europe is often such a very sorry affair that a fair-minded American will have it on his

77

conscience to call attention to a rainless and radiant October.

The echoes of the electoral strife kept me company for a while after starting upon that abbreviated journey to Turin, which, as you leave Paris at night, in a train unprovided with encouragements to slumber, is a singular mixture of the odious and the charming. The charming, however, I think, prevails; for the dark half of the journey is, in fact, the least interesting. The morning light ushers you into the romantic gorges of the Jura, and after a big bowl of *café au lait* at Culoz you may compose yourself comfortably for the climax of your spectacle. The day before leaving Paris I met a French friend who had just returned from a visit to a Tuscan country-seat, where he had been watching the vintage. "Italy," he said, "is more lovely than words can tell, and France, steeped in this electoral turmoil, seems no better than a bear-garden." That part of the bear-garden through which you travel as you approach the Mont-Cenis seemed to me that day very beautiful. The autumn colouring, thanks to the absence of rain, had been vivid and crisp, and the vines that swung their low garlands between the mulberries, in the neighbourhood of Chambéry, looked like long festoons of coral and amber. The frontier station of Modane, on the farther side of the Mont-Cenis tunnel, is a very ill-regulated place; but even the most irritable of tourists, meeting it on his way southward, will be disposed to consider it good-naturedly. There is far too much bustling and scrambling, and the facilities afforded you for the obligatory process of ripping

78

open your luggage before the officers of the Italian custom-house are much scantier than should be; but, for myself, there is something that deprecates irritation in the shabby green and gray uniforms of all the Italian officials who stand loafing about and watching the northern invaders scramble back into marching order. Wearing an administrative uniform does not necessarily spoil a man's temper, as in France one is sometimes led to believe; for these excellent under-paid Italians carry theirs as lightly as possible, and their answers to your inquiries do not in the least bristle with rapiers, buttons, and cockades. After leaving Modane you slide straight downhill into the Italy of your desire; and there is something very impressive in the way the road edges along those great precipices which stand shoulder to shoulder, in a long perpendicular file, until they finally admit you to a distant glimpse of the ancient capital of Piedmont.

Turin is not a city to make, in vulgar parlance, a fuss about, and I pay an extravagant tribute to subjective emotion in speaking of it as ancient. But if the place is not so peninsular as Florence and Rome, at least it is more so than New York and Paris; and while the traveller walks about the great arcades and looks at the fourth-rate shop windows, he does not scruple to cultivate a shameless optimism. Relatively speaking, Turin is diverting; but there is, after all, no reason in a large collection of shabbily-stuccoed houses, disposed in a rigidly rectangular manner, for passing a day of deep, still gaiety. The only reason, I am afraid, is the old superstition of Italy—that property in the very look of the written word, the evocation of a myriad images, that makes any lover of the arts take Italian satisfactions upon easier terms than any other. Italy is an idea to conjure with, and we play tricks upon our credulity even with such inferior apparatus as is offered to our hand at Turin. I walked about all the morning under the tall porticoes, thinking it sufficient entertainment to take note of the soft, warm air, of that colouring of things in Italy that is at once broken and harmonious, and of the comings and goings, the physiognomy and manners, of the excellent Turinese. I had opened the old book again; the old charm was in the style; I was in a more delightful world. I saw nothing surpassingly beautiful or curious; but the appreciative traveller finds a vividness in nameless details. And I must add that on the threshold of Italy he tastes of one solid and perfectly definable pleasure, in finding himself among the traditions of the grand style in architecture. It must be said that we have still to come to Italy to see great houses. (I am speaking more particularly of town-architecture.) In northern cities there are beautiful houses, picturesque and curious houses; sculptured gables that hang over the street, charming bay-windows, hooded doorways, elegant proportions, and a profusion of delicate ornament; but a good specimen of an old Italian palazzo has a nobleness that is all its own. We laugh at Italian "palaces," at their peeling paint, their nudity, their dreariness; but they have the great palatial quality—elevation and extent. They make smaller houses seem beggarly; they round their great arches and interspace their huge windows with a noble indifference to the cost of materials. These grand proportions—the colossal basements, the doorways that seem meant for cathedrals, the far-away cornices—impart by contrast a humble and *bourgeois* expression to those less exalted dwellings in which the air of grandeur depends largely upon the help of the upholsterer. At Turin my first feeling was really one of shame for the architectural manners of our northern lands. I have heard people who know the Italians well say that at bottom they despise all the rest of mankind and regard them as barbarians. I doubt of it, for the Italians strike me as having less national vanity than any other people in Europe; but if the charge had its truth there would be some ground for the feeling in the fact that they live in palaces.

An impression which, on coming back to Italy, I find even stronger than when it was first received is that of the contrast between the fecundity of the great artistic period and the vulgarity of the Italian genius of to-day. The first few hours spent on Italian soil are sufficient to renew it, and the phenomenon that I allude to is surely one of the most singular in human history. That the people who but three hundred years ago had the best taste in the world should now have the worst; that having produced the noblest, loveliest, costliest works, they should now be given up to the manufacture of objects at once ugly and paltry; that the race of which Michael Angelo and Raphael, Leonardo and Titian were characteristic should have no other title to distinction than third-rate *genre* pictures and catchpenny statues—all this is a frequent perplexity to the observer of actual Italian life. The flower of art in these latter years has ceased to bloom very powerfully anywhere; but nowhere does it seem so drooping and withered as in the shadow of the immortal embodiments of the old Italian genius. You go into a church or a gallery and feast your fancy upon a splendid picture or an exquisite piece of sculpture, and on issuing from the door that has admitted you to the beautiful past you are confronted with something that has all the effect of a very bad joke. The aspect of your lodging (the carpets, the curtains, the upholstery in general, with their crude and violent colouring and their vulgar material), the third-rate look of the shops, the extreme bad taste of the dress of the women, the cheapness and baseness of every attempt at decoration in the cafés and railway stations, the hopeless frivolity of everything that pretends to be a work of art—all this modern crudity runs riot over the relics of the great period.

We can do a thing for the first time but once; it is but once for all that we can have a pleasure in its freshness. This is a law which is not on the whole, I think, to be regretted, for we sometimes learn to know things better by not enjoying them too much. It is certain, however, at the same time, that a traveller who has worked off the primal fermentation of his relish for this inexhaustibly interesting country has by no means entirely drained the cup. After thinking of Italy as historical and artistic, it will do him no great harm to think of her, for a while, as modern, an idea supposed (as a general thing correctly) to be fatally at variance with the Byronic, the Ruskinian, the artistic, poetic, æsthetic manner of considering this fascinating peninsula. He may grant—I don't say it is absolutely necessary—that modern Italy is ugly, prosaic, provokingly out of relation to the diary and the album; it is nevertheless true that, at the point things have come to, modern Italy in a manner imposes herself. I had not been many hours in the country before I became conscious of this circumstance; and I may add that, the first irritation past, I found myself able to accept it. And if we think of it, nothing is more easy to understand than a certain displeasure on the part of the young Italy of to-day at being looked at by all the world as a kind of soluble pigment. Young Italy, preoccupied with its economical and political future, must be heartily tired of being admired for its eyelashes and its pose In one of Thackeray's novels there is mention of a young artist who sent to the ˜Royal Academy a picture representing " A Contadino dancing with a Trasteverina at the door of a Locanda, to the music of a Pifferaro." It is in this attitude and with these conventional accessories that the world has hitherto seen fit to represent young Italy, and I do not wonder that, if the youth has any spirit, he should at last begin to resent our insufferable æsthetic patronage. He has established a line of tram-cars in Rome, from the Porta del Popolo to the Ponte Molle, and it is on one of these democratic vehicles that I seem to see him taking his triumphant course down the vista of the future. I will not pretend to rejoice with him any more than I really do; I will not pretend, as the sentimental

83

tourists say about it all, as if it were the setting
of an intaglio or the border of a Roman scarf, to
"like" it. Like it or not, as we may, it is evidently
destined to be ; I see a new Italy in the future
which in many important respects will equal, if not
surpass, the most enterprising sections of our native
land. Perhaps by that time Chicago and San Fran-
cisco will have acquired a pose, and their sons and
daughters will dance at the doors of *locande*. However this may be, a vivid impression of an accomplished schism between the old Italy and the new
is, as the French say, *le plus clair* of a new visit
to this ever-suggestive part of the world. The old
Italy has become more and more of a museum,
preserved and perpetuated in the midst of the new,
but without any further relation to it—it must be
admitted, indeed, that such a relation is considerable—than that of the stock on his shelves to the
shopkeeper, or of the Siren of the South to the
showman who stands before his booth. More than
once, as we move about nowadays in the Italian
cities, there seems to pass before our eyes a vision
of the coming years. It represents to our satisfaction an Italy united and prosperous, but altogether commercial. The Italy, indeed, that we
sentimentalise and romance about was an ardently
mercantile country ; though I suppose it loved not
its ledgers less, but its frescoes and altar-pieces
more. Scattered through this brilliantly economical
community—this country of a thousand ports—we
see a large number of beautiful buildings, in which
an endless series of dusky pictures are darkening,
dampening, fading, failing, through the years. At

the doors of the beautiful buildings are little turn-
stiles, at which there sit a great many men in
uniform, to whom the visitor pays a ten-penny fee.
Inside, in the vaulted and frescoed chambers, the
art of Italy lies buried, as in a thousand mauso-
leums. It is well taken care of; it is constantly
copied; sometimes it is "restored"—as in the case
of that beautiful boy-figure of Andrea del Sarto, at
Florence, which may be seen at the gallery of the
Uffizi, with its honourable duskiness quite peeled
off and heaven knows what raw, bleeding cuticle
laid bare. One evening lately, in Florence, in the
soft twilight, I took a stroll among those encircling
hills on which the massive villas are mingled with
the vaporous olives. Presently I arrived where three
roads met at a wayside shrine, in which, before
some pious daub of an old-time Madonna, a little
votive lamp glimmered through the evening air.
The hour, the lovely evening, the place, the twinkling taper, the sentiment of the observer, the thought
that some one had been rescued here from an
assassin, or from some other peril, and had set up a
little grateful altar in consequence, in the yellow-
plastered wall of a tangled *podere ;* all this led me
to approach the shrine with a reverent, an emotional
step. I drew near it, but after a few steps I paused.
I became conscious of an incongruous odour; it
seemed to me that the evening air was charged
with a perfume which, although to a certain extent
familiar, had not hitherto associated itself with
rustic frescoes and wayside altars. I gently interro-
gated the atmosphere, and the operation left me no
doubts. The odour was that of petroleum; the

votive taper was nourished with the national fluid
of Pennsylvania. I confess that I burst out laughing, and a picturesque contadino, wending his homeward way in the dusk, stared at me as if I were an
iconoclast. If he noticed the petroleum, it was only,
I imagine, to sniff it gratefully; but to me the thing
served as a symbol of the Italy of the future. There
is a horse-car from the Porta del Popolo to the
Ponte Molle, and the Tuscan shrines are fed with
kerosene.

II.

If it is very well to come to Turin first, it is
still better to go to Genoa afterwards. Genoa is
the queerest place in the world, and even a second
visit helps you little to straighten it out. In the
wonderful crooked, twisting, climbing, soaring, bur-
rowing Genoese alleys the traveller is really up to
his neck in the old Italian sketchability. Genoa is,
I believe, a port of great capacity, and the bequest
of the late Duke of Galliera, who left four millions
of dollars for the purpose of improving and enlarging
it, will doubtless do much toward converting it into
one of the great commercial stations of Europe. But
as, after leaving my hotel the afternoon I arrived,
I wandered for a long time at hazard through the
tortuous byways of the city, I said to myself, not
without an accent of private triumph, that here
was something it would be almost impossible to
modernise. I had found my hotel, in the first
place, extremely entertaining—the Croce di Malta,
as it was called, established in a gigantic palace
on the edge of the swarming and not over-clean

harbour. It was the biggest house I had ever
entered, and the basement alone would have contained a dozen American caravansaries. I met an
American gentleman in the vestibule who (as he
had indeed a perfect right to be) was annoyed by
its troublesome dimensions—one was a quarter of
an hour ascending out of the basement—and desired
to know whether it was a "fair sample" of the
Genoese inns. It appeared to be an excellent
specimen of Genoese architecture generally; so far
as I observed, there were few houses perceptibly
smaller than this Titanic tavern. I lunched in a
dusky ballroom, whose ceiling was vaulted, frescoed
and gilded with the fatal facility of a couple of
centuries ago, and which looked out upon another
ancient house-front, equally huge and equally
battered, from which it was separated only by a
little wedge of dusky space (one of the principal
streets, I believe, of Genoa), out of the bottom of
which the Genoese populace sent up to the windows
— I had to crane out very far to see it—a perpetual clattering, shuffling, chaffering sound. Issuing forth, presently, into this crevice of a street, I
found an abundance of that soft local colour for the
love of which one revisits Italy. It offered itself,
indeed, in a variety of tints, some of which were
not remarkable for their freshness or purity. But
their combined effect was highly pictorial, and the
picture was a very rich and various representation
of southern low-life. Genoa is the crookedest and
most incoherent of cities; tossed about on the
sides and crests of a dozen hills, it is seamed with
gullies and ravines that bristle with those innumer-

able palaces for which we have heard from our
earliest years that the place is celebrated. These
great edifices, with their mottled and faded complexions, lift their big ornamental cornices to a
tremendous height in the air, where, in a certain
indescribably forlorn and desolate fashion, over-
topping each other, they seem to reflect the twinkle
and glitter of the warm Mediterranean. Down
about the basements, in the little dim, close alleys,
the people are for ever moving to and fro, or standing in their cavernous doorways and their dusky,
crowded shops, calling, chattering, laughing, scrambling, living their lives in the conversational Italian
fashion. For a long time I had not received such
an impression of the human agglomeration. I
had not for a long time seen people elbowing each
other so closely, or swarming so thickly out of
populous hives. A traveller is very often disposed
to ask himself whether it has been worth while to
leave his home—whatever his home may have
been—only to see new forms of human suffering,
only to be reminded that toil and privation, hunger
and sorrow and sordid effort, are the portion of the
great majority of his fellow-men. To travel is, as
it were, to go to the play, to attend a spectacle ;
and there is something heartless in stepping forth
into the streets of a foreign town to feast upon
novelty when the novelty consists simply of the
slightly different costume in which hunger and
labour present themselves. These reflections were
forced upon me as I strolled about in those crepus-
cular, stale-smelling alleys of Genoa; but after a
time they ceased to bear me company. The reason

of this, I think, is because (at least to foreign eyes) the sum of Italian misery is, on the whole, less than the sum of the Italian knowledge of life. That people should thank you, with a smile of striking sweetness, for the gift of twopence is a proof, certainly, of an extreme and constant destitution; but (keeping in mind the sweetness) it is also a proof of an enviable ability not to be depressed by circumstances. I know that this may possibly be great nonsense; that half the time that we are admiring the brightness of the Italian smile the romantic natives may be, in reality, in a sullen frenzy of impatience and pain. Our observation in any foreign land is extremely superficial, and our remarks are happily not addressed to the inhabitants themselves, who would be sure to exclaim upon the impudence of the fancy-picture. The other day I visited a very picturesque old city upon a mountain-top, where, in the course of my wanderings, I arrived at an old disused gate in the ancient town-wall. The gate had not been absolutely forfeited; but the recent completion of a modern road down the mountain led most vehicles away to another egress. The grass-grown pavement, which wound into the plain by a hundred graceful twists and plunges, was now given up to ragged contadini and their donkeys, and to such wayfarers as were not alarmed at the disrepair into which it had fallen. I stood in the shadow of the tall old gateway admiring the scene, looking to right and left at the wonderful walls of the little town, perched on the edge of a shaggy precipice; at the circling mountains over against them; at the road dipping

89

downward among the chestnuts and olives. There was no one within sight but a young man, who was slowly trudging upward, with his coat slung over his shoulder and his hat upon his ear, like a cavalier in an opera. Like an operatic performer, too, he was singing as he came; the spectacle, generally, was operatic, and as his vocal flourishes reached my ear I said to myself that in Italy accident was always picturesque, and that such a figure had been exactly what was wanted to set off the landscape. It suggested in a high degree that knowledge of life for which I just now commended the Italians. I was turning back, under the old gateway, into the town, when the young man overtook me, and, suspending his song, asked me if I could favour him with a match to light the hoarded remnant of a cigar. This request led, as I walked back to the inn, to my having some conversation with him. He was a native of the ancient city, and answered freely all my inquiries as to its manners and customs and the state of public opinion there. But the point of my anecdote is that he presently proved to be a brooding young radical and communist, filled with hatred of the present Italian government, raging with discontent and crude political passion, professing a ridiculous hope that Italy would soon have, as France had had, her " '89," and declaring that he, for his part, would willingly lend a hand to chop off the heads of the king and the royal family. He was an unhappy, underfed, unemployed young man, who took a hard, grim view of everything, and was operatic only quite in spite of himself. This made it very absurd of me to have looked at him simply as a graceful ornament to the prospect, an harmonious little figure in the middle distance. " Damn the prospect, damn the middle distance!" would have been all *his* philosophy. Yet, but for the accident of my having a little talk with him, I should have made him do service, in memory, as an example of sensuous optimism!

I am bound to say, however, that I believe that a great deal of the sensuous optimism that I noticed in the Genoese alleys and beneath the low, crowded arcades along the port was very real. Here every one was magnificently sunburnt, and there were plenty of those queer types, mahogany-coloured, bare-chested mariners, with earrings and crimson girdles, that make a southern seaport entertaining. But it is not fair to speak as if at Genoa there were nothing but low-life to be seen, for the place is the residence of some of the grandest people in the world. Nor are all the palaces ranged upon dusky alleys; the handsomest and most impressive form a splendid series on each side of a couple of very proper streets, in which there is plenty of room for a coach-and-four to approach the big doorways. Many of these doorways are open, revealing great marble staircases, with couchant lions for balustrades, and ceremonious courts surrounded by walls of sun-softened yellow. One of the palaces is coloured a goodly red, and contains, in particular, the grand people I just now spoke of. They live, indeed, in the third story; but here they have suites of wonderful painted and gilded chambers, in which there are many foreshortened frescoes in

91

the vaulted ceilings, and the walls are embossed
with the most florid mouldings. These distinguished
tenants bear the name of Vandyke, though they are
members of the noble family of Brignole-Sale, one
of whose children (the Duchess of Galliera) has
lately given proof of nobleness in presenting the
gallery of the Red Palace to the city of Genoa.

III.

On leaving Genoa I repaired to Spezia, chiefly
with a view of accomplishing a sentimental pilgrimage, which I, in fact, achieved, in the most agreeable
conditions. The Gulf of Spezia is now the headquarters of the Italian fleet, and there were several
big iron-plated frigates riding at anchor in front of
the town. The streets were filled with lads in blue
flannel, who were receiving instruction at a school-
ship in the harbour, and in the evening—there
was a brilliant moon—the little breakwater which
stretched out into the Mediterranean offered a promenade to the naval functionaries. But this fact
is, from the tourist's point of view, of little account,
for since it has become prosperous Spezia has grown
ugly. The place is filled with long, dull stretches
of dead wall and great raw expanses of artificial
land. It wears that look of monstrous, of more
than Occidental, newness which distinguishes all
the creations of the young Italian state. Nor did
I find any great compensation in an immense new
inn, which has lately been deposited by the edge
of the sea, in anticipation of a *passeggiata* which is
to come that way some five years hence, the region

being in the meantime of the most primitive forma-
tion. The inn was filled with grave English people,
who looked respectable and bored, and there was of
course a Church of England service in the gaudily-
frescoed parlour. Neither was it the drive to Porto
Venere that chiefly pleased me—a drive among vines
and olives — over the hills and beside the sea, to
a queer little crumbling village on a headland, as
sweetly desolate and superannuated as the name it
bears. There is a ruined church near the village,
which occupies the site (according to tradition) of
an ancient temple of Venus; and if Venus ever
revisits her desecrated shrines she must sometimes
pause a moment in that sunny stillness, and listen
to the murmur of the tideless sea at the base of
the narrow promontory. If Venus sometimes comes
there, Apollo surely does as much; for close to the
temple is a gateway, surmounted by an inscription
in Italian and English, which admits you to a curious
(and it must be confessed rather cockneyfied) cave
among the rocks. It was here, says the inscription,
that the great Byron, swimmer and poet, "defied the
waves of the Ligurian sea." The fact is interesting,
though not supremely so; for Byron was always defy-
ing something, and if a slab had been put up where-
ever this performance came off, these commemorative
tablets would be, in many parts of Europe, as thick
as milestones. No; the great merit of Spezia, to
my eye, is that I engaged a boat there of a lovely
October afternoon, and had myself rowed across
the gulf—it took about an hour and a half—to the
little bay of Lerici, which opens out of it. This
bay of Lerici is charming; the bosky gray-green

hills close it in, and on either side of the entrance, perched upon a bold headland, a wonderful old crumbling castle keeps ineffectual guard. The place is classic for all English travellers, for in the middle of the curving shore is the now desolate little villa in which Shelley spent the last months of his short life. He was living at Lerici when he started on that short southern cruise from which he never returned. The house he occupied is strangely shabby, and as sad as you may choose to find it. It stands directly upon the beach, with scarred and battered walls, and a loggia of several arches opening upon a little terrace with a rugged parapet, which, when the wind blows, must be drenched with the salt spray. The place is very lonely—all overwearied with sun and breeze and brine—very close to nature, as it was Shelley's passion to be. I can fancy a great lyric poet sitting on the terrace, of a warm evening, far from England, in the early years of the century. In that place, and with his genius, he would, as a matter of course, have heard in the voice of nature a sweetness which only the lyric movement could translate. It is a place where an English-speaking traveller may very honestly be sentimental and feel moved, himself, to lyric utterance. But I must content myself with saying in halting prose that I remember few episodes of Italian travel more sympathetic, as they have it here, than that perfect autumn afternoon; the half-hour's station on the little battered terrace of the villa ; the climb to the singularly picturesque old castle that hangs above Lerici ; the meditative lounge, in the fading light, on the vine-decked platform that looked out toward

the sunset and the darkening mountains, and, far
below, upon the quiet sea, beyond which the pale-
faced villa stared up at the brightening moon.

IV.

I had never known Florence more charming
than I found her for a week in that brilliant
October. She sat in the sunshine beside her yellow
river like the little treasure-city that she has always
seemed, without commerce, without other industry
than the manufacture of mosaic paper-weights and
alabaster Cupids, without actuality, or energy, or
earnestness, or any of those rugged virtues which
in most cases are deemed indispensable for civic
robustness; with nothing but the little unaug-
mented stock of her mediæval memories, her tender-
coloured mountains, her churches and palaces, pictures and statues. There were very few strangers;
one's detested fellow sight-seer was infrequent; the
native population itself seemed scanty; the sound
of wheels in the streets was but occasional; by
eight o'clock at night, apparently, every one had
gone to bed, and the wandering tourist, still wandering, had the place to himself—had the thick
shadow-masses of the great palaces, and the shafts
of moonlight striking the polygonal paving-stones,
and the empty bridges, and the silvered yellow of the
Arno, and the stillness broken only by a homeward
step, accompanied by a snatch of song from a warm
Italian voice. My room at the inn looked out on
the river, and was flooded all day with sunshine.
There was an absurd orange-coloured paper on the

walls; the Arno, of a hue not altogether different, flowed beneath; and on the other side of it rose a line of sallow houses, of extreme antiquity, crumbling and mouldering, bulging and protruding over the stream. (I seem to speak of their fronts; but what I saw was their shabby backs, which were exposed to the cheerful flicker of the river, while the fronts stood for ever in the deep, damp shadow of a narrow mediæval street.) All this brightness and yellowness was a perpetual delight; it was a part of that indefinably charming colour which Florence always seems to wear as you look up and down at it from the river, from the bridges and quays. This is a kind of grave brilliancy—a harmony of high tints—which I know not how to describe. There are yellow walls and green blinds and red roofs, and intervals of brilliant brown and natural-looking blue; but the picture is not spotty nor gaudy, thanks to the colours being distributed in large and comfortable masses, and to its being washed over, as it were, by some happy softness of sunshine. The river-front of Florence is, in short, a delightful composition. Part of its charm comes, of course, from the generous aspect of those high-based Tuscan palaces which a renewal of acquaintance with them has again commended to me as the most dignified dwellings in the world. Nothing can be finer than that look of giving up the whole immense ground-floor to simple purposes of vestibule and staircase, of court and high-arched entrance; as if this were all but a massive pedestal for the real habitation, and people were not properly housed unless, to begin with, they should be lifted fifty feet above the pavement. The great blocks of the basement; the great intervals, horizontally and vertically, from window to window (telling of the height and breadth of the rooms within); the armorial shield hung forward at one of the angles; the wide-brimmed roof, overshadowing the narrow street; the rich old browns and yellows of the walls—these definite elements are put together with admirable art.

Take one of these noble structures out of its oblique situation in the town; call it no longer a palace, but a villa; set it down upon a terrace, on one of the hills that encircle Florence, with a row of high-waisted cypresses beside it, a grassy courtyard, and a view of the Florentine towers and the valley of the Arno, and you will think it perhaps even more worthy of your esteem. It was a Sunday noon, and brilliantly warm, when I arrived in Florence; and after I had looked from my windows a while at that quietly-basking river-front I have spoken of, I took my way across one of the bridges and then out of one of the gates—that immensely tall Roman Gate, in which the space from the top of the arch to the cornice (except that there is scarcely a cornice, it is all a plain, massive piece of wall) is as great (or seems to be) as that from the ground to the former point. Then I climbed a steep and winding way—much of it a little dull, if one likes, being bounded by mottled, mossy garden-walls—to a villa on a hill-top, where I found various things that touched me with almost too fine a point. Seeing them again, often, for a week, both by sunlight and moonshine, I never quite learned not to covet them; not to feel that not being a part of them was somehow to miss an exquisite chance. What a tranquil, contented life it seemed, with romantic beauty as a part of its daily texture!—the sunny terrace, with its tangled *podere* beneath it; the bright gray olives against the bright blue sky; the long, serene, horizontal lines of other villas, flanked by their upward cypresses, disposed upon the neighbouring hills; the richest little city in the world in a softly-scooped hollow at one's feet, and beyond it the most appealing of views, the most majestic, yet the most familiar. Within the villa was a great love of art and a painting-room full of successful work, so that if human life there seemed very tranquil, the tranquillity meant simply contentment and devoted occupation. A beautiful occupation in that beautiful position, what could possibly be better? That is what I spoke just now of envying—a way of life that is not afraid of a little isolation and tolerably quiet days. When such a life presents itself in a dull or an ugly place, we esteem it, we admire it, but we do not feel it to be the ideal of good fortune. When, however, the people who lead it move as figures in an ancient, noble landscape, and their walks and contemplations are like a turning of the leaves of history, we seem to have before us an admirable case of virtue made easy; meaning here by virtue, contentment and concentration, the love of privacy and study. One need not be exacting if one lives among local conditions that are of themselves constantly suggestive. It is true, indeed, that I might, after a certain time, grow weary of a regular afternoon stroll among the Florentine lanes;

of sitting on low parapets, in intervals of flower-topped wall, and looking across at Fiesole, or down the rich-hued valley of the Arno; of pausing at the open gates of villas and wondering at the height of cypresses and the depth of loggias; of walking home in the fading light and noting on a dozen westward-looking surfaces the glow of the opposite sunset. But for a week or so all this was delightful. The villas are innumerable, and if one is a stranger half the talk is about villas. This one has a story; that one has another; they all look as if they had stories. Most of them are offered to rent (many of them for sale) at prices unnaturally low; you may have a tower and a garden, a chapel and an expanse of thirty windows, for five hundred dollars a year. In imagination, you hire three or four; you take possession, and settle, and live there. About the finest there is something very grave and stately; about two or three of the best there is something even solemn and tragic. From what does this latter impression come? You gather it it as you stand there in the early dusk, looking at the long, pale-brown façade, the enormous windows, the iron cages fastened upon the lower ones. Part of the brooding expression of these great houses comes, even when they have not fallen into decay, from their look of having outlived their original use. Their extraordinary largeness and massiveness are a satire upon their present fate. They were not built with such a thickness of wall and depth of embrasure, such a solidity of staircase and super-fluity of stone, simply to afford an economical winter residence to English and American families.

I know not whether it was the appearance of these stony old villas, which seemed so dumbly conscious of a change of manners, that threw a tinge of melancholy over the general prospect; certain it is that, having always found this plaintive note in the view of Florence, it seemed to me now particularly distinct. "Lovely, lovely, but it makes me blue," the fanciful stranger could not but murmur to himself as, in the late afternoon, he looked at the landscape from over one of the low parapets, and then, with his hands in his pockets, turned away indoors to candles and dinner.

V.

Below, in the city, in wandering about in the streets and churches and museums, it was impossible not to have a good deal of the same feeling; but here the impression was more easy to analyse. It came from a sense of the perfect separateness of all the great productions of the Renaissance from the present and the future of the place, from the actual life and manners, the native ideal. I have already spoken of the way in which the great aggregation of beautiful works of art in the Italian cities strikes the visitor nowadays (so far as present Italy is concerned) as the mere stock-in-trade of an impecunious but thrifty people. It is this metaphysical desertedness and loneliness of the great works of architecture and sculpture that deposits a certain weight upon the heart; when we see a great tradition broken we feel something of the pain with which we hear a stifled cry. But regret is one thing and resentment is another. Seeing one morning, in a shop-window, the series of *Mornings in Florence*, published a few years since by Mr. Ruskin, I made haste to enter and purchase these amusing little books, some passages of which I remembered formerly to have read. I could not turn over many pages without observing that the " separateness" of the new and old which I just mentioned had produced in their author the liveliest irritation. With the more acute phases of this sentiment it was difficult to sympathise, for the simple reason, it seems to me, that it savours of arrogance to demand of any people, as a right of one's own, that they shall be artistic. " Be artistic yourselves ! " is the very natural reply that young Italy has at hand for English critics and censors. When a people produces beautiful statues and pictures it gives us something more than is set down in the bond, and we must thank it for its generosity ; and when it stops producing them or caring for them we may cease thanking, but we hardly have a right to begin and abuse it. The wreck of Florence, says Mr. Ruskin, " is now too ghastly and heart-breaking to any human soul that remembers the days of old ; " and these desperate words are an allusion to the fact that the little square in front of the cathedral, at the foot of Giotto's Tower, with the grand Baptistery on the other side, is now the resort of a number of hackney-coaches and omnibuses. This fact is doubtless lamentable, and it would be a hundred times more agreeable to see among people who have been made the heirs of so priceless a work of art as the sublime campanile some such feeling about it as would keep it free even from the danger of defilement. A cab-stand is a very ugly and dirty thing, and Giotto's Tower should have nothing in common with such conveniences. But there is more than one way of taking such things, and a quiet traveller, who has been walking about for a week with his mind full of the sweetness and suggestiveness of a hundred Florentine places, may feel at last, in looking into Mr. Ruskin's little tracts that, discord for discord, there is not much to choose between the importunity of the author's personal ill-humour and the incongruity of horse-pails and bundles of hay. And one may say this without being at all a partisan of the doctrine of the inevitableness of new desecrations. For my own part, I believe there are few things in this line that the new Italian spirit is not capable of, and not many, indeed, that we are not destined to see. Pictures and buildings will not be completely destroyed, because in that case foreigners with full pockets would cease to visit the country, and the turn-stiles at the doors of the old palaces and convents, with the little patented slit for absorbing your half-franc, would grow quite rusty, and creak with disuse. But it is safe to say that the new Italy, growing into an old Italy again, will continue to take her elbow-room wherever she finds it.

I am almost ashamed to say what I did with Mr. Ruskin's little books. I put them into my pocket and betook myself to Santa Maria Novella. There I sat down, and after I had looked about for a while at the beautiful church, I drew them forth one by one, and read the greater part of them. Occupying one's self with light literature in a great

religious edifice is perhaps as bad a piece of profanation as any of those rude dealings which Mr. Ruskin
justly deplores; but a traveller has to make the
most of odd moments, and I was waiting for a friend
in whose company I was to go and look at Giotto's
beautiful frescoes in the cloister of the church. My
friend was a long time coming, so that I had an
hour with Mr. Ruskin, whom I called just now a
light *littérateur*, because in these little Mornings in
Florence he is for ever making his readers laugh.
I remembered, of course, where I was; and, in spite
of my latent hilarity, I felt that I had rarely got
such a snubbing. I had really been enjoying the
good old city of Florence; but I now learned from
Mr. Ruskin that this was a scandalous waste of
charity. I should have gone about with an impre-
cation on my lips, I should have worn a face three
yards long. I had taken great pleasure in certain
frescoes by Ghirlandaio, in the choir of that very
church; but it appeared from one of the little books
that these frescoes were as naught. I had much
admired Santa Croce, and I had thought the Duomo
a very noble affair; but I had now the most positive
assurance I knew nothing about it. After a while,
if it was only ill-humour that was needed for doing
honour to the city of the Medici, I felt that I had
risen to a proper level; only now it was Mr. Ruskin
himself I had lost patience with, and not the stupid
Brunelleschi and the vulgar Ghirlandaio. Indeed, I
lost patience altogether, and asked myself by what
right this informal votary of form pretended to run
riot through a quiet traveller's relish for the noblest
of pleasures—his wholesome enjoyment of the love-

liest of cities. The little books seemed invidious and insane, and it was only when I remembered that I had been under no obligation to buy them that I checked myself in repenting of having done so. Then, at last, my friend arrived, and we passed together out of the church, and through the first cloister beside it, into a smaller enclosure, where we stood a while to look at the tomb of the Marchesa Strozzi-Ridolfi, upon which the great Giotto has painted four superb little pictures. It was easy to see the pictures were superb; but I drew forth one of my little books again, for I had observed that Mr. Ruskin spoke of them. Hereupon I recovered my tolerance; for what could be better in this case, I asked myself, than Mr. Ruskin's remarks? They are, in fact, excellent and charming, and full of appreciation of the deep and simple beauty of the great painter's work. I read them aloud to my companion; but my companion was rather, as the phrase is, "put off" by them. One of the frescoes (it is a picture of the birth of the Virgin) contains a figure coming through a door. "Of ornament," I quote, "there is only the entirely simple outline of the vase which the servant carries; of colour two or three masses of sober red and pure white, with brown and gray. That is all," Mr. Ruskin continues. "And if you are pleased with this you can see Florence. But if not, by all means amuse yourself there, if you find it amusing, as long as you like; you can never see it." *You can never see it.* This seemed to my friend insufferable, and I had to shuffle away the book again, so that we might look at the fresco with the unruffled geniality it deserves.

We agreed afterwards, when in a more convenient place I read aloud a good many more passages from Mr. Ruskin's tracts, that there are a great many ways of seeing Florence, as there are of seeing most beautiful and interesting things, and that it is very dry and pedantic to say that the happy vision depends upon our squaring our toes with a certain particular chalk-mark. We see Florence wherever and whenever we enjoy it, and for enjoying it we find a great many more pretexts than Mr. Ruskin seems inclined to allow. My friend and I agreed also, however, that the little books were an excellent purchase, on account of the great charm and felicity of much of their incidental criticism; to say nothing, as I hinted just now, of their being extremely amusing. Nothing, in fact, is more comical than the familiar asperity of the author's style and the pedagogic fashion in which he pushes and pulls his unhappy pupils about, jerking their heads toward this, rapping their knuckles for that, sending them to stand in corners, and giving them Scripture texts to copy. But it is neither the felicities nor the aberrations of detail, in Mr. Ruskin's writings, that are the main affair for most readers; it is the general tone that, as I have said, puts them off or draws them on. For many persons he will never bear the test of being read in this rich old Italy, where art, so long as it really lived at all, was spontaneous, joyous, irresponsible. If the reader is in daily contact with those beautiful Florentine works which do still, in a way, force themselves into notice through the vulgarity and cruelty of modern profanation, it will seem to him that Mr. Ruskin's little books are pitched in the strangest falsetto key. "One may read a hundred pages of this sort of thing," said my friend, "without ever dreaming that he is talking about *art*. You can say nothing worse about it than that." And that is very true. Art is the one corner of human life in which we may take our ease. To justify our presence there the only thing that is demanded of us is that we shall have a passion for representation. In other places our passions are conditioned and embarrassed; we are allowed to have only so many as are consistent with those of our neighbours; with their convenience and well-being, with their convictions and prejudices, their rules and regulations. Art means an escape from all this. Wherever her brilliant standard floats the need for apologies and exonerations is over; there it is enough simply that we please or that we are pleased. There the tree is judged only by its fruits. If these are sweet, one is welcome to pluck them.

One may read a great many pages of Mr. Ruskin without getting a hint of this delightful truth; a hint of the not unimportant fact that art, after all, is made for us, and not we for art. This idea of the value of a work of art being the amount of illusion it yields is conspicuous by its absence. And as for Mr. Ruskin's world of art being a place where we may take life easily, woe to the luckless mortal who enters it with any such disposition. Instead of a garden of delight, he finds a sort of assize-court, in perpetual session. Instead of a place in which human responsibilities are lightened and suspended, he finds a region governed by a kind of Draconic

legislation. His responsibilities, indeed, are tenfold
increased; the gulf between truth and error is for
ever yawning at his feet; the pains and penalties
of this same error are advertised, in apocalyptic ter-
minology, upon a thousand sign-posts; and the poor
wanderer soon begins to look back with infinite
longing to the lost paradise of the artless. There
can be no greater want of tact in dealing with those
things with which men attempt to ornament life
than to be perpetually talking about "error." A
truce to all rigidities is the law of the place; the
only thing that is absolute there is sensible charm.
The grim old bearer of the scales excuses herself; she
feels that this is not her province. Differences here
are not iniquity and righteousness; they are simply
variations of temperament and of point of view. We
are not under theological government.

VI.

It was very charming, in the bright, warm days,
to wander from one corner of Florence to another,
paying one's respects again to remembered master-
pieces. It was pleasant also to find that memory
had played no tricks, and that the beautiful things
of an earlier year were as beautiful as ever. To
enumerate these beautiful things would take a great
deal of space; for I never had been more struck with
the mere quantity of brilliant Florentine work. Even
giving up the Duomo and Santa Croce to Mr. Ruskin
as very ill-arranged edifices, the list of the Florentine
treasures is almost inexhaustible. Those long outer
galleries of the Uffizi had never seemed to me more

delectable; sometimes there were not more than two or three figures standing there, Baedeker in hand, to break the charming perspective. One side of this upstairs-portico, it will be remembered, is entirely composed of glass; a continuity of old-fashioned windows, draped with white curtains of rather primitive fashion, which hang there till they acquire a perceptible "tone." The light, passing through them, is softly filtered and diffused; it rests mildly upon the old marbles—chiefly antique Roman busts—which stand in the narrow intervals of the casements. It is projected upon the numerous pictures that cover the opposite wall, and that are not by any means, as a general thing, the gems of the great collection; it imparts a faded brightness to the old ornamental arabesques upon the painted wooden ceiling, and it makes a great soft shining upon the marble floor, in which, as you look up and down, you see the strolling tourists and the motionless copyists almost reflected. I don't know why I should find all this very pleasant, but, in fact, I have seldom gone into the Uffizi without walking the length of this third-story cloister, between the (for the most part) third-rate pictures and the faded cotton curtains. Why is it that in Italy we see a charm in things in regard to which in other countries we always take vulgarity for granted? If in the city of New York a great museum of the arts were to be provided, by way of decoration, with a species of verandah inclosed on one side by a series of small-paned windows, draped in dirty linen, and furnished on the other with an array of pictorial feebleness, the place being surmounted by a thinly-painted wooden roof, strongly suggestive of summer heat, of winter cold, of frequent leakage, those amateurs who had had the advantage of foreign travel would be at small pains to conceal their contempt. Contemptible or respectable, to the judicial mind, this quaint old loggia of the Uffizi admitted me into twenty chambers where I found as great a number of ancient favourites. I do not know that I had a warmer greeting for any old friend than for Andrea del Sarto, that most touching of painters who is not one of the first. But it was on the other side of the Arno that I found him in force, in those dusky drawing-rooms of the Pitti Palace, to which you take your way along the tortuous tunnel that wanders through the houses of Florence, and is supported by the little goldsmiths' booths on the Ponte Vecchio. In the rich, insufficient light of these beautiful rooms, where, to look at the pictures, you sit in damask chairs and rest your elbows on tables of malachite, Andrea del Sarto becomes peculiarly effective. Before long you feel a real affection for him. But the great pleasure, after all, was to revisit the earlier masters, in those specimens of them chiefly that bloom so unfadingly on the big, plain walls of the Academy. Fra Angelico and Filippo Lippi, Botticelli, and Lorenzo di Credi are the sweetest and best of all painters ; as I sat for an hour in their company, in the cold great hall of the institution I have mentioned — there are shabby rafters above and an immense expanse of brick tiles below, and many bad pictures as well as good ones—it seemed to me more than ever that if one really had to choose one could not do better than choose here. You may sit very quietly and

comfortably at the Academy, in this big first room—
at the upper end, especially, on the left—because
more than many other places it savours of old Florence. More for instance, in reality, than the Bargello, though the Bargello makes great pretensions.
Beautiful and picturesque as the Bargello is, it smells
too strongly of restoration, and, much of old Italy as
still lurks in its furbished and renovated chambers,
it speaks even more distinctly of the ill-mannered
young kingdom that has (as unavoidably as you
please) lifted down a hundred delicate works of
sculpture from the convent-walls where their pious
authors placed them. If the early Tuscan painters
are exquisite, I can think of no praise generous
enough for the sculptors of the same period, Dona-
tello and Luca della Robbia, Matteo Civitale and
Mino da Fiesole, who, as I refreshed my memory of
them, seemed to me to leave absolutely nothing to
be desired in the way of purity of inspiration and
grace of invention. The Bargello is full of early
Tuscan sculpture, most of the pieces of which have
come from suppressed convents; and even if the
visitor be an ardent liberal, he is uncomfortably
conscious of the rather brutal process by which it
has been collected. One can hardly envy young
Italy the number of disagreeable things she has had
to do.

The railway journey from Florence to Rome has
been altered both for the better and for the worse;
for the better, in that it has been shortened by a
couple of hours; for the worse, inasmuch as, when
about half the distance has been traversed, the train
deflects to the west, and leaves the beautiful old

cities of Assisi, Perugia, Terni, Narni, unvisited. Of old, it was possible to visit these places, in a manner, from the window of the train; even if you did not stop, as you probably could not, every time you passed, the picturesque fashion in which, like a loosened belt on an aged and shrunken person, their old red walls held them easily together was something well worth noting. Now, however, by way of compensation, the express-train to Rome stops at Orvieto, and in consequence . . . In consequence what? What is the consequence of an express train stopping at Orvieto? As I glibly wrote that sentence I suddenly paused, with a sense of the queer stuff I was uttering. That an express train would graze the base of the horrid purple mountain from the apex of which this dark old Catholic city uplifts the glittering front of its cathedral—that might have been foretold by a keen observer of contemporary manners. But that it would really have the grossness to stop there, this is a fact over which, as he records it, a sentimental chronicler may well make what is vulgarly called an ado. The train does stop at Orvieto, not very long, it is true, but long enough to let you out. The same phenomenon takes place on the following day, when, having visited the city, you get in again. I availed myself of both of these occasions, having formerly neglected to drive to Orvieto in a post-chaise. And really, the railway-station being in the plain, and the town on the summit of an extraordinary hill, you have time to forget all about the triumphs of steam, while you wind upwards to the city-gate. The position of Orvieto is superb; it is worthy of the " middle distance " of

111

a last-century landscape.   But, as every one knows,
the beautiful cathedral is the proper attraction of the
place, which, indeed, save for this fine monument,
and for its craggy and crumbling ramparts, is a
meanly arranged and, as Italian cities go, not particularly impressive little town.   I spent a beautiful
Sunday there, and I looked at the charming church.
I looked at it a great deal—a great deal considering
that on the whole I found it inferior to its fame.
Intensely brilliant, however, is the densely carved
front; densely covered with the freshest-looking
mosaics.   The old white marble of the sculptured
portions is as softly yellow as ancient ivory; the
large, exceedingly bright pictures above them flashed
and twinkled in the splendid weather.   Very beautiful and interesting are the theological frescoes of Luca
Signorelli, though I have seen pictures that struck
me as more attaching.   Very enchanting, finally,
are the clear-faced saints and seraphs, in robes of
pink and azure, whom Fra Angelico has painted upon
the ceiling of the great chapel, along with a noble
sitting figure—more expressive of movement than
most of the creations of this pictorial peace-maker—
of Christ in judgment.   But the interest of the
cathedral of Orvieto is mainly not the visible result,
but the historical process that lies behind it; those
three hundred years of devoted popular labour of
which an American scholar has written an admirable
account.[1]

[1] Charles Eliot Norton: *Study and Travel in Italy*

Occasional Paris

IT is hard to say exactly what is the profit of comparing one race with another, and weighing in opposed
groups the manners and customs of neighbouring
countries; but it is certain that as we move about the
world we constantly indulge in this exercise. This is
especially the case if we happen to be infected with
the baleful spirit of the cosmopolite—that uncomfortable consequence of seeing many lands and
feeling at home in none. To be a cosmopolite is
not, I think, an ideal; the ideal should be to be a
concentrated patriot. Being a cosmopolite is an
accident, but one must make the best of it. If you
have lived about, as the phrase is, you have lost
that sense of the absoluteness and the sanctity of
the habits of your fellow-patriots which once made
you so happy in the midst of them. You have
seen that there are a great many *patriæ* in the
world, and that each of these is filled with excellent
people for whom the local idiosyncrasies are the
only thing that is not rather barbarous. There
comes a time when one set of customs, wherever it

115

may be found, grows to seem to you about as provincial as another; and then I suppose it may be said of you that you have become a cosmopolite. You have formed the habit of comparing, of looking for points of difference and of resemblance, for present and absent advantages, for the virtues that go with certain defects, and the defects that go with certain virtues. If this is poor work compared with the active practice, in the sphere to which a discriminating Providence has assigned you, of the duties of a tax-payer, an elector, a juryman or a diner-out, there is nevertheless something to be said for it. It is good to think well of mankind, and this, on the whole, a cosmopolite does. If you limit your generalisations to the sphere I mentioned just now, there is a danger that your occasional fits of pessimism may be too sweeping. When you are out of humour the whole country suffers, because at such moments one is never discriminating, and it costs you very little bad logic to lump your fellow-citizens together. But if you are living about, as I say, certain differences impose themselves. The worst you can say of the human race is, for instance, that the Germans are a detestable people. They do not represent the human race for you, as in your native town your fellow-citizens do, and your unflattering judgment has a flattering reverse. If the Germans are detestable, you are mentally saying, there are those admirable French, or those charming Americans, or those interesting English. (Of course it is simply by accident that I couple the German name here with the unfavourable adjective. The epithets may be transposed at will.) Nothing can

116

well be more different from anything else than the
English from the French, so that, if you are acquainted
with both nations, it may be said that on any special
point your agreeable impression of the one implies
a censorious attitude toward the other, and *vice versâ*
This has rather a shocking sound; it makes the
cosmopolite appear invidious and narrow-minded.
But I hasten to add that there seems no real reason
why even the most delicate conscience should take
alarm. The consequence of the cosmopolite spirit
is to initiate you into the merits of all peoples; to
convince you that national virtues are numerous,
though they may be very different, and to make
downright preference really very hard. I have, for
instance, every disposition to think better of the
English race than of any other except my own.
There are things which make it natural I should;
there are inducements, provocations, temptations,
almost bribes. There have been moments when I
have almost burned my ships behind me, and declared that, as it simplified matters greatly to pin
one's faith to a chosen people, I would henceforth
cease to trouble my head about the lights and
shades of the foreign character. I am convinced
that if I had taken this reckless engagement, I
should greatly have regretted it. You may find a
room very comfortable to sit in with the window
open, and not like it at all when the window has been
shut. If one were to give up the privilege of comparing the English with other people, one would
very soon, in a moment of reaction, make once for
all (and most unjustly) such a comparison as would
leave the English nowhere. Compare then, I say,

117

as often as the occasion presents itself. The result as regards any particular people, and as regards the human race at large, may be pronounced agreeable, and the process is both instructive and entertaining.

So the author of these observations finds it on returning to Paris after living for upwards of a year in London. He finds himself comparing, and the results of comparison are several disjointed reflections, of which it may be profitable to make a note. Certainly Paris is a very old story, and London is a still older one ; and there is no great reason why a journey across the channel and back should quicken one's perspicacity to an unprecedented degree. I therefore will not pretend to have been looking at Paris with new eyes, or to have gathered on the banks of the Seine a harvest of extraordinary impressions. I will only pretend that a good many old impressions have recovered their freshness, and that there is a sort of renovated entertainment in looking at the most brilliant city in the world with eyes attuned to a different pitch. Never, in fact, have those qualities of brightness and gaiety that are half the stock-in-trade of the city by the Seine seemed to me more uncontestable. The autumn is but half over, and Paris is, in common parlance, empty. The private houses are closed, the lions have returned to the jungle, the Champs Elysées are not at all "mondains." But I have never seen Paris more Parisian, in the pleasantest sense of the word ; better humoured, more open-windowed, more naturally entertaining. A radiant September helps the case ; but doubtless the matter is, as I hinted above, in a large degree "subjective." For when

one comes to the point there is nothing very particular just now for Paris to rub her hands about.
The Exhibition of 1878 is looming up as large as a
mighty mass of buildings on the Trocadéro can make
it. These buildings are very magnificent and fan-
tastical; they hang over the Seine, in their sudden
immensity and glittering newness, like a palace in
a fairy-tale. But the trouble is that most people
appear to regard the Exhibition as in fact a fairy-
tale. They speak of the wonderful structures on the
Champ de Mars and the Trocadéro as a predestined
monument to the folly of a group of gentlemen
destitute of a sense of the opportune. The moment
certainly does not seem very well chosen for inviting
the world to come to Paris to amuse itself. The
world is too much occupied with graver cares—with
reciprocal cannonading and chopping, with cutting
of throats and burning of homes, with murder of
infants and mutilation of mothers, with warding off
famine and civil war, with lamenting the failure of
its resources, the dulness of trade, the emptiness of
its pockets. Rome is burning altogether too fast
for even its most irresponsible spirits to find any
great satisfaction in fiddling. But even if there is
(as there very well may be) a certain scepticism
at headquarters as to the accomplishment of this
graceful design, there is no apparent hesitation, and
everything is going forward as rapidly as if mankind
were breathless with expectation. That familiar
figure, the Parisian *ouvrier,* with his white, chalky
blouse, his attenuated person, his clever face, is more
familiar than ever, and I suppose, finding plenty of
work to his hand, is for the time in a comparatively

119

rational state of mind. He swarms in thousands, not only in the region of the Exhibition, but along the great thoroughfare—the Avenue de l'Opéra— which has just been opened in the interior of Paris. This is an extremely Parisian creation, and as it is really a great convenience—it will save a great many steps and twists and turns—I suppose it should be spoken of with gratitude and admiration. But I confess that to my sense it belongs primarily to that order of benefits which during the twenty years of the Empire gradually deprived the streets of Paris of nine-tenths of their ancient individuality. The deadly monotony of the Paris that M. Hauss-mann called into being—its huge, blank, pompous, featureless sameness—sometimes comes over the wandering stranger with a force that leads him to devote the author of these miles of architectural commonplace to execration. The new street is quite on the imperial system; it must make the late Napoleon III. smile with beatific satisfaction as he looks down upon it from the Bonapartist corner of Paradise. It stretches straight away from the pompous façade of the Opera to the doors of the Théâtre Français, and it must be admitted that there is something fine in the vista that is closed at one end by the great sculptured and gilded mass of the former building. But it smells of the modern asphalt; it is lined with great white houses that are adorned with machine-made arabesques, and each of which is so exact a copy of all the rest that even the little white porcelain number on a blue ground, which looks exactly like all the other num-bers, hardly constitutes an identity. Presently there will be a long succession of milliners' and chocolate-makers' shops in the basement of this homogeneous row, and the pretty bonnets and bonbonnières in the shining windows will have their ribbons knotted with a *chic* that you must come to Paris to see. Then there will be little glazed sentry-boxes at regular intervals along the curbstone, in which churlish old women will sit selling half a dozen copies of each of the newspapers; and over the hardened bitumen the young Parisian of our day will constantly circulate, looking rather pallid and wearing very large shirt-cuffs. And the new avenue will be a great success, for it will place in symmetrical communication two of the most important establishments in France—the temple of French music and the temple of French comedy.

I said just now that no two things could well be more unlike than England and France; and though the remark is not original, I uttered it with the spontaneity that it must have on the lips of a traveller who, having left either country, has just disembarked in the other. It is of course by this time a very trite observation, but it will continue to be made so long as Boulogne remains the same lively antithesis of Folkestone. An American, conscious of the family-likeness diffused over his own huge continent, never quite unlearns his surprise at finding that so little of either of these two almost contiguous towns has rubbed off upon the other. He is surprised at certain English people feeling so far away from France, and at all French people feeling so far away from England. I travelled from Boulogne the other day in the same railway-carriage with a couple of amiable and ingenuous young Britons, who had come over to spend ten days in Paris. It was their first landing in France; they had never yet quitted their native island; and in the course of a little conversation that I had with them I was struck with the scantiness of their information in regard to French manners and customs. They were very intelligent lads; they were apparently fresh from a university; but in respect to the interesting country they were about to enter, their minds were almost a blank. If the conductor, appearing at the carriage door to ask for our tickets, had had the leg of a frog sticking out of his pocket, I think their only very definite preconception would have been confirmed. I parted with them at the Paris station, and I have no doubt that they very soon began to make precious discoveries; and I have alluded to them not in the least to throw ridicule upon their "insularity"—which indeed, being accompanied with great modesty, I thought a very pretty spectacle—but because having become, since my last visit to France, a little insular myself, I was more conscious of the emotions that attend on an arrival.

The brightness always seems to begin while you are still out in the channel, when you fairly begin to see the French coast. You pass into a region of intenser light—a zone of clearness and colour. These properties brighten and deepen as you approach the land, and when you fairly stand upon that good Boulognese quay, among the blue and red douaniers and soldiers, the small ugly men in cerulean blouses, the charming fishwives, with their folded kerchiefs and their crisp cap-frills, their short striped petticoats, their tightly-drawn stockings, and their little clicking sabots—when you look about you at the smokeless air, at the pink and yellow houses, at the white-fronted café, close at hand, with its bright blue letters, its mirrors and marble-topped tables, its white-aproned, alert, undignified waiter, grasping a huge coffee-pot by a long handle—when you perceive all these things you feel the additional savour that foreignness gives to the picturesque; or feel rather, I should say, that simple foreignness may itself make the picturesque; for certainly the elements in the picture I have just sketched are not especially exquisite. No matter; you are amused, and your amusement continues — being sensibly stimulated by a visit to the buffet at the railway-station, which is better than the refreshment-room at Folkestone. It is a pleasure to have people offering you soup again, of their own movement; it is a pleasure to find a little pint of Bordeaux standing naturally before your plate ; it is a pleasure to have a napkin; it is a pleasure, above all, to take up one of the good long sticks of French bread—as bread is called the staff of life, the French bake it literally in the shape of staves—and break off a loose, crisp, crusty morsel.

There are impressions, certainly, that imperil your good-humour. No honest Anglo-Saxon can like a French railway-station; and I was on the point of adding that no honest Anglo-Saxon can like a French railway-official. But I will not go so far as that; for after all I cannot remember any great harm that such a functionary has ever done me—except in locking me up as a malefactor. It is necessary to say, however, that the honest Anglo-Saxon, in a French railway-station, is in a state of chronic irritation—an irritation arising from his sense of the injurious effect upon the genial French nature of the possession of an administrative uniform. I believe that the consciousness of brass buttons on his coat and stripes on his trousers has spoiled many a modest and amiable Frenchman, and the sight of these aggressive insignia always stirs within me a moral protest. I repeat that my aversion to them is partly theoretic, for I have found, as a general thing, that an inquiry civilly made extracts a civil answer from even the most official-looking personage. But I have also found that such a personage's measure of the civility due to him is inordinately large; if he places himself in any degree at your service, it is apparently from the sense that true greatness can afford to unbend. You are constantly reminded that you must not presume. In England these intimations never proceed from one's "inferiors." In France the "administration" is the first thing that touches you; in a little while you get used to it, but you feel somehow that, in the process, you have lost the flower of your self-respect. Of course you are under some obligation to it. It has taken you off the steamer at Folkestone; made you tell your name to a gentleman with a sword, stationed at the farther end of the plank—not a drawn sword, it is true, but still, at the best, a very nasty weapon; marshalled you into the railway-station; assigned you to a carriage—I was going to say to a seat; transported you to Paris, marshalled you again out of the train, and under a sort of military surveillance, into an enclosure containing a number of human sheep-pens, in one of which it has imprisoned you for some half-hour. I am always on the point, in these places, of asking one of my gaolers if I may not be allowed to walk about on parole. The administration at any rate has finally taken you out of your pen, and, through the medium of a functionary who "inscribes" you in a little book, transferred you to a cab selected by a logic of its own. In doing all this it has certainly done a great deal for you ; but somehow its good offices have made you feel sombre and resentful. The other day, on arriving from London, while I was waiting for my luggage, I saw several of the porters who convey travellers' impedimenta to the cab come up and deliver over the coin they had just received for this service to a functionary posted *ad hoc* in a corner, and armed with a little book in which he noted down these remittances. The *pour-boires* are apparently thrown into a common fund and divided among the guild of porters. The system is doubtless an excellent one, excellently carried out; but the sight of the poor round-shouldered man of burdens dropping his coin into the hand of the official arithmetician was to my fancy but another reminder that the individual, as an individual, loses by all that the administration assumes.

After living a while in England you observe the individual in Paris with quickened attention ; and I think it must be said that at first he makes an indifferent figure. You are struck with the race being physically and personally a poorer one than that great family of largely-modelled, fresh-coloured people you have left upon the other side of the channel. I remember that in going to England a year ago and disembarking of a dismal, sleety Sunday evening at Folkestone, the first thing that struck me was the good looks of the railway porters— their broad shoulders, their big brown beards, their well-cut features. In like manner, landing lately at Boulogne of a brilliant Sunday morning, it was impossible not to think the little men in numbered caps who were gesticulating and chattering in one's path, rather ugly fellows. In arriving from other countries one is struck with a certain want of dignity in the French face. I do not know, however, whether this is anything worse than the fact that the French face is expressive ; for it may be said that, in a certain sense, to express anything is to compromise with one's dignity, which likes to be understood without taking trouble. As regards the lower classes, at any rate, the impression I speak of always passes away ; you perceive that the good looks of the French working-people are to be found in their look of intelligence. These people, in Paris, strike me afresh as the cleverest, the most perceptive, and, intellectually speaking, the most human of their kind. The Paris *ouvrier*, with his democratic blouse, his expressive, demonstrative, agreeable eye, his meagre limbs, his irregular, pointed features, his sallow complexion, his face at once fatigued and animated, his light, nervous organisation, is a figure that I always encounter again with pleasure. In some cases he looks depraved and perverted, but at his worst he looks refined , he is full of vivacity of perception, of something that one can appeal to.

126

It takes some courage to say this, perhaps, after reading *L'Assommoir;* but in M. Emile Zola's extraordinary novel one must make the part, as the French say, of the horrible uncleanness of the author's imagination. *L'Assommoir*, I have been told, has had great success in the lower walks of Parisian life; and if this fact is not creditable to the delicacy of M. Zola's humble readers, it proves a good deal in favour of their intelligence. With all its grossness the book in question is essentially a literary performance; you must be tolerably clever to appreciate it. It is highly appreciated, I believe, by the young ladies who live in the region of the Latin Quarter—those young ladies who thirty years ago were called grisettes, and now are called I don't know what. They know long passages by heart; they repeat them with infinite gusto. " Ce louchon d'Augustine "—the horrible little girl with a squint, who is always playing nasty tricks and dodging slaps and projectiles in Gervaise's shop, is their particular favourite; and it must be admitted that " ce louchon d'Augustine " is, as regards reality, a wonderful creation.

If Parisians, both small and great, have more of the intellectual stamp than the people one sees in London, it is striking, on the other hand, that the people of the better sort in Paris look very much less " respectable." I did not know till I came back to Paris how used I had grown to the English *cachet;* but I immediately found myself missing it. You miss it in the men much more than in the women; for the well-to-do Frenchwoman of the lower orders, as one sees her in public, in the streets and in shops, is always a delightfully comfortable and creditable person. I must confess to the highest admiration for her, an admiration that increases with acquaintance. She, at least, is essentially respectable ; the neatness, compactness, and sobriety of her dress, the decision of her movement and accent suggest the civic and domestic virtues—order, thrift, frugality, the moral necessity of making a good appearance. It is, I think, an old story that to the stranger in France the women seem greatly superior to the men. Their superiority, in fact, appears to be conceded ; for wherever you turn you meet them in the forefront of action. You meet them, indeed, too often ; you pronounce them at times obtrusive. It is annoying when you go to order your boots or your shirts, to have to make known your desires to even the most neat-waisted female attendant; for the limitations to the feminine intellect are, though few in number, distinct, and women are not able to understand certain masculine needs. Mr. Worth makes ladies' dresses; but I am sure there will never be a fashionable tailoress. There are, however, points at which, from the commercial point of view, feminine assistance is invaluable. For insisting upon the merits of an article that has failed to satisfy you, talking you over, and making you take it; for defending a disputed bill, for paying the necessary compliments or supplying the necessary impertinence—for all these things the neat-waisted sex has peculiar and precious faculties. In the commercial class in Paris the man always appeals to the woman; the woman always steps forward. The woman always proposes the conditions of a bargain. Go about and look for furnished rooms, you always encounter a concierge and his wife. When you ask the price of the rooms, the woman takes the words out of her husband's mouth, if indeed he have not first turned to her with a questioning look. She takes you in hand; she proposes conditions; she thinks of things he would not have thought of.

What I meant just now by my allusion to the absence of the "respectable" in the appearance of the Parisian population was that the men do not look like gentlemen, as so many Englishmen do. The average Frenchman that one encounters in public is of so different a type from the average Englishman that you can easily believe that to the end of time the two will not understand each other. The Frenchman has always, comparatively speaking, a Bohemian, empirical look; the expression of his face, its colouring, its movement, have not been toned down to the neutral complexion of that breeding for which in English speech we reserve the epithet of "good." He is at once more artificial and more natural; the former where the Englishman is positive, the latter where the Englishman is negative. He takes off his hat with a flourish to a friend, but the Englishman never bows. He ties a knot in the end of a napkin and thrusts it into his shirt-collar, so that, as he sits at breakfast, the napkin may serve the office of a pinafore. Such an operation as that seems to the Englishman as *naïf* as the flourishing of one's hat is pretentious.

I sometimes go to breakfast at a café on the Boulevard, which I formerly used to frequent with considerable regularity. Coming back there the other day, I found exactly the same group of habitués at their little tables, and I mentally exclaimed as I looked at them over my newspaper, upon their unlikeness to the gentlemen who confront you in the same attitude at a London club. Who are they? what are they? On these points I have no information; but the stranger's imagination does not seem to see a majestic social order massing itself behind them as it usually does in London. He goes so far as to suspect that what is behind them is not adapted for exhibition; whereas your Englishmen, whatever may be the defects of their personal character, or the irregularities of their conduct, are pressed upon from the rear by an immense body of private proprieties and comforts, of domestic conventions and theological observances. But it is agreeable all the same to come back to a café of which you have formerly been an habitué. Adolphe or Edouard, in his long white apron and his large patent-leather slippers, has a perfect recollection of " les habitudes de Monsieur." He remembers the table you preferred, the wine you drank, the newspaper you read. He greets you with the friendliest of smiles, and remarks that it is a long time since he has had the pleasure of seeing Monsieur. There is something in this simple remark very touching to a heart that has suffered from that incorruptible dumbness of the British domestic. But in Paris such a heart finds consolation at every step; it is reminded of that most classic quality of the French nature—its sociability; a sociability which operates here as it never does

in England, from below upward. Your waiter
utters a greeting because, after all, something human
within him prompts him; his instinct bids him
say something, and his taste recommends that it
be agreeable. The obvious reflection is that a
waiter must not say too much, even for the sake
of being human. But in France the people always
like to make the little extra remark, to throw in
something above the simply necessary. I stop
before a little man who is selling newspapers at
a street-corner, and ask him for the *Journal des
Débats*. His answer deserves to be literally given:
" Je ne l'ai plus, Monsieur; mais je pourrai vous
donner quelquechose à peu près dans le même genre
—la *République Française*." Even a person of his
humble condition must have had a lurking sense of
the comicality of offering anything as an equivalent
for the "genre" of the venerable, classic, academic
Débats. But my friend could not bear to give me
a naked, monosyllabic refusal.

There are two things that the returning observer
is likely to do with as little delay as possible.
One is to dine at some *cabaret* of which he retains a
friendly memory; another is to betake himself to the
Théâtre Français. It is early in the season; there
are no new pieces; but I have taken great pleasure
in seeing some of the old ones. I lost no time in
going to see Mademoiselle Sarah Bernhardt in
Andromaque. *Andromaque* is not a novelty, but
Mademoiselle Sarah Bernhardt has a perennial
freshness. The play has been revived, to enable
her to represent not the great part, the injured and
passionate Hermione, but that of the doleful

131

funereal widow of Hector. This part is a poor
one; it is narrow and monotonous, and offers few
brilliant opportunities. But the actress knows how
to make opportunities, and she has here a very
sufficient one for crossing her thin white arms over
her nebulous black robes, and sighing forth in silver
accents her dolorous rhymes. Her rendering of the
part is one more proof of her singular intelligence
—of the fineness of her artistic nature. As there
is not a great deal to be done with it in the way of
declamation, she has made the most of its plastic
side. She understands the art of motion and attitude as no one else does, and her extraordinary
personal grace never fails her. Her Andromaque
has postures of the most poetic picturesqueness—
something that suggests the broken stem and drooping head of a flower that had been rudely plucked.
She bends over her classic confidant like the figure
of Bereavement on a bas-relief, and she has a
marvellous manner of lifting and throwing back
her delicate arms, locking them together, and passing
them behind her hanging head.

The *Demi-Monde* of M. Dumas *fils* is not a novelty
either; but I quite agree with M. Francisque Sarcey
that it is on the whole, in form, the first comedy of
our day. I have seen it several times, but I never
see it without being forcibly struck with its merits.
For the drama of our time it must always remain
the model. The interest of the story, the quiet art
with which it is unfolded, the naturalness and
soberness of the means that are used, and by which
great effects are produced, the brilliancy and richness of the dialogue—all these things make it a

singularly perfect and interesting work. Of course
it is admirably well played at the Théâtre Français.
Madame d'Ange was originally a part of too great
amplitude for Mademoiselle Croizette; but she is
gradually filling it out and taking possession of it;
she begins to give a sense of the "calme infernal,"
which George Sand somewhere mentions as the
leading attribute of the character. As for Delau-
nay, he does nothing better, more vividly and
gallantly, than Olivier de Jalin. When I say
gallantry I say it with qualification; for what a
very queer fellow is this same M. de Jalin! In
seeing the *Demi-Monde* again I was more than
ever struck with the oddity of its morality and
with the way that the ideal of fine conduct differs
in different nations. The *Demi-Monde* is the
history of the eager, the almost heroic, effort of a
clever and superior woman, who has been guilty of
what the French call "faults," to pass from the
irregular and equivocal circle to which these faults
have consigned her into what is distinctively termed
"good society." The only way in which the passage can be effected is by her marrying an honourable man; and to induce an honourable man to
marry her, she must suppress the more discredit-
able facts of her career. Taking her for an honest
woman, Raymond de Nanjac falls in love with her,
and honestly proposes to make her his wife. But
Raymond de Nanjac has contracted an intimate
friendship with Olivier de Jalin, and the action of
the play is more especially De Jalin's attempt—a
successful one—to rescue his friend from the igno-
miny of a union with Suzanne d'Ange. Jalin

133

knows a great deal about her, for the simple reason that he has been her lover. Their relations have been most harmonious, but from the moment that Suzanne sets her cap at Nanjac, Olivier declares war. Suzanne struggles hard to keep possession of her suitor, who is very much in love with her, and Olivier spares no pains to detach him. It is the means that Olivier uses that excite the wonderment of the Anglo-Saxon spectator. He takes the ground that in such a cause all means are fair, and when, at the climax of the play, he tells a thumping lie in order to make Madame d'Ange compromise herself, expose herself, he is pronounced by the author "le plus honnête homme que je connaisse." Madame d'Ange, as I have said, is a superior woman; the interest of the play is in her being a superior woman. Olivier has been her lover; he himself is one of the reasons why she may not marry Nanjac; he has given her a push along the downward path. But it is curious how little this is held by the author to disqualify him from fighting the battle in which she is so much the weaker combatant. An English-speaking audience is more "moral" than a French, more easily scandalised; and yet it is a singular fact that if the *Demi-Monde* were represented before an English-speaking audience, its sympathies would certainly not go with M. de Jalin. It would pronounce him rather a coward. Is it because such an audience, although it has not nearly such a pretty collection of pedestals to place under the feet of the charming sex, has, after all, in default of this degree of gallantry, a tenderness more fundamental? Madame d'Ange has stained herself, and it is doubtless not at all proper that such ladies should be led to the altar by honourable young men. The point is not that the English-speaking audience would be disposed to condone Madame d'Ange's irregularities, but that it would remain perfectly cold before the spectacle of her ex-lover's masterly campaign against her, and quite fail to think it positively admirable, or to regard the fib by which he finally clinches his victory as a proof of exceptional honesty. The ideal of our own audience would be expressed in some such words as, " I say, that's not fair game. Can't you let the poor woman alone ? "

A Little Tour

IT was a very little tour, but the charm of the three or four old towns and monuments that it embraced, the beauty of the brilliant October, the pleasure of reminding one's self how much of the interest, strength and dignity of France is to be found outside of that huge pretentious caravansary called Paris (a reminder often needed), these things deserve to be noted. I went down to Rheims to see the famous cathedral, and to reach Rheims I travelled through the early morning hours along the charming valley of the Marne. The Marne is a pretty little green river, the vegetation upon whose banks, otherwise unadorned, had begun to blush with the early frosts in a manner that suggested the autumnal tints of American scenery. The trees and bushes were scarlet and orange; the light was splendid and a trifle harsh; I could have fancied myself immersed in an American "fall," if at intervals some gray old large-towered church had not lifted a sculptured front above a railway-station, to dispel the fond illusion. One of these church-fronts (I saw it only from the train) is particularly impressive; the little cathedral of Meaux, of which the great Bossuet was bishop, and along whose frigid nave he set his eloquence rolling with an impetus which it has not wholly lost to this day. It was entertaining, moreover, to enter the country of champagne; for Rheims is in the ancient province whose later fame is syllabled the world over in popping corks. A land of vineyards is not usually accounted sketchable; but the country about Epernay seemed to me to have a charm of its own. It stretched away in soft undulations that were pricked all over with little stakes muffled in leaves. The effect at a distance was that of vast surfaces, long, subdued billows, of pincushion; and yet it was very pretty. The deep blue sky was over the scene; the undulations were half in sun and half in shade; and here and there, among their myriad bristles, were groups of vintagers, who, though they are in reality, doubtless, a prosaic and mercenary body of labourers, yet assumed, to a fancy that glanced at them in the cursory manner permitted by the passage of the train, the appearance of joyous and disinterested votaries of Bacchus. The blouses of the men, the white caps of the women, were gleaming in the sunshine; they moved about crookedly among the tiny vine-poles. I thought them full of a charming suggestiveness. Of all the delightful gifts of France to the world, this was one of the most agreeable—the keen, living liquid in which the finest flower of sociability is usually dipped. It came from these sunny places; this little maze of curling-sticks supplied the world with half the world's gaiety. I call it little only in relation to the immense number of bottles with gilded necks in which this gaiety is annually stored up. The acreage of the champagne seemed to me, in fact, large ; the bristling slopes went rolling away to new horizons in a manner that was positively reassuring. Making the handsomest allowance for the wine manufactured from baser elements, it was apparent that this big corner of a province represents a very large number of bottles.

As you draw near to Rheims the vineyards become sparser, and finally disappear, a fact not to be regretted, for there is something incongruous in the juxtaposition of champagne and gothic architecture. It may be said, too, that for the proper appreciation of a structure like the cathedral of Rheims you have need of all your head. As, after my arrival, I sat in my window at the inn, gazing up at the great façade, I found something dizzying in the mere climbing and soaring of one's astonished vision ; and later, when I came to wander about in the upper regions of the church, and to peep down through the rugged lacework of the towers at the little streets and the small spots of public places, I found myself musing upon the beauty of soberness. My window at the Lion d'Or was like a proscenium-box at the play ; to admire the cathedral at my leisure I had only to perch myself in the casement with a good opera-glass. I sat there for a long time watching the great architectural drama. A drama I may call it, for no church-front that I have seen is more animated, more richly figured. The density of the sculptures, the immense scale of the images, detract, perhaps, at first, in a certain sense, from the impressiveness of the cathedral of Rheims; the absence of large surfaces, of ascending lines, deceives you as to the elevation of the front, and the dimensions of some of the upper statues bring them unduly near the eye. But little by little you perceive that this great figured and storied screen has a mass proportionate to its detail, and that it is the grandest part of a structure which, as a whole, is one of the noblest works of man's hands. Most people remember to have seen some print or some photograph of this heavily-charged façade of Rheims, which is usually put forward as the great example of the union of the purity and the possible richness of gothic. I must first have seen some such print in my earliest years, for I have always thought of Rheims as the typical gothic cathedral. I had vague associations with it; it seemed to me that I had already stood there in the little overwhelmed *place*. One's literary associations with Rheims are indeed very vivid and impressive; they begin with the picture of the steel-clad Maid passing under the deeply-sculptured portal, with a banner in her hand which she has no need to lower, and while she stands amid the incense and the chants, the glitter of arms and the glow of coloured lights, asking leave of the young king whom she has crowned to turn away and tend her flocks. And after that there is the sense of all the kings of France having travelled down to Rheims in their splendour to be consecrated; the great groups on the front of the church must have looked down on groups almost as stately—groups full of colour and movement—assembled in the square. (The square of Rheims, it must be confessed, is rather shabby. It is singular that the august ceremony of the *sacre* should not have left its mark upon the disposition of the houses, should not have kept them at a respectful distance. Louis XIV., smoothing his plumage before he entered the church, can hardly have had space to swing the train of his coronation-robe.) But when in driving into the town I reached the small precinct, such as it is, and saw the cathedral lift its spireless towers above the long rows of its carven saints, the huge wheel of its window, the three great caverns of its portals, with the high acute pediments above each arch, and the sides abutting outward like the beginning of a pyramid; when I looked at all this I felt that I had carried it in my mind from my earliest years, and that the stately vision had been implanted there by some forgotten glimpse of an old-fashioned water-colour sketch, in which the sky was washed in with expressive splashes, the remoter parts of the church tinted with a fascinating blueness, and the foundations represented as encumbered with little gabled and cross-timbered houses, inhabited by women in red petticoats and curious caps.

I shall not attempt any regular enumeration of the great details of the façade of Rheims; I cannot profess even to have fully apprehended them. They are a glorious company, and here and there, on its high-hung pedestal, one of the figures detaches itself with peculiar effectiveness. Over the central portal sits the Virgin Mary, meekly submitting her head to the ponderous crown which her Son prepares to place

upon it; the attitude and movement of Christ are full
of a kind of splendid politeness. The three great doorways are in themselves a museum of imagery, disposed in each case in five close tiers, the statues in
each of the tiers packed perpendicularly against their
comrades. The effect of these great hollowed and
chiselled recesses is extremely striking; they are a
proper vestibule to the dusky richness of the interior.
The cathedral of Rheims, more fortunate than many of
its companions, appears not to have suffered from the
iconoclasts of the Revolution; I noticed no absent
heads nor broken noses. It is very true that these
members may have had adventures to which they
do not, as it were, allude. But, like many of its
companions, it is so pressed upon by neighbouring
houses that it is not easy to get a general view of
the sides and the rear. You may walk round it,
and note your walk as a long one; you may observe
that the choir of the church travels back almost into
another quarter of the city; you may see the far-
spreading mass lose itself for a while in parasitic
obstructions, and then emerge again with all its
buttresses flying; but you miss that wide margin of
space and light which should enable it to present
itself as a consistent picture. Pictures have their
frames, and poems have their margins; a great work
of art, such as a gothic cathedral, should at least
have elbow-room. You may, however, stroll beneath
the walls of Rheims, along a narrow, dark street,
and look up at the mighty structure and see its
higher parts foreshortened into all kinds of delusive
proportions. There is a grand entertainment in the
view of the church which you obtain from the

farthermost point to which you may recede from it in the rear, keeping it still within sight. I have never seen a cathedral so magnificently buttressed. The buttresses of Rheims are all double; they have a tremendous spring, and are supported upon pedestals surmounted by immense crocketed canopies containing statues of wide-winged angels. A great balustrade of gothic arches connects these canopies one with another, and along this balustrade are perched strange figures of sitting beasts, unicorns and mermaids, griffins and monstrous owls. Huge, terrible gargoyles hang far over into the street, and doubtless some of them have a detail which I afterwards noticed at Laon. The gargoyle represents a grotesque beast—a creature partaking at once of the shape of a bird, a fish, and a quadruped. At Laon, on either side of the main entrance, a long-bellied monster cranes forth into the air with the head of a hippopotamus; and under its belly crouches a little man, hardly less grotesque, making up a rueful grimace and playing some ineffectual trick upon his terrible companion. One of these little figures has plunged a sword, up to the hilt, into the belly of the monster above him, so that when he draws it forth there will be a leak in the great stone gutter; another has suspended himself to a rope that is knotted round the neck of the gargoyle, and is trying in the same manner to interrupt its functions by pulling the cord as tight as possible. There was sure to be a spirit of life in an architectural conception that could range from the combination of clustering towers and opposing fronts to this infinitely minute play of humour.

145

There is no great play of humour in the interior of Rheims, but there is a great deal of beauty and solemnity. This interior is a spectacle that excites the sensibility, as our forefathers used to say; but it is not an easy matter to describe. It is no description of it to say that it is four hundred and sixty-six feet in length, and that the roof is one hundred and twenty-four feet above the pavement; nor is there any very vivid portraiture in the statement that if there is no coloured glass in the lower windows, there is, *per contra*, a great deal of the most gorgeous and most ancient in the upper ones. The long sweep of the nave, from the threshold to the point where the coloured light-shafts of the choir lose themselves in the gray distance, is a triumph of perpendicular perspective. The white light in the lower part of Rheims really contributes to the picturesqueness of the interior. It makes the gloom above look richer still, and throws that part of the roof which rests upon the gigantic piers of the transepts into mysterious remoteness. I wandered about for a long time; I sat first in one place and then in another; I attached myself to that most fascinating part of every great church, the angle at which the nave and transept divide. It was the better to observe this interesting point, I think, that I passed into the side gate of the choir—the gate that stood ajar in the tall gilded railing. I sat down on a stool near the threshold; I leaned back against the side of one of the stalls; the church was empty, and I lost myself in the large perfection of the place. I lost myself, but the beadle found me; he stood before me, and with a silent, imperious gesture, motioned me to

146

depart. I risked an argumentative glance, whereupon he signified his displeasure, repeated his gesture, and pointed to an old gentleman with a red cape, who had come into the choir softly, without my seeing him, and had seated himself in one of the stalls. This old gentleman seemed plunged in pious thoughts; I was not, after all, very near him, and he did not look as if I disturbed him. A canon is at any time, I imagine, a more merciful man than a beadle. But of course I obeyed the beadle, and eliminated myself from this peculiarly sacred precinct. I found another chair, and I fell to admiring the cathedral again. But this time I think it was with a difference—a difference which may serve as an excuse for the triviality of my anecdote. Sundry other old gentlemen in red capes emerged from the sacristy and went into the choir; presently, when there were half a dozen, they began to chant, and I perceived that the impending vespers had been the reason of my expulsion. This was highly proper, and I forgave the beadle; but I was not so happy as before, for my thoughts had passed out of the architectural channel into—what shall I say?—into the political. Here they found nothing so sweet to feed upon. It was the 5th of October; ten days later the elections for the new Chamber were to take place—the Chamber which was to replace the Assembly dissolved on the 16th of May by Marshal MacMahon, on a charge of "latent" radicalism. Stranger though one was, it was impossible not to be much interested in the triumph of the republican cause; it was impossible not to sympathise with this supreme effort of a brilliant and generous people to learn the lesson

147

of national self-control and self-government. It was impossible by the same token, not to have noted and detested the alacrity with which the Catholic party had rallied to the reactionary cause, and the unction with which the clergy had converted itself into the go-betweens of Bonapartism. The clergy was giving daily evidence of its devotion to arbitrary rule and to every iniquity that shelters itself behind the mask of " authority." These had been frequent and irritating reflections; they lurked in the folds of one's morning paper. They came back to me in the midst of that tranquil grandeur of Rheims, as I listened to the droning of the old gentlemen in the red capes. Some of the canons, it was painful to observe, had not been punctual; they came hurrying out of the sacristy after the service had begun. They looked like amiable and venerable men; their chanting and droning, as it spread itself under the great arches, was not disagreeable to listen to; I could certainly bear them no grudge. But their presence there was distracting and vexatious; it had spoiled my enjoyment of their church, in which I doubtless had no business. It had set me thinking of the activity and vivacity of the great organisation to which they belonged, and of all the odious things it would have done before the 15th of October. To what base uses do we come at last! It was this same organisation that had erected the magnificent structure around and above me, and which had then seemed an image of generosity and benignant power. Such an edifice might at times make one feel tenderly sentimental toward the Catholic church—make one remember how many of the great achievements of

the past we owe to her. To lapse gently into this
state of mind seems indeed always, while one strolls
about a great cathedral, a proper recognition of its
hospitality; but now I had lapsed gently out of it,
and it was one of the exasperating elements of the
situation that I felt, in a manner, called upon to de-
cide how far such a lapse was unbecoming. I found
myself even extending the question a little, and
picturing to myself that conflict which must often
occur at such a moment as the present—which is
actually going on, doubtless, in many thousands of
minds—between the actively, practically liberal instinct and what one may call the historic, æsthetic
sense, the sense upon which old cathedrals lay a
certain palpable obligation. How far should a lover
of old cathedrals let his hands be tied by the sanctity
of their traditions? How far should he let his
imagination bribe him, as it were, from action? This
of course is a question for each man to answer for
himself; but as I sat listening to the drowsy old
canons of Rheims, I was visited, I scarcely know
why, by a kind of revelation of the anti-catholic
passion, as it must burn to-day in the breasts of
certain radicals. I felt that such persons must
be intent upon war to the death; how that must
seem the most sacred of all duties. Can anything,
in the line of action, for a votary of the radical
creed, be more sacred? I asked myself; and can any
instruments be too trenchant? I raised my eyes
again to the dusky splendour of the upper aisles and
measured their enchanting perspective, and it was
with a sense of doing them full justice that I gave
my fictive liberal my good wishes.

This little operation restored my equanimity, so that I climbed several hundred steps and wandered lightly over the roof of the cathedral. Climbing into cathedral-towers and gaping at the size of the statues that look small from the street has always seemed to me a rather brutal pastime; it is not the proper way to treat a beautiful building; it is like holding one's nose so close to a picture that one sees only the grain of the canvas. But when once I had emerged into the upper wilderness of Rheims the discourse of a very urbane and appreciative old bell-ringer, whom I found lurking behind some gigantic excrescence, gave an æsthetic complexion to what would otherwise have been a rather vulgar feat of gymnastics. It was very well to see what a great cathedral is made of, and in these high places of the immensity of Rheims I found the matter very impressively illustrated. I wandered for half an hour over endless expanses of roof, along the edge of sculptured abysses, through hugely-timbered attics and chambers that were in themselves as high as churches. I stood knee-high to strange images, of unsuspected proportions, and I followed the topmost staircase of one of the towers, which curls upward like the groove of a corkscrew, and gives you at the summit a hint of how a sailor feels at the masthead. The ascent was worth making to learn the fulness of beauty of the church, the solidity and perfection, the mightiness of arch and buttress, the latent ingenuity of detail. At the angles of the balustrade which ornaments the roof of the choir are perched a series of huge sitting eagles, which from below, as you look up at them, produce a great effect. They

are immense, grim-looking birds, and the sculptor
has given to each of them a pair of very neatly
carved human legs, terminating in talons. Why did
he give them human legs ? Why did he indulge in
this ridiculous conceit ? I am unable to say, but the
conceit afforded me pleasure. It seemed to tell of
an imagination always at play, fond of the unexpected and delighting in its labour.

Apart from its cathedral Rheims is not an interesting city. It has a prosperous, modern, mercantile
air. The streets look as if at one time M. Hauss-
mann, in person, may have taken a good deal of
exercise in them ; they prove, however, that a French
provincial town may be a wonderfully fresh, clean,
comfortable-looking place. Very different is the
aspect of the ancient city of Laon, to which you may,
by the assistance of the railway, transfer yourself
from Rheims in a little more than an hour. Laon
is full of history, and the place, as you approach it,
reminds you of a quaint woodcut in the text of an
ancient folio. Out of the midst of a smiling plain
rises a goodly mountain, and on the top of the mountain is perched the old feudal *commune,* from the
centre of which springs, with infinite majesty, the
many-towered cathedral. At Laon you are in the
midst of old France; it is one of the most interesting chapters of the past. Ever since reading in the
pages of M. Thierry the story of the fierce struggle
for municipal independence waged by this ardent
little city against its feudal and ecclesiastical lords,
I had had the conviction that Laon was worthy of a
visit. All the more so that her two hundred years
of civic fermentation had been vainly spent, and

that in the early part of the fourteenth century she
had been disfranchised without appeal. M. Thierry's
readers will remember the really thrilling interest of
the story which he has selected as the most complete
and typical among those of which the records of the
mediæval communities are full; the complications
and fluctuations of the action, its brilliant episodes,
its sombre, tragic *dénoûment.* I did not visit Laon
with the *Lettres sur l'Histoire de France* in my pocket,
nor had I any other historic texts for reference;
but a vague notion of the vigorous manner in which
for a couple of centuries the stubborn little town
had attested its individuality supplied my observations with an harmonious background. Nothing can
well be more picturesque than the position of this
interesting city. The tourist who has learned his
trade can tell a " good " place at a glance. The
moment Laon became visible from the window of
the train I perceived that Laon was good. And then
I had the word for it of an extremely intelligent
young officer of artillery, who shared my railway-
carriage in coming from Rheims, and who spoke with
an authority borrowed from three years of garrison-
life on that windy hill-top. He affirmed that the
only recreation it afforded was a walk round the
ramparts which encircle the town ; people went down
the hill as little as possible—it was such a dreadful
bore to come up again. But he declared, nevertheless, that, as an intelligent traveller, I should be
enchanted with the place; that the cathedral was
magnificent, the view of the surrounding country
a perpetual entertainment, and the little town full
of originality. After I had spent a day there I

thought of this pleasant young officer and his familiar walk upon the city-wall; he gave a point to my inevitable reflections upon the degree to which at the present hour, in France, the front of the stage is occupied by the army. Inevitable reflections, I say, because the net result of any little tour that one may make just now is a vivid sense of red trousers and cropped heads. Wherever you go you come upon a military quarter, you stumble upon a group of young citizens in uniform. It is always a pretty spectacle; they enliven the scene; they touch it here and there with an effusion of colour. But this is not the whole of the matter, and when you have admitted that it is pictorial to be always *sous les armes*, you fall to wondering whether it is not very expensive. A million of defenders take up a good deal of room, even for defenders. It must be very uncomfortable to be always defending. How do the young men bear it; how does France bear it; how long will she be able to keep it up? Every young Frenchman, on reaching maturity, has to give up five years of his life to this bristling Minotaur of military service. It is hard for a nation of shameless civilians to understand how life is arranged among people who come into the world with this heavy mortgage upon the freshest years of their strength; it seems like drinking the wine of life from a vessel with a great leak in the bottom. Is such a *régime* inspiring, or is it demoralising? Is the effect of it to quicken the sentiment of patriotism, the sense of the dangers to which one's country is exposed and of what one owes to the common cause, or to take the edge from all ambition that is not purely military, to force

153

young men to say that there is no use trying, that nothing is worth beginning, and that a young fellow condemned to pay such a tax as that has a right to refund himself in any way that is open to him? Reminded as one is at every step of the immensity of the military burden of France, the most interesting point seems to me not its economical but its moral bearing. Its effect upon the finances of the country may be accurately computed; its effect upon the character of the young generation is more of a mystery. As the analytic tourist wanders of an autumn afternoon upon the planted rampart of an ancient town and meets young soldiers strolling in couples or leaning against the parapet and looking off at the quiet country, he is apt to take the more genial view of the dreadful trade of arms. He is disposed to say that it teaches its votaries something that is worth knowing and yet is not learned in several other trades—the hardware, say, or the dry-goods business. Five years is a good deal to ask of a young life as a sacrifice; but the sacrifice is in some ways a gain. Certainly, apart from the question of material defence, it may be said that no European nation, at present, can afford, morally, not to pass her young men, the hope of the country, through the military mill. It does for them something indispensable; it toughens, hardens, solidifies them; gives them an ideal of honour, of some other possibility in life than making a fortune. A country in which the other trades I spoke of have it all their own way appears, in comparison, less educated.

So I mused, as I strolled in the afternoon along the charming old city-wall at Laon; and if my

meditations seem pretentious or fallacious, I must
say in justice that I had been a good while coming
to them. I had done a great many things first. I
had climbed up the long straight staircase which has
been dropped like a scaling-ladder from one of the
town-gates to the bottom of the hill. Laon still has
her gates as she still has her wall, and one of these,
the old Porte d'Ardon, is a really precious relic of
mediæval architecture. I had repaired to the sign
of the *Hure*—a portrait of this inhospitable beast is
swung from the front of the inn—and bespoken a
a lodging ; I had spent a long time in the cathedral,
in it and before it, beside it, behind it ; I had walked
all over the town, from the citadel, at one end of
the lofty plateau on which it stands, to the artillery-
barracks and the charming old church of St. Martin
at the other. The cathedral of Laon has not the
elaborate grandeur of that of Rheims ; but it is a
very noble and beautiful church. Nothing can be
finer than its position ; it would set off any church
to stand on such a hill-crest. Laon has also a
facade of many sculptures, which, however, has suffered greater violence than that of Rheims, and is
now being carefully and delicately restored. Whole
figures and bas-reliefs have lately been replaced by
exact imitations in that fresh white French stone
which looks at first like a superior sort of plaster.
They were far gone, and I suppose the restorer's
hand was imperiously called for. I do not know
that it has been too freely used. But half the charm
of Laon is the magnificent colouring of brownish,
weather-battered gray which it owes to the great
exposure of its position, and it will be many a year

before the chalky scars and patches will be wrought into dusky harmony with the rest of the edifice. Fortunately, however, they promise not to be very numerous; the principal restorations have taken place inside. I know not what all this labour costs; but I was interested in learning from the old bell-ringer at Rheims that the sum voted by the Chamber for furbishing up his own church was two millions of francs, to be expended during ten years. That is what it is to have "national monuments" to keep up. One is apt to think of the fourteenth century as a rather ill-appointed and comfortless period; but the fact that at the present time the mere repair of one of its buildings costs forty thousand dollars a year would indicate that the original builders had a great deal of money to spend. The cathedral of Laon was intended to be a wonderful cluster of towers, but only two of these ornaments—the couple above the west front—have been carried to a great altitude; the pedestals of the rest, however, detach themselves with much vigour, and contribute to the complicated and somewhat fantastic look which the church wears at a distance, and which makes its great effectiveness. The finished towers are admirably light and graceful; with the sky shining through their large interstices they suggest an imitation of timber in masonry. They have one very quaint feature. From their topmost portions, at each angle, certain carven heads of oxen peep forward with a startling naturalness—a tribute to the patient, powerful beasts who dragged the material of the building up the long zig-zags of the mountain. We perhaps treat our dumb creatures

156

better to-day than was done five hundred years ago ; but I doubt whether a modern architect, in settling his accounts, would have " remembered," as they say, the oxen.

The whole precinct of the cathedral of Laon is picturesque. There is a charming Palais de Justice beside it, separated from it by a pleasant, homely garden, in which, as you walk about, you have an excellent view of the towering back and sides of the great church. The Palais de Justice, which is an ancient building, has a fine old gothic arcade, and on the other side, directly upon the city-wall, a picturesque, irregular rear, with a row of painted windows, through which, from the *salle d'audience*, the judge on the bench and the prisoner in the dock may enjoy a prospect, admonitory, inspiring, or depressing, as the case may be, of the expanded country. This great sea-like plain that lies beneath the town on all sides constitutes, for Laon, a striking resemblance to those Italian cities —Siena, Volterra, Perugia—which the traveller remembers so fondly as a dark silhouette lifted high against a glowing sunset. There is something Italian, too, in the mingling of rock and rampart in the old foundations of the town, and in the generous verdure in which these are muffled. At one end of the hill-top the plateau becomes a narrow ridge ; the slope makes a deep indentation, which contributes to the effect of a thoroughly Italian picture. A line of crooked little red-roofed houses stands on the edge of this indentation, with their feet in the tangled verdure that blooms in it ; and above them rises a large, florid, deserted-looking church, which you may be sure has a little empty, grass-grown, out-of-the-way *place* before it. Almost opposite, on another spur of the hill, the gray walls of a suppressed convent peep from among the trees. I might have been at Perugia.

There came in the evening to the inn of the Hure a very worthy man who had vehicles to hire. The Hure was decidedly a provincial hostelry, and I compared it mentally with certain English establishments of a like degree, of which I had lately had observation. In England I should have had a waiter in an old evening-suit and a white cravat, who would have treated me to cold meat and bread and cheese. There would have been a musty little inn-parlour and probably a very good fire in the grate, and the festally-attired waiter would have been my sole entertainer. At Laon I was in perpetual intercourse with the landlord and his wife, and a large body of easy-going, confidential domestics. Our intercourse was carried on in an old darksome stone kitchen, with shining copper vessels hanging all over the walls, in which I was free to wander about and take down my key in one place and rummage out my candlestick in another, while the domestics sat at table eating *pot-au-feu*. The landlord cooked the dinner; he wore a white cap and apron; he brought in the first dish at the table d'hôte. Of course there was a table d'hôte, with several lamps and a long array of little dessert-dishes, for the benefit of two commercial travellers, who tucked their napkins into their necks, and the writer of these lines. Every country has its manners. In England the benefits—whatever they are—represented by the evening dress of the waiter would have been most apparent; in France one was more sensible of the blessings of which the white cap and apron of the host were a symbol. In England, certainly, one is treated more as a gentleman. It is too often forgotten, however, that even a gentleman partakes of nourishment. But I am forgetting my dispenser of vehicles, concerning whom, however, and whose large red cheeks and crimson cravat, I have left myself room to say no more than that they were witnesses of a bargain that I should be driven early on the morrow morning, in an " Américaine," to the Château de Coucy. The Américaine proved to be a vehicle of which I should not have been eager to claim the credit for my native land; but with the aid of a ragged but resolute little horse, and a driver so susceptible as regards his beast's appearance that, referring to the exclamation of dismay with which I had greeted it, he turned to me at the end of each successive kilometre with a rancorous " *Now*, do you say he can't go ? "—with these accessories, I say, it conveyed me more than twenty miles. It was entertaining to wind down the hillside from Laon in the early morning of a splendid autumn day; to dip into the glistening plain, all void of hedges and fences, and sprinkled with light and dew; to jog along the straight white roads, between the tall, thin poplars; to rattle through the half-waked villages and past the orchards heavy with sour-looking crimson apples. The Château de Coucy is a well-known monument; it is one of the most considerable ruins in France, and it is in some respects the most extraordinary. As you come from Laon a turn in the road suddenly, at last, reveals it to you. It is still at a distance; you will not reach it for half an hour; but its huge white donjon stands up like some gigantic lighthouse at sea. Coucy is altogether on a grand scale, but this colossal, shining cylinder is a wonder of bigness. As M. Viollet-le-Duc says, it seems to have been built by giants for a race of giants. The very quaint little town of Coucy-le-Château nestles at the foot of this strange, half-substantial, half-spectral structure; it was, together with a goodly part of the neighbouring country, the feudal appanage of those terrible lords who erected the present indestructible edifice, and whose "boastful motto" (I quote from Murray) was

> "Roi je ne suis,
> Prince ni comte aussi ;
> Je suis le Sire de Coucy."

Coucy is a sleepy little borough, still girdled with its ancient wall, entered by its old gateways, and supported on the verdurous flanks of a hill-top. I interviewed the host of the Golden Apple in his kitchen; I breakfasted—*ma foi, fort bien,* as they would say in the indigenous tongue—in his parlour; and then I visited the château, which is at five minutes' walk. This very interesting ruin is the property of the state, and the state is represented by a very civil and intelligent woman, who divests the trade of custodian of almost all its grossness. Any feudal ruin is a charming affair, and Coucy has much of the sweet melancholy of its class. There are four great towers, connected by a massive curtain and enclosing the tremendous donjon of which I just now spoke. All this is very crumbling and silvery; the enclosure is a tangle of wild verdure, and the pigeons perch upon the inaccessible battlements exactly where the sketcher would wish them. But the place lacked, to my sense, the peculiar softness and venerableness, the ivied mellowness, of a great English ruin. At Coucy there is no ivy to speak of; the climate has not caressed and embroidered the rugged masses of stone. This is what I meant by speaking of the famous donjon as spectral; the term is an odd one to apply to an edifice whose walls are thirty-four feet thick. Its vast, pale surface has not a speck nor a stain, not a clinging weed nor a creeping plant. It looks like a tower of ivory.

I took my way from Coucy to the ancient town of Soissons, where I found another cathedral, from which, I think, I extracted all the entertainment it could legitimately yield. There is little other to be had at Soissons, in spite of the suggestiveness of its name, which is redolent of history and local colour. The truth is, I suppose, that Soissons looks so new, precisely because she is so old. She is in her second youth; she has renewed herself. The old city was worn out; it could no longer serve; it has been succeeded by another. The new one is a quiet, rather aristocratic-looking little *ville de province*—a collection of well-conditioned, sober-faced abodes of gentility, with high-walled gardens behind them and very carefully closed portes-cochère in front. Occasionally a porte-cochère opens; an elderly lady in black emerges and paces discreetly away. An old gentleman has come to the door with her. He is comfortably corpulent; he wears gold spectacles and embroidered slippers. He looks up and down the dull street, and sees nothing at all; then he retires, closing the porte-cochère very softly and firmly. But he has stood there long enough to give an observant stranger the impression of a cautious provincial bourgeoisie that has a solid fortune well invested, and that marries its daughters only *à bon escient*. This latter ceremony, however, whenever it occurs, probably takes place in the cathedral, and though resting on a prosaic foundation must borrow a certain grace from that charming building. The cathedral of Soissons has a statueless front and only a single tower; but it is **full of a certain** natural elegance.

Chartres

THE spring, in Paris, since it has fairly begun, has been enchanting. The sun and the moon have been blazing in emulation, and the difference between the blue sky of day and of night has been as slight as possible. There are no clouds in the sky, but there are little thin green clouds, little puffs of raw, tender verdure, entangled among the branches of the trees. All the world is in the streets; the chairs and tables which have stood empty all winter before the doors of the cafés are at a premium; the theatres have become intolerably close; the puppet-shows in the Champs Elysées are the only form of dramatic entertainment which seems consistent with the season. By way of doing honour, at a small cost, to this ethereal mildness, I went out the other day to the ancient town of Chartres, where I spent several hours, which I cannot consent to pass over as if nothing had happened. It is the experience of the writer of these lines, who likes nothing so much as moving about to see the world, that if one has been for a longer time than usual resident and stationary, there is a kind of overgrown entertainment in taking the train, even for a suburban goal; and that if one takes it on a charming April day, when there is a sense, almost an odour, of change in the air, the innocent pleasure is as nearly as possible complete. My accessibility to emotions of this kind amounts to an infirmity, and the effect of it was to send me down to Chartres in a shamelessly optimistic state of mind. I was so prepared to be entertained and pleased with everything that it is only a mercy that the cathedral happens really to be a fine building. If it had not been, I should still have admired it inordinately, at the risk of falling into heaven knows what æsthetic heresy. But I am almost ashamed to say how soon my entertainment began. It began, I think, with my hailing a little open carriage on the Boulevard and causing myself to be driven to the Gare de l'Ouest—far away across the river, up the Rue Bonaparte, of art-student memories, and along the big, straight Rue de Rennes to the Boulevard Montparnasse. Of course, at this rate, by the time I reached Chartres—the journey is of a couple of hours—I had almost drained the cup of pleasure. But it was replenished at the station, at the buffet, from the pungent bottle of wine I drank with my breakfast. Here, by the way, is another excellent excuse for being delighted with any day's excursion in France—that wherever you are, you may breakfast to your taste. There may, indeed, if the station is very small, be no buffet; but if there is a buffet, you may be sure that civilisation—in the persons of a sympathetic young woman in a well-made black dress, and a rapid, zealous, grateful waiter—presides at it. It was quite the least, as the French say, that after my breakfast I should have thought the cathedral, as I saw it from the top of the steep hill on which the town stands, rising high above the clustered houses and seeming to make of their red-roofed agglomeration a mere pedestal for its immense beauty, promised remarkably well. You see it so as you emerge from the station, and then, as you climb slowly into town, you lose sight of it. You perceive Chartres to be a rather shabby little *ville de province*, with a few sunny, empty open *places*, and crooked shady streets, in which two or three times you lose your way, until at last, after more than once catching a glimpse, high above some slit between the houses, of the clear gray towers shining against the blue sky, you push forward again, risk another short cut, turn another interposing corner, and stand before the goal of your pilgrimage.

I spent a long time looking at this monument. I revolved around it, like a moth around a candle; I went away and I came back; I chose twenty different standpoints; I observed it during the different hours of the day, and saw it in the moonlight as well as the sunshine. I gained, in a word, a certain sense of familiarity with it; and yet I despair of giving any coherent account of it. Like most French cathedrals, it rises straight out of the street, and is destitute of that setting of turf and trees and deaneries and canonries which contribute so largely to the impressiveness of the great English churches. Thirty years ago a row of old houses

167

was glued to its base and made their back walls of its sculptured sides. These have been plucked away, and, relatively speaking, the church is fairly isolated. But the little square that surrounds it is deplorably narrow, and you flatten your back against the opposite houses in the vain attempt to stand off and survey the towers. The proper way to look at them would be to go up in a balloon and hang poised, face to face with them, in the blue air. There is, however, perhaps an advantage in being forced to stand so directly under them, for this position gives you an overwhelming impression of their height. I have seen, I suppose, churches as beautiful as this one, but I do not remember ever to have been so fascinated by superpositions and vertical effects. The endless upward reach of the great west front, the clear, silvery tone of its surface, the way three or four magnificent features are made to occupy its serene expanse, its simplicity, majesty, and dignity— these things crowd upon one's sense with a force that makes the act of vision seem for the moment almost all of life. The impressions produced by architecture lend themselves as little to interpretation by another medium as those produced by music. Certainly there is an inexpressible harmony in the facade of Chartres.

The doors are rather low, as those of the English cathedrals are apt to be, but (standing three together) are set in a deep framework of sculpture—rows of arching grooves, filled with admirable little images, standing with their heels on each other's heads. The church, as it now exists, except the northern tower, dates from the middle of the thirteenth century, and

these closely-packed figures are full of the grotesqueness of the period. Above the triple portals is a
vast round-topped window, in three divisions, of the
grandest dimensions and the stateliest effect. Above
this window is a circular aperture, of huge circumference, with a double row of sculptured spokes
radiating from its centre and looking on its lofty field
of stone as expansive and symbolic as if it were
the wheel of Time itself. Higher still is a little
gallery with a delicate balustrade, supported on a
beautiful cornice and stretching across the front
from tower to tower; and above this is a range of
niched statues of kings—fifteen, I believe, in number.
Above the statues is a gable, with an image of the
Virgin and Child on its front, and another of Christ
on its apex. In the relation of all these parts there
is such a high felicity that while on the one side the
eye rests on a great many large blanks there is no
approach on the other to poverty. The little gallery
that I have spoken of, beneath the statues of the
kings, had for me a peculiar charm. Useless, at its
tremendous altitude, for other purposes, it seemed
intended for the little images to step down and walk
about upon. When the great façade begins to glow
in the late afternoon light, you can imagine them
strolling up and down their long balcony in couples,
pausing with their elbows on the balustrade, resting
their stony chins in their hands, and looking out,
with their little blank eyes, on the great view of the
old French monarchy they once ruled, and which
now has passed away. The two great towers of the
cathedral are among the noblest of their kind. They
rise in solid simplicity to a height as great as the

eye often troubles itself to travel, and then suddenly they begin to execute a magnificent series of feats in architectural gymnastics. This is especially true of the northern spire, which is a late creation, dating from the sixteenth century. The other is relatively quiet; but its companion is a sort of tapering bouquet of sculptured stone. Statues and buttresses, gargoyles, arabesques and crockets pile themselves in successive stages, until the eye loses the sense of everything but a sort of architectural lacework. The pride of Chartres, after its front, is the two portals of its transepts — great dusky porches, in three divisions, covered with more images than I have time to talk about. Wherever you look, along the sides of the church, a time-worn image is niched or perched. The face of each flying buttress is garnished with one, with the features quite melted away.

The inside of the cathedral corresponds in vastness and grandeur to the outside—it is the perfection of gothic in its prime. But I looked at it rapidly, the place was so intolerably cold. It seemed to answer one's query of what becomes of the winter when the spring chases it away. The winter hereabouts has sought an asylum in Chartres cathedral, where it has found plenty of room and may reside in a state of excellent preservation until it can safely venture abroad again. I supposed I had been in cold churches before, but the delusion had been an injustice to the temperature of Chartres. The nave was full of the little padded chairs of the local bourgeoisie, whose faith, I hope for their comfort, is of the good old red-hot complexion. In a higher temperature I should have done more justice to the magnificent old glass of the windows—which glowed through the icy dusk like the purple and orange of a winter sunset—and to the immense sculptured external casing of the choir. This latter is an extraordinary piece of work. It is a high gothic screen, shutting in the choir, and covered with elaborate bas-reliefs of the sixteenth and seventeenth centuries, representing scenes from the life of Christ and of the Virgin. Some of the figures are admirable, and the effect of the whole great semicircular wall, chiselled like a silver bowl, is superb. There is also a crypt of high antiquity and, I believe, great interest, to be seen; but my teeth chattered a respectful negative to the sacristan who offered to guide me to it. It was so agreeable to stand in the warm outer air again, that I spent the rest of the day in it.

Although, besides its cathedral, Chartres has no very rare architectural treasures, the place is pictorial, in a shabby, third-rate, poverty-stricken degree, and my observations were not unremunerative. There is a little church of Saint-Aignan, of the sixteenth century, with an elegant, decayed façade, and a small tower beside it, lower than its own roof, to which it is joined, in unequal twinship, by a single long buttress. Standing there with its crumbling Renaissance doorway, in a kind of grass-grown alcove, it reminded me of certain monuments that the tourist encounters in small Italian towns. Most of the streets of Chartres are crooked lanes, winding over the face of the steep hill, the summit of the hill being occupied by half a dozen little open squares, which seem like reservoirs of the dulness and stillness that flow through the place. In the midst of one of them rises an old dirty brick obelisk, commemorating the glories of the young General Marceau, of the first Republic—" Soldier at 16, general at 23, he died at 27." Such memorials, when one comes upon them unexpectedly, produce in the mind a series of circular waves of feeling, like a splash in a quiet pond. Chartres gives us an impression of extreme antiquity, but it is an antiquity that has gone down in the world. I saw very few of those stately little hôtels, with pilastered fronts, which look so well in the silent streets of provincial towns. The houses are mostly low, small, and of sordid aspect, and though many of them have overhanging upper stories, and steep, battered gables, they are rather wanting in character. I was struck, as an American always is in small French and English towns, with the immense number of shops, and their brilliant appearance, which seems so out of proportion to any visible body of consumers. At Chartres the shopkeepers must all feed upon each other, for, whoever buys, the whole population sells. This population appeared to consist mainly of several hundred brown old peasant women, in the seventies and eighties, with their faces cross-hatched with wrinkles and their quaint white coifs drawn tightly over their weather-blasted eye-brows. Labour-stricken grandams, all the world over, are the opposite of lovely, for the toil that wrestles for its daily bread, morsel by morsel, is not beautifying; but I thought I had never seen the possibilities of female ugliness so variously embodied as in the crones of Chartres. Some of them were leading small children by the hand—little red-cheeked girls, in the close black caps and black pinafores of humble French infancy—a costume which makes French children always look like orphans. Others were guiding along the flinty lanes the steps of small donkeys, some of them fastened into little carts, some with well-laden backs. These were the only quadrupeds I perceived at Chartres. Neither horse nor carriage did I behold, save at the station the omnibuses of the rival inns—the " Grand Monarque " and the " Duc de Chartres" —which glare at each other across the Grande Place. A friend of mine told me that a few years ago, passing through Chartres, he went by night to call upon a gentleman who lived there. During his visit it came on to rain violently, and when the hour for his departure arrived the rain had made the streets impassable. There was no vehicle to be had, and my friend was resigning himself to a soaking. " You can be taken of course in the sedan-chair," said his host with dignity. The sedan-chair was produced, a couple of serving-men grasped the handles, my friend stepped into it, and went swinging back—through the last century—to the " Grand Monarque." This little anecdote, I imagine, still paints Chartres socially.

Before dinner I took a walk on the planted promenade which encircles the town—the Tour-de-ville it is called—much of which is extremely picturesque. Chartres has lost her walls as a whole, but here and there they survive, and play a desultory part in holding the town together. In one place the rampart is really magnificent—smooth, strong and lofty, curtained with ivy, and supporting on its summit an old convent and its garden. Only one of the city-gates remains—a narrow arch of the fourteenth century, flanked by two admirable round towers, and preceded by a fosse. If you stoop a little, as you stand outside, the arch of this hoary old gate makes a capital setting for the picture of the interior of the town, and, on the inner hill-top, against the sky, the large gray mass of the cathedral. The ditch is full, and to right and to left it flows along the base of the mouldering wall, through which the shabby backs of houses extrude, and which is garnished with little wooden galleries, lavatories of the town's soiled linen. These little galleries are filled with washerwomen, who crane over and dip their many-coloured rags into the yellow stream. The old patched and interrupted wall, the ditch with its weedy edges, the spots of colour, the white-capped laundresses in their little wooden cages—one lingers to look at it all.

Rouen

IT is quite in the nature of things that a Parisian correspondence should have flagged during the last few weeks; for even the most brilliant of capitals, when the summer has fairly begun to be summer, affords few topics to the chronicler. To a chronicle of small beer such a correspondence almost literally finds itself reduced. The correspondent consumes a goodly number of those magnified thimblefuls of this fluid, known in Paris as "bocks," and from the shadiest corner of the coolest café he can discover watches the softened bitumen grow more largely interspaced. There is little to do or to see, and therefore little to write about. There is in fact only one thing to do, namely, to get out of Paris. The lively imagination of the correspondent anticipates his departure and takes flight to one of the innumerable watering-places whose charms at this season are set forth in large yellow and pink placards on all the empty walls. They order this matter, like so many others, much better in France. Here you have not, as in America, to hunt up the "summer retreat" about which you desire information in a dense alphabetical list in the columns of a newspaper; you are familiar with its merits for weeks before you start —you have seen them half a dozen times a day emblazoned on the line of your customary walk, over the hand and seal of the company that runs, as we should say in America, the Casino. If you are detained in Paris, however, after luckier mortals have departed—your reflections upon the fate of the luckless mortals who do not depart at all are quite another question, demanding another chapter—it does not perhaps make you much happier to peruse these lyrical advertisements, which seem to flutter with the breezes of Houlgate and Etretat. You must take your consolation where you can find it, and it must be added that of all great cities Paris is the most tolerable in hot weather. It is true that the asphalt liquifies, and it is true that the brilliant limestone of which the city is built reflects the sun with uncomfortable fierceness. It is also true that of a summer evening you pay a penalty for living in the best-lighted capital in the world. The inordinate amount of gas in the streets makes the atmosphere hot and thick, so that even under the dim constellations you feel of a July night as if you were in a big music-hall. If you look down at such a time upon the central portions of Paris from a high window in a remoter quarter, you see them wrapped in a lurid haze, of the devil's own brewing. But, on the other hand, there are a hundred facilities for remaining out of doors. You are not obliged to sit on a " stoop " or on a curb-stone, as in New-York. The Boulevards are a long chain of cafés, each one with its little

178

promontory of chairs and tables projecting into the
sea of asphalt. These promontories are doubtless not
exactly islands of the blessed, peopled though some
of them may be with sirens addicted to beer, but
they may help you to pass a hot evening. Then you
may dine in the Champs Elysées, at a table spread
under the trees, beside an ivied wall, and almost
believe you are in the country. This illusion, im-
perfect as it is, is a luxury, and must be paid for
accordingly; the dinner is not so good as at a restaurant on the Boulevard, and is considerably dearer,
and there is after all not much difference in sitting
with one's feet in dusty gravel or on a sanded floor.
But the whole situation is more idyllic. I indulged
in a cheap idyl the other day by taking the penny
steamer down the Seine to Auteuil (a very short sail),
and dining at what is called in Parisian parlance a
guingette on the bank of the stream. It was a very
humble style of entertainment, but the most ambitious pursuit of pleasure can do no more than succeed,
and this was a success. The Seine at Auteuil is wide,
and is spanned by a stately viaduct of two tiers of
arches, which stands up against the sky in a picturesque and monumental manner. Your table is
spread under a trellis which scratches your head—
spread chiefly with fried fish—and an old man who
looks like a political exile comes and stands before
it and sings a doleful ditty on the respect due to
white hairs. You testify by the bestowal of copper
coin the esteem with which his own inspire you, and
he is speedily replaced by a lad with one arm, who
treats you to something livelier:

"A la bonne heure ; parlez-moi de ça !"

179

You eventually return to Paris on the top of a tram-car. It is a very different affair to go out and dine at the Bois de Boulogne, at the charming restaurant which is near the cascade and the Longchamp race-course. Here are no ballad-singers, but stately trees majestically grouped and making long evening sha-dows on a lawn, and irreproachable tables, and car-riages rolling up behind high-stepping horses and depositing all sorts of ladies. The drive back through the wood at night is most charming, and the coolness of the air extreme, however hot you may still be certain to find the city.

The best thing, therefore, is not to go back. I write these lines at an inn at Havre, before a window which frames the picture of the seaward path of the transatlantic steamers. One of the great black ships is at this moment painted on the canvas, very near, and beginning its outward journey. I watch it to the right-hand ledge of the window, which is as far as so poor a sailor need be expected to follow it. The hotel at Havre is called, for mysterious reasons, " Frascati "—reasons which I give up the attempt to fathom, so undiscoverable are its points of analogy with the lovely village of the same name which nestles among the olives of the Roman hills. The locality has its charms, however. It is very agreeable, for instance, at the end of a hot journey, to sit down to dinner in a great open cage, hung over the Atlantic, and, while the sea-breeze cools your wine. watch the swiftly-moving ships pass before you like the figures on the field of a magic lantern. It is pleasant also to open your eyes in the early dawn, before the light is intense, and without moving your head on the

pillow, enjoy the same clear vision of the ocean high-
way. In the vague dusk, with their rapid gliding,
the passing vessels look like the ghosts of wrecked
ships. Most seaports are picturesque, and Havre is
not the least so ; but my enjoyment has been not of
my goal, but of my journey.

My head is full of the twenty-four hours I have
just passed at Rouen, and of the charming sail down
the Seine to Honfleur. Rouen is a city of very
ancient renown, and yet I confess I was not prepared
to find a little town of so much expression. The
traveller who treads the Rouen streets at the present day sees but the shadow of their former characteristics; for the besom of M. Haussmann has
swept through the city, and a train of " embellish-
ments " has followed in its track. The streets have
been widened and straightened, and the old houses
—gems of mediæval domestic architecture—which
formed the peculiar treasure of the place, have been
more than decimated. A great deal remains, however, and American eyes are quick to make discoveries. The cathedral, the churches, the Palais de
Justice, are alone a splendid group of monuments,
and a stroll through the streets reveals a collection of
brown and sculptured façades, of quaintly-timbered
gables, of curious turrets and casements, of doorways which still may be called rich. Every now
and then a considerable stretch of duskiness and
crookedness delights the sentimental tourist who is
to pass but a couple of nights at Rouen, and who
does not care if his favourite adjective happen to
imply another element which also is spelled with a
p. It is nothing to him that the picturesque is

pestiferous. It is everything to him that the great front of the cathedral is magnificently battered, heavy, impressive. It has been defaced immensely, and is now hardly more than a collection of empty niches. I do not mean, of course, that the wanton tourist rejoices in the absence of the statues which once filled them, but up to the present moment, at least, he is not sorry that the façade has not been restored. It consists of a sort of screen, pierced in the centre with a huge wheel-window, crowned with a pyramid of chiselled needles and spires, flanked with two turrets capped with tall empty canopies, and covered, generally, with sculptures — friezes, statues, excrescences. On each side of it rises a great tower; one a rugged mass of early Norman work, with little ornament save its hatcheted closed arches, and its great naked base, as huge and white as the bottom of a chalk-cliff; the other a specimen of sixteenth century gothic, extremely flamboyant and confounding to the eye. The sides of the cathedral are as yet more or less imbedded in certain black and dwarfish old houses, but if you pass around them by a long détour, you arrive at two superb lateral porches. The so-called Portail des Libraires, in especial, on the northern side, is a magnificent affair, sculptured from summit to base (it is now restored), and preceded by a long forecourt, in which the guild of booksellers used to hold its musty traffic. From here you see the immense central tower, perched above the junction of the transepts and the nave, and crowned with a gigantic iron spire, lately erected to replace one which was destroyed by lightning in the early part of the century. This gaunt pyramid has the drawback, to American eyes, of resembling too much the tall fire-towers which are seen in transatlantic cities, and its dimensions are such that, viewed from a distance, it fairly makes little Rouen look top-heavy. Behind the choir, within, is a beautiful lady-chapel, and in this chapel are two enchanting works of art. The larger and more striking of these is the tomb of the two Cardinals d'Amboise, uncle and nephew—the elder, if I mistake not, minister of Louis XII. It consists of a shallow, oblong recess in the wall, lined with gilded and fretted marble, and corniced with delicate little statues. Within the recess the figures of the two cardinals are kneeling, with folded hands and ruggedly earnest faces, their long robes spread out behind them with magnificent amplitude. They are full of life, dignity, and piety; they look like portraits of Holbein transferred into marble. The base of the monument is composed of a series of admirable little images representing the cardinal and other virtues, and the effect of the whole work is wonderfully grave and rich. The discreet traveller will never miss an opportunity to come into a great church at eventide—the hour when his fellow-travellers, less discreet, are lingering over the table d'hôte, when the painted windows glow with a deeper splendour, when the long wand of the beadle, slowly tapping the pavement, or the shuffle of the old sacristan, has a ghostly resonance along the empty nave, and three or four work-weary women, before a dusky chapel, are mumbling for the remission of unimaginable sins. At this hour, at Rouen, the tomb of the Duke of Brézé, husband of Diana of Poitiers, placed opposite to the monument

I have just described, seemed to me the most beautiful thing in the world. It is presumably the work of the delightful Jean Goujon, and it bears the stamp of his graceful and inventive talent. The deceased is lying on his back, almost naked, with a part of his shroud bound in a knot about his head— a realistic but not a repulsive image of death. At his head kneels the amiable Diana, in sober garments, all decency and devotion; at his feet stands the Virgin, a charming young woman with a charming child. Above, on another tier, the subject of the monument is represented in the fulness of life, dressed as for a tournament, bestriding a high-stepping war-horse, riding forth like a Roland or a Galahad. The architecture of the tomb is exceedingly graceful and the subordinate figures admirable, but the image of the dead Duke is altogether a masterpiece. The other evening, in the solemn stillness and the fading light of the great cathedral, it seemed irresistibly human and touching. The spectator felt a sort of impulse to smooth out the shroud and straighten the helpless hands.

The second church of Rouen, Saint-Ouen, the beautiful and harmonious, has no monuments of this value, but it offers within a higher interest than the Cathedral. Without, it looks like an English abbey, scraped and restored, disencumbered of huddling neighbours and surrounded on three sides by a beautiful garden. Seen to this excellent advantage it is one of the noblest of churches; but within, it is one of the most fascinating. My taste in architecture greatly resembles my opinions in fruit; the particular melon or pear or peach that I am eating appears to me to place either peaches, pears, or melons, beyond all other succulent things. In the same way, in a fine building the present impression is the one that convinces me most. This is deplorable levity; yet I risk the affirmation *à propos* of Saint-Ouen. I can imagine no happier combination of lightness and majesty. Its proportions bring tears to the eyes. I have left myself space only to recommend the sail down the Seine from Rouen to the mouth of the stream; but I recommend it in the highest terms. The heat was extreme and the little steamer most primitive, but the river is as entertaining as one could wish. It makes an infinite number of bends and corners and angles, rounded off by a charming vegetation. Abrupt and rocky hills go with it all the way—hills with cornfields lying in their hollows and deep woods crowning their tops. Out of the woodland peep old manors, and beneath, between the hills and the stream, are high-thatched farmsteads, lying deep in their meadows and orchards, cottages pallisaded with hollyhocks, gray old Norman churches and villas flanked with big horse-chestnuts. It is a land of peace and plenty, and remarkable to Anglo-Saxon eyes for the English-looking details of its scenery. I noticed a hundred places where one might have been in Kent as well as in Normandy. In fact it is almost better than Kent, for Kent has no Seine. At the last the river becomes unmistakably an arm of the sea, and as a river, therefore, less interesting. But crooked little Honfleur, with its miniature port, clinging to the side of a cliff as luxuriant as one of the headlands of the Mediterranean, gratifies in a high degree the tourist with a propensity for sketching.

Etretat

THE coast of Normandy and Picardy, from Trouville to Boulogne, is a chain of *stations balnéaires*, each with its particular claim to patronage. The grounds of the claim are in some cases not especially obvious ; but they are generally found to reside in the fact that if one's spirits, on arriving, are low, so also are the prices. There are the places that are dear and brilliant, like Trouville and Dieppe, and places that are cheap and dreary, like Fécamp and Cabourg. Then there are the places that are both cheap and pleasant. This delightful combination of qualities may be found at the modest *plage* from which I write these lines. At Etretat you may enjoy some of the finest cliff-scenery it has been my fortune to behold, and you may breakfast and dine at the principal hotel for the sum of five and a half francs a day. You may engage a room in the town over the butcher's, the baker's, the cobbler's, at a rate that will depend upon your talent for driving a bargain, but that in no case will be exorbitant. Add to this that there are no other opportunities at Etretat to

189

spend money. You wear old clothes, you walk about in canvas shoes, you deck your head with a fisherman's cap (when made of white flannel these articles may be extolled for their coolness, convenience, and picturesqueness), you lie on the pebbly strand most of the day, watching the cliffs, the waves, and the bathers; in the evening you converse with your acquaintance on the terrace of the Casino, and you keep monkish hours. Though Etretat enjoys great and deserved popularity, I see no symptoms of the decline of these simple fashions — no menace of the invasion of luxury. A little more luxury, indeed, might be imported without doing any harm; though after all we soon learn that it is an idle enough prejudice that has hitherto prevented us from keeping our soap in a sugar-dish and regarding a small rock, placed against a door, as an efficient substitute for a key. From a Parisian point of view, Etretat is certainly primitive, but it would be affectation on the part of an American to pretend that he was not agreeably surprised to find a "summer resort," in which he had been warned that he would have to rough it, so elaborately appointed and organised. Etretat may be primitive, but Etretat is French, and therefore Etretat is "administered."

Like most of the French watering-places, the place has a limited past. Twenty years ago it was but a cluster of fishing-huts. A group of artists and literary people were its first colonists, and Alphonse Karr became the mouthpiece of their enthusiasm. In vulgar phrase, he wrote up Etretat, and he lives in legend, at the present hour, as the *genius loci*. The main street is named after him; the gable of the

chief inn—the classic Hôtel Blanquet—is adorned
with a coloured medallion representing his cropped
head and long beard; the shops are stocked with his
photographs and with pictures of his villa. Like
the magician who has evoked the spirit, he has made
his bow and retired; but the artistic fraternity, his
disciples, still haunt the place, and it enjoys also the
favour of theatrical people, three or four of whom,
having retired upon their laurels, possess villas here.
From my open window, as I write these lines, I look
out beyond a little cluster of clean housetops at the
long green flank of the down, as it slopes to the
village from the summit of the cliff. To the right
is the top of an old storm-twisted grove of oaks, in
the heart of which stands a brown old farmhouse;
then comes the sharp, even outline of the down, with
its side spotted with little flat bushes and wrinkled
with winding paths, along which here and there I
see a bright figure moving; on the left, above the
edge of the cliff, stands a bleak little chapel, dedicated to our Lady of the fishing-folk. Just here a
provoking chimney starts up and cuts off my view
of the downward plunge of the cliff, showing me,
with a bar of blue ocean beyond, but a glimpse of
its white cheek—its fantastic profile is to the left.
But there is not far to go to see without impedi-
ments. Three minutes' walk along the Rue Alphonse
Karr, where every house is a shop, and every shop
has lodgers above it, who scramble bedward by a
ladder and trap-door, brings you to the little pebbly
bay where the cliffs are perpendicular and the foreign
life of Etretat goes forward. At one end are the
small fishing-smacks, with their green sides and their

black sails, resting crookedly upon the stones; at the other is the Casino, and the two or three tiers of bathing-houses on the slope of the beach in front of it. This beach may be said to be Etretat. It is so steep and stony as to make circulation impossible; one's only course is to plant a camp-chair among the stones or to look for a soft spot in the pebbles, and to abide in the position so chosen. And yet it is the spot in Etretat most sacred to tranquil pleasure.

The French do not treat their beaches as we do ours—as places for a glance, a dip, or a trot, places animated simply during the balneary hours, and wrapped in natural desolation for the rest of the twenty-four. They love them, they adore them, they take possession of them, they live upon them. The people here sit upon the beach from morning to night; whole families come early and establish themselves, with umbrellas and rugs, books and work. The ladies get sunburnt and don't mind it; the gentlemen smoke interminably; the children roll over on the pointed pebbles and stare at the sun like young eagles. (The children's lot I rather commiserate; they have no wooden spades and pails; they have no sand to delve and grub in; they can dig no trenches and canals, nor see the creeping tide flood them.) The great occupation and amusement is the bathing, which has many entertaining features (I allude to it as a spectacle), especially for strangers who keep an eye upon national idiosyncrasies. The French take their bathing very seriously; supplemented by opéra-bouffe in the evening at the Casino, it is their most preferred form of communion with nature. The spectators and the bathers commingle

in graceful promiscuity; it is the freedom of the
golden age. The whole beach becomes a large
family party, in which the sweetest familiarities
prevail. There is more or less costume, but the
minimum rather than the maximum is found the
more comfortable. Bathers come out of their dress-
ing-houses wrapped in short white sheets, which they
deposit on the stones, taking an air-bath for some
minutes before entering the water. Like everything
in France, the bathing is excellently managed, and
you feel the firm hand of a paternal and overlooking
government the moment you issue from your hut.
The Government will on no consideration consent to
your being rash. There are six or eight worthy old
sons of Neptune on the beach—perfect amphibious
creatures—who, if you are a new-comer, immediately
accost you and demand pledges that you know how
to swim. If you do not, they give you much excellent advice, and keep an eye on you while you
are in the water. They are moreover obliged to
render you any service you may demand—to pour
buckets of water over your head, to fetch your bath-
ing-sheet and your slippers, to carry your wife and
children into the sea, to dip them, cheer them, sustain
them, to teach them how to swim and how to dive,
to hover about, in short, like ministering and trickling
angels. At a short distance from the shore are two
boats, freighted with sundry other marine divinities,
who remain there perpetually, taking it as a personal
offence if you venture out too far.

The French themselves have every pretext for
venturing, being in general excellent swimmers.
Every one swims, and swims indefatigably—men,

women, and children.   I have been especially struck
with the prowess of the ladies, who take the neatest
possible headers from the two long plunging-boards
which are rigged in the water upon high wheels.
As you recline upon the beach you may observe
Mademoiselle X. issue from her cabin—Mademoiselle X., the actress of the Palais Royal Theatre,
whom you have seen and applauded behind the
footlights.   She wears a bathing-dress in which, as
regards the trousers, even what I have called the
minimum has been appreciably scanted; but she
trips down, surveying her liberated limbs.   " *C'est
convenable, j'espère, hein ?*" says Mademoiselle, and
trots up the spring-board which projects over the
waves with one end uppermost, like a great see-saw.
She balances a moment, and then gives a great aerial
dive, executing on the way the most graceful of
somersaults.   This performance the star of the
Palais Royal repeats during the ensuing hour, at
intervals of five minutes, and leaves you, as you lie
tossing little stones into the water, to consider the
curious and delicate question why a lady may go so
far as to put herself into a single scant clinging
garment and take a straight leap, head downward,
before three hundred spectators, without violation of
propriety—and why impropriety should begin only
when she turns over in the air in such a way that
for five seconds her head is upwards.   The logic of
the matter is mysterious ; white and black are
divided by a hair.   But the fact remains that virtue
is on one side of the hair and vice on the other.
There are some days here so still and radiant, however, that it seems as if vice itself, steeped in such

194

an air and such a sea, might be diluted into inno-
cence. The sea is as blue as melted sapphires, and
the rugged white faces of the bordering cliffs make
a silver frame for the picture. Every one is idle,
amused, good-natured; the bathers take to the water
as easily as mermen and mermaids. The bathing-
men in the two *bateaux de surveillance* have in their
charge a freight of rosy children, more or less chub-
bily naked, and they have nailed a gay streamer and
a rude nosegay to their low mastheads. The swimmers dip and rise, circling round the boats and playing with the children. Every now and then they
grasp the sides of the boats and cling to them in a
dozen harmonious attitudes, making one fancy that
Eugène Delacroix's great picture of Dante and Virgil
on the Styx, with the damned trying to scramble
into Charon's bark, has been repainted as a scene
on one of the streams of Paradise. The swimmers
are not the damned, but the blessed, and the demonstrative French babies are the cherubs.

The Casino at Etretat is a modest but respectable
establishment, with a sufficiently capacious terrace,
directly upon the beach, a café, a billiard-room, a
ballroom—which may also be used as a theatre, a
reading-room, and a *salon de conversation*. It is in
very good taste, without any attempt at gilding or
mirrors; the ballroom, in fact, is quite a masterpiece, with its charm of effect produced simply by
unpainted woods and happy proportions. Three
evenings in the week a blond young man in a white
necktie plays waltzes on a grand piano; but the
effect is not that of an American "hop," owing to
the young ladies of France not being permitted to

dance in public places. They may only sit wistfully beside their mammas. Imagine a " hop" at which sweet seventeen is condemned to immobility. The burden of the gaiety is sustained by three or four rosy English maidens and as many of their American sisters. On the other evenings a weak little operatic troupe gives light specimens of the lyric drama, the privilege of enjoying which is covered by your subscription to the Casino. The French hurry in joyously (four times a week in July and August!) at the sound of the bell, but I can give no report of the performances. Sometimes I look through the lighted windows and see, on the diminutive stage, a short-skirted young woman with one hand on her heart and the other persuasively extended. Through the hot unpleasant air comes a little ghost of a roulade. I turn away and walk on the terrace and listen to the ocean vocalising to the stars.

But there are (by daylight) other walks at Etretat than the terrace, and no account of the place is complete without some commemoration of the admirable cliffs. They are the finest I have seen; their fantastic needles and buttresses, at either end of the little bay, give to careless Etretat an extreme distinction. In spite of there being no sands, a persistent admirer of nature will walk a long distance upon the tiresome sea-margin of pebbles for the sake of being under them and visiting some of their quiet caves and embrowned recesses, varnished by the ocean into splendid tones. Seen in this way from directly below, they look stupendous; they hold up their heads with attitudes quite Alpine. They are marvellously white and straight and smooth; they have the tint and something of the surface of time-yellowed marble, and here and there, at their summits, they break into quaint little pinnacles and turrets. But to be on the top of them is even better; here you may walk over miles of grassy, breezy down, with the woods, contorted and sea-stunted, of old farmsteads on your land-side (the farmhouses here have all a charming way of being buried in a wood, like the castle of the Sleeping Beauty), coming every little while upon a weather-blackened old shepherd and his flock (their conversation—the shepherds'—is delightful), or on some little seaward-plunging valley, holding in its green hollow a diminutive agricultural village, curtained round from the sea-winds by a dense stockade of trees. So you may go southward or northward, without impediment, to Havre or to Dieppe.

An English Easter

It may be said of the English, as is said of the council of war in Sheridan's farce of *The Critic* by one of the spectators of the rehearsal, that when they *do* agree, their unanimity is wonderful. They differ among themselves greatly just now as regards the machinations of Russia, the derelictions of Turkey, the merits of the Reverend Arthur Tooth, the genius of Mr. Henry Irving, and a good many other matters; but neither just now nor at any other time do they fail to conform to those social observances on which respectability has set her seal. England is a country of curious anomalies, and this has much to do with her being so interesting to foreign observers. The English individual character is very positive, very independent, very much made up according to its own sentiment of things, very prone to startling eccentricities; and yet at the same time it has beyond any other this peculiar gift of squaring itself with fashion and custom. In no

other country, I imagine, are so many people to be
found doing the same thing, in the same way, at
the same time — using the same slang, wearing the
same hats and neckties, collecting the same china-
plates, playing the same game of lawn-tennis or of
polo, admiring the same professional beauty. The
monotony of such a spectacle would soon become
oppressive if the foreign observer were not conscious
of this latent capacity in the performers for great
freedom of action; he finds a good deal of entertainment in wondering how they reconcile the traditional insularity of the individual with this perpetual tribute to usage. Of course, in all civilised
societies, the tribute to usage is constantly paid; if
it is less apparent in America than elsewhere the
reason is not, I think, because individual independence
is greater, but because usage is more sparsely established. Where custom can be ascertained people
certainly follow it; but for one definite precedent
in American life there are fifty in English. I am
very far from having discovered the secret; I have
not in the least learned what becomes of that
explosive personal force in the English character
which is compressed and corked down by social
conformity. I look with a certain awe at some of
the manifestations of the conforming spirit, but the
fermenting idiosyncrasies beneath it are hidden from
my vision. The most striking example, to foreign
eyes, of the power of custom in England is, of
course, the universal church-going. In the sight of
the English people getting up from its tea and toast
of a Sunday morning and brushing its hat, and
drawing on its gloves, and taking its wife on its

202

arm, and making its offspring march before, and so, for decency's, respectability's, propriety's sake, taking its way to a place of worship appointed by the State, in which it repeats the formulas of a creed to which it attaches no positive sense, and listens to a sermon over the length of which it explicitly haggles and grumbles—in this exhibition there is something very striking to a stranger, something which he hardly knows whether to regard as a great force or as a great infirmity. He inclines, on the whole, to pronounce the spectacle sublime, because it gives him the feeling that whenever it may become necessary for a people trained in these manœuvres to move all together under a common direction, they will have it in them to do so with tremendous weight and cohesiveness. We hear a good deal about the effect of the Prussian military system in consolidating the German people and making them available for a particular purpose; but I really think it not fanciful to say that the military punctuality which characterises the English observance of Sunday ought to be appreciated in the same fashion. A nation which has passed through the mill will certainly have been stamped by it. And here, as in the German military service, it is really the whole nation. When I spoke just now of paterfamilias and his *entourage* I did not mean to limit the statement to him. The young unmarried men go to church, the gay bachelors, the irresponsible members of society. (That last epithet must be taken with a grain of allowance. No one in England is literally irresponsible; that perhaps is the shortest way of describing the nation.

Every one is free and every one is responsible.
To say what it is people are responsible to is of
course a great extension of the question : briefly, to
social expectation, to propriety, to morality, to
"position," to the classic English conscience, which
is, after all, such a powerful factor. With us there
is infinitely less responsibility ; but there is also,
I think, less freedom.)

The way in which the example of the more
luxurious classes imposes itself upon the less luxurious may of course be noticed in smaller matters
than church-going ; in a great many matters which
it may seem trivial to mention. If one is bent
upon observation, nothing, however, is trivial. So
I may cite the practice of banishing the servants
from the room at breakfast. It is the fashion,
and accordingly, through the length and breadth of
England, every one who has the slightest pretension
to standing high enough to feel the way the social
breeze is blowing conforms to it. It is awkward,
unnatural, troublesome for those at table, it involves
a vast amount of leaning and stretching, of waiting
and perambulating, and it has just that vice against
which, in English history, all great movements have
been made—it is arbitrary. But it flourishes for
all that, and all genteel people, looking into each
other's eyes with the desperation of gentility, agree
to endure it for gentility's sake. My instance may
seem feeble, and I speak honestly when I say I
might give others, forming part of an immense body
of prescriptive usage, to which a society possessing
in the largest manner, both by temperament and
education, the sense of the "inalienable" rights and

comforts of the individual, contrives to accommodate itself.   I do not mean to say that usage in England is always uncomfortable and arbitrary.   On the contrary, few strangers can be unfamiliar with that sensation (a most agreeable one) which consists in perceiving in the rigidity of a tradition which has struck one at first as mechanical, a reason existing in the historic " good sense " of the English race. The sensation is frequent, though in saying so I do not mean to imply that even superficially the presumption is against the usages of English society. It is not, for instance, necessarily against the custom of which I had it more especially in mind to speak in writing these lines.   The stranger in London is forewarned that at Easter all the world goes out of town, and that if he have no mind to be left as lonely as Marius on the ruins of Carthage, he, too, had better make arrangements for a temporary absence.   It must be admitted that there is a sort of unexpectedness in this prompt re-emigration of a body of people who, but a week before, were apparently devoting much energy to settling down for the season.   Half of them have but lately come back from the country, where they have been spending the winter, and they have just had time, it may be supposed, to collect the scattered threads of town-life.   Presently, however, the threads are dropped and society is dispersed, as if it had taken a false start.   It departs as Holy Week draws to a close, and remains absent for the following ten days.   Where it goes is its own affair; a good deal of it goes to Paris.   Spending last winter in that city, I remember how, when I woke up on Easter

Monday and looked out of my window, I found the street covered, overnight, with a sort of snow-fall of disembarked Britons. They made, for other people, an uncomfortable week of it. One's customary table at the restaurant, one's habitual stall at the Théâtre Français, one's usual fiacre on the cab-stand, were very apt to have suffered pre-emption. I believe that the pilgrimage to Paris was this year of the usual proportions ; and you may be sure that people who did not cross the Channel were not without invitations to quiet old places in the country, where the pale, fresh primroses were beginning to light up the dark turf and the purple bloom of the bare tree-masses to be freckled here and there with verdure In England country-life is the obverse of the medal, town-life the reverse, and when an occasion comes for quitting London there are few members of what the French call the " easy class " who have not a collection of dull, moist, verdant resorts to choose from. Dull I call them, and I fancy not without reason, though at the moment I speak of, their dulness must have been mitigated by the unintermittent presence of the keenest and liveliest of east winds. Even in mellow English country homes Easter-tide is a period of rawness and atmospheric acridity— the moment at which the frank hostility of winter, which has at last to give up the game, turns to peevishness and spite. This is what makes it arbitrary, as I said just now, for " easy " people to go forth to the wind-swept lawns and the shivering parks. But nothing is more striking to an American than the frequency of English holidays and the large way in which occasions for " a little change " are made use of. All this speaks to Americans of three things which they are accustomed to see allotted in scantier measure. The English have more time than we, they have more money, and they have a much higher relish for active leisure. Leisure, fortune, and the love of sport—these things are implied in English society at every turn. It was a very small number of weeks before Easter that Parliament met, and yet a ten days' recess was already, from the luxurious Parliamentary point of view, a necessity. A short time hence we shall be having the Whitsuntide holidays, which I am told are even more of a season of revelry than Easter, and from this point to midsummer, when everything stops, it is an easy journey. The men of business and the professional men partake in equal measure of these agreeable diversions, and I was interested in hearing a lady whose husband was an active member of the bar say that, though he was leaving town with her for ten days, and though Easter was a very nice "little break," they really amused themselves more during the later festival, which would come on toward the end of May. I thought this highly probable, and admired so dramatic an interfusion of work and play. If my phrase has a slightly ironical sound, this is purely accidental. A large appetite for holidays, the ability not only to take them but to know what to do with them when taken, is the sign of a robust people, and judged by this measure we Americans are rather incompetent. Such holidays as we take are taken very often in Europe, where it is sometimes noticeable that our privilege is rather heavy on our hands. Acknowledgment made of English industry, however (our own stands in no need of compliments), it must be added that for those same easy classes I just spoke of things are very easy indeed. The number of persons obtainable for purely social purposes at all times and seasons is infinitely greater than among ourselves; and the ingenuity of the arrangements permanently going forward to disembarrass them of their superfluous leisure is as yet in America an undeveloped branch of civilisation. The young men who are preparing for the stern realities of life among the gray-green cloisters of Oxford are obliged to keep their terms but half the year; and the rosy little cricketers of Eton and Harrow are let loose upon the parental home for an embarrassing number of months. Happily the parental home is apt to be an affair of gardens, lawns, and parks.

II.

Passion Week, in London, is distinctly an ascetic period; there is really an approach to sackcloth and ashes. Private dissipation is suspended; most of the theatres and music-halls are closed; the huge dusky city seems to take on a still sadder colouring and a sort of hush steals over its mighty uproar. At such a time, for a stranger, London is not cheerful. Arriving there, during the past winter, about Christmas-time, I encountered three British Sundays in a row—a spectacle to strike terror into the stoutest heart. A Sunday and a "bank-holiday," if I remember aright, had joined hands with a Christ-

mas-day, and produced the portentous phenomenon
to which I allude. I betrayed, I suppose, some
apprehension of its oppressive character, for I remember being told in a consolatory way that I needn't
fear; it would not come round again for another
year. This information was given me on the
occasion of that surprising interruption of one's
relations with the laundress which is apparently
characteristic of the period. I was told that all the
washerwomen were intoxicated, and that, as it would
take them some time to revive, I must not count
upon a relay of "fresh things." I shall not forget
the impression made upon me by this statement; I
had just come from Paris and it almost sent me
spinning back. One of the incidental *agréments* of
life in the latter city had been the knock at my
door on Saturday evenings of a charming young
woman with a large basket covered with a snowy
napkin on her arm, and on her head a frilled and
fluted muslin cap, which was an irresistible adver-
tisement of her art. To say that my admirable
blanchisseuse was not in liquor is altogether too gross
a compliment; but I was always grateful to her for
her russet cheek, her frank, expressive eye, her talkative smile, for the way her charming cap was poised
upon her crisp, dense hair, and her well-made dress
was fitted to her well-made waist. I talked with
her; I *could* talk with her; and as she talked she
moved about and laid out her linen with a delightful modest ease. Then her light step carried her off
again, talking, to the door, and with a brighter smile
and an "Adieu, monsieur!" she closed it behind her,
leaving one to think how stupid is prejudice and how

209

poetic a creature a washerwoman may be. London, in December, was livid with sleet and fog, and against this dismal background was offered me the vision of a horrible old woman in a smoky bonnet, lying prone in a puddle of whisky! She seemed to assume a kind of symbolic significance, and she almost frightened me away.

I mention this trifle, which is doubtless not creditable to my fortitude, because I found that the information given me was not strictly accurate, and that at the end of three months I had another array of London Sundays to face. On this occasion, however, nothing occurred to suggest again the dreadful image I have just sketched, though I devoted a good deal of time to observing the manners of the lower orders. From Good Friday to Easter Monday, inclusive, they were very much *en évidence*, and it was an excellent occasion for getting an impression of the British populace. Gentility had retired to the background, and in the West End all the blinds were lowered; the streets were void of carriages, and well-dressed pedestrians were rare; but the "masses" were all abroad and making the most of their holiday, and I strolled about and watched them at their gambols. The heavens were most unfavourable, but in an English "outing" there is always a margin left for a drenching, and throughout the vast smoky city, beneath the shifting gloom of the sky, the grimy crowds trooped about with a kind of weather-proof stolidity. The parks were full of them, the railway stations overflowed, and the Thames embankment was covered. The "masses," I think, are usually an entertaining spectacle, even when observed

210

through the distorting medium of London bad weather. There are indeed few things in their way more impressive than a dusky London holiday; it suggests a variety of reflections. Even looked at superficially, the British capital is one of the most interesting of cities, and it is perhaps on such occasions as this that I have most felt its interest. London is ugly, dusky, dreary, more destitute than any European city of graceful and decorative incident; and though on festal days, like those I speak of, the populace is massed in large numbers at certain points, many of the streets are empty enough of human life to enable you to perceive their intrinsic want of charm. A Christmas-day or a Good Friday uncovers the ugliness of London. As you walk along the streets, having no fellow-pedestrians to look at, you look up at the brown brick house-walls, corroded with soot and fog, pierced with their straight stiff window-slits, and finished, by way of a cornice, with a little black line resembling a slice of curbstone. There is not an accessory, not a touch of architectural fancy, not the narrowest concession to beauty. If I were a foreigner it would make me rabid; being an Anglo-Saxon I find in it what Thackeray found in Baker Street—a delightful proof of English domestic virtue, of the sanctity of the British home. There are miles and miles of these edifying monuments, and it would seem that a city made up of them should have no claim to that larger effectiveness of which I just now spoke. London, however, is not made up of them; there are architectural combinations of a statelier kind, and the impression moreover does not rest on details.

London is pictorial in spite of details—from its dark-green, misty parks, the way the light comes down leaking and filtering from its cloud-ceiling, and the softness and richness of tone which objects put on in such an atmosphere as soon as they begin to recede. Nowhere is there such a play of light and shade, such a struggle of sun and smoke, such aërial gradations and confusions. To eyes addicted to such contemplations this is a constant diversion, and yet this is only part of it. What completes the effect of the place is its appeal to the feelings, made in so many ways, but made above all by agglomerated immensity. At any given point London looks huge; even in narrow corners you have a sense of its hugeness, and petty places acquire a certain interest from their being parts of so mighty a whole. Nowhere else is so much human life gathered together, and nowhere does it press upon you with so many suggestions. These are not all of an exhilarating kind; far from it. But they are of every possible kind, and that is the interest of London. Those that were most forcible during the showery Easter season were certain of the more perplexing and depressing ones; but even with these was mingled a brighter strain.

I walked down to Westminster Abbey on Good Friday afternoon—walked from Piccadilly across the Green Park and through that of St. James. The parks were densely filled with the populace—the elder people shuffling about the walks and the poor little smutty-faced children sprawling over the dark damp turf. When I reached the Abbey I found a dense group of people about the entrance, but I

squeezed my way through them and succeeded in
reaching the threshold. Beyond this it was impossible to advance, and I may add that it was not
desirable. I put my nose into the church and
promptly withdrew it. The crowd was terribly
compact, and beneath the gothic arches the odour
was not that of incense. I slowly eliminated myself, with that very modified sense of disappointment
that one feels in London at being crowded out of a
place. This is a frequent disappointment, for you
very soon find out that there are, selfishly speaking,
too many people. Human life is cheap; your
fellow-mortals are too numerous. Wherever you go
you make the observation. Go to the theatre, to a
concert, to an exhibition, to a reception; you always
find that, before you arrive, there are people enough
in the field. You are a tight fit in your place, wherever you find it; you have too many companions
and competitors. You feel yourself at times in
danger of thinking meanly of the human personality;
numerosity, as it were, swallows up quality, and perpetual association is rather irritating. This is the
reason why the perfection of luxury in England is to
own a "park"—an artificial solitude. To get one's
self into the middle of a few hundred acres of oak-
studded turf and to keep off the crowd by the breadth,
at least, of this grassy cincture, is to enjoy a comfort
which circumstances make peculiarly precious. But
I walked back through the profane pleasure-grounds
of London, in the midst of "superfluous herds,"
and I found that entertainment which I never fail
to derive from a great English assemblage. The
English are, to my eyes, so much the handsomest

213

people in Europe that it takes some effort of the
imagination to believe that the fact requires proof.
I never see a large number of them without feeling
this impression confirmed; though I hasten to add
that I have sometimes felt it to be rather shaken
in the presence of a limited group. I suspect that
a great English crowd would yield a larger percent-
age of handsome faces and figures than any other.
With regard to the upper class I suppose this is
generally granted; but I should extend it to the
whole people. Certainly, if the English populace
strike the observer by their good looks, they must be
very good-looking indeed. They are as ill-dressed
as their betters are well-dressed, and their garments
have that sooty-looking surface which has nothing
in common with some of the more romantic forms
of poverty. It is the hard prose of misery—an
ugly and hopeless imitation of respectable attire.
This is especially noticeable in the battered and be-
draggled bonnets of the women, which look as if their
husbands had stamped on them in hobnailed boots,
as a hint of what is in store for their wearers. Then
it is not too much to say that two-thirds of the
London faces, among the "masses," bear in some
degree or other the traces of alcoholic action. The
proportion of flushed, empurpled, eruptive counten-
ances is very striking; and the ugliness of the sight
is not diminished by the fact that many of the faces
thus disfigured were evidently meant to please. A
very large allowance is to be made, too, for the
people who bear the distinctive stamp of that physical and mental degradation which comes from the
slums and purlieus of this dusky Babylon—the

pallid, stunted, misbegotten, and in every way miserable figures. These people swarm in every London crowd, and I know of none in any other place that suggest an equal degree of misery. But when these abatements are made, the observer is still liable to be struck by the frequency of well-moulded faces and bodies well put together; of strong, straight brows and handsome mouths and noses, of rounded, finished chins and well-poised heads, of admirable complexions and well-disposed limbs.

The capacity of an Englishwoman for being handsome strikes me as absolutely unlimited, and even if (I repeat) it is in the luxurious class that it is most freely exercised, yet among the daughters of the people one sees a great many fine points. Among the men fine points are strikingly numerous—especially among the younger ones. Here the same distinction is to be made—the gentlemen are certainly handsomer than the vulgarians. But taking one young Englishman with another, they are physically very well turned out. Their features are finished, composed, as it were, more harmoniously than those of many of their nearer and remoter neighbours, and their figures are apt to be both powerful and compact. They present to view very much fewer accidental noses and inexpressive mouths, fewer sloping shoulders and ill-planted heads of hair, than their American kinsmen. Speaking always from the sidewalk, it may be said that as the spring increases in London and the symptoms of the season multiply, the beautiful young men who adorn the West End pavements, and who advance before you in couples, arm-in-arm, fair-haired, gray-eyed, athletic, slow-strolling, ambrosial, are among the most brilliant features of the brilliant period. I have it at heart to add that if the English are handsomer than ourselves, they are also very much uglier. Indeed I think that all the European peoples are uglier than the American; we are far from producing those magnificent types of facial eccentricity which flourish among older civilisations. American ugliness is on the side of physical poverty and meanness; English on that of redundancy and monstrosity. In America there are few grotesques; in England there are many —and some of them have a high pictorial value.

III.

The element of the grotesque was very noticeable to me in the most striking collection of the shabbier English types that I had seen since I came to London. The occasion of my seeing them was the funeral of Mr. George Odger, which befell some four or five weeks before the Easter period. Mr. George Odger, it will be remembered, was an English radical agitator of humble origin, who had distinguished himself by a perverse desire to get into Parliament. He exercised, I believe, the useful profession of shoemaker, and he knocked in vain at the door that opens but to the refined. But he was a useful and honourable man, and his own people gave him an honourable burial. I emerged accidentally into Piccadilly at the moment they were so engaged, and the spectacle was one I should have been sorry to miss. The crowd was enormous, but I managed to squeeze through it and to get into a hansom cab

216

that was drawn up beside the pavement, and here I looked on as from a box at the play. Though it was a funeral that was going on I will not call it a tragedy; but it was a very serious comedy. The day happened to be magnificent—the finest of the year. The funeral had been taken in hand by the classes who are socially unrepresented in Parliament, and it had the character of a great popular "manifestation." The hearse was followed by very few carriages, but the *cortège* of pedestrians stretched away in the sunshine, up and down the classic gentility of Piccadilly, on a scale that was highly impressive. Here and there the line was broken by a small brass band—apparently one of those bands of itinerant Germans that play for coppers beneath lodging-house windows; but for the rest it was compactly made up of what the newspapers call the dregs of the population. It was the London rabble, the metropolitan mob, men and women, boys and girls, the decent poor and the indecent, who had scrambled into the ranks as they gathered them up on their passage, and were making a sort of solemn "lark" of it. Very solemn it all was—perfectly proper and undemonstrative. They shuffled along in an interminable line, and as I looked at them out of the front of my hansom I seemed to be having a sort of panoramic view of the under side, the wrong side, of the London world. The procession was filled with figures which seemed never to have "shown out," as the English say, before; of strange, pale, mouldy paupers who blinked and stumbled in the Piccadilly sunshine. I have no space to describe them more minutely, but I found the whole affair

217

rather suggestive. My impression rose not simply
from the radical, or, as I may say for the sake of
colour, the revolutionary, emanation of this dingy
concourse, lighted up by the ironical sky; but from
the same causes that I had observed a short time
before, on the day the Queen went to open Parliament, when in Trafalgar Square, looking straight
down into Westminster and over the royal procession, were gathered a group of banners and festoons
inscribed in big staring letters with mottoes and
sentiments which a sensitive police department might
easily have found seditious. They were mostly in
allusion to the Tichborne claimant, whose release
from his dungeon they peremptorily demanded, and
whose cruel fate was taken as a pretext for several
sweeping reflections on the social arrangements of
the time and country. These impertinent standards
were allowed to sun themselves as freely as if they
had been the manifestoes of the Irish Giant or the
Oriental Dwarf at a fair. I had lately come from
Paris, where the police-department is more sensitive,
and where revolutionary placards are not observed
to adorn the base of the obelisk in the Place de la
Concorde. I was, therefore, the more struck on both
of the occasions I speak of with the admirable English practice of letting people alone—with the good
sense and the good humour and even the good taste
of it. It was this that I found impressive, as I
watched the "manifestation" of Mr. Odger's underfed partisans—the fact that the mighty mob could
march along and do its errand, while the excellent
quiet policemen stood by simply to see that the
channel was kept clear and comfortable.

When Easter Monday came it was obvious that every one (save Mr. Odger's friends—three or four million or so) had gone out of town. There was hardly a pair of shutters in the West End that was not closed; there was not a bell that it was any use to pull. The weather was detestable, the rain incessant, and the fact that all one's friends were away gave one plenty of leisure to reflect that the country must be the reverse of enlivening. But all one's friends had gone thither (this is the unanimity I began by talking about), and to restrict as much as possible the proportions of that game of hide-and-seek of which, at the best, so much of London social life consists, it seemed wise to bring within the limits of the dull season any such excursion as one might have projected in commemoration of the first days of spring. After due cogitation I paid a little visit to Canterbury and Dover, taking Rochester by the way, and it was of this momentous journey that I proposed, in beginning these remarks, to give an account. But I have dallied so much by the way that I have come almost to my rope's end without reaching my first stage. I should have begun, artistically, by relating that I put myself in the humour for remote adventure by going down the Thames on a penny steamboat to—the Tower. This was on the Saturday before Easter, and the City was as silent as the grave. The Tower was a memory of my childhood, and having a theory that from such memories the dust of the ages had better not be shaken, I had not retraced my steps to its venerable walls. But the Tower is very good—much less cockneyfied than I supposed it would seem to my maturer vision;

very gray and historical, with the look that vivifies
—rather lividly indeed—the past. I could not get
into it, as it had been closed for Passion Week, but
I was consequently relieved from the obligation to
march about with a dozen fellow-starers in the train
of a didactic beef-eater, and I strolled at will through
the courts and the garden, sharing them only with
the lounging soldiers of the garrison, who seemed to
connect the place with important events.

IV.

At Rochester I stopped for the sake of its castle,
which I espied from the railway-train, perched on a
grassy bank beside the widening Medway. There
were other reasons as well; the place has a small
cathedral, and one has read about it in Dickens,
whose house of Gadshill was a couple of miles from
the town. All this Kentish country, between London and Dover, figures indeed repeatedly in Dickens;
he is to a certain extent, for our own time, the spirit
of the land. I found this to be quite the case at
Rochester. I had occasion to go into a little shop
kept by a talkative old woman who had a photograph
of Gadshill lying on her counter. This led to my
asking her whether the illustrious master of the
house often made his appearance in the town. "Oh,
bless you, sir," she said, "we every one of us knew
him to speak to. He was in this very shop on the
Tuesday with a party of foreigners—as he was dead
in his bed on the Friday." (I should remark that I
probably do not repeat the days of the week as she
gave them.) "He 'ad on his black velvet suit, and

it always made him look so 'andsome. I said to my
'usband, ' I *do* think Charles Dickens looks so nice
in that black velvet suit.' But he said he couldn't
see as he looked any way particular. He was in
this very shop on the Tuesday, with a party of
foreigners." Rochester consists of little more than
one long street, stretching away from the castle and
the river toward neighbouring Chatham, and edged
with low brick houses, of intensely provincial aspect,
most of which have some small, dull quaintness of
gable or window. Nearly opposite to the shop of
the old lady with the dissentient husband is a little
dwelling with an inscribed slab set into its face,
which must often have provoked a smile in the great
master of laughter. The slab relates that in the
year 1579 Richard Watts here established a charity
which should furnish " six poor travellers, not rogues
or proctors," one night's lodging and entertainment
gratis, and four pence in the morning to go on their
way withal, and that in memory of his " munificence "
the stone has lately been renewed. The inn at
Rochester was poor, and I felt strongly tempted to
knock at the door of Mr. Watts's asylum, under plea
of being neither a rogue nor a proctor. The poor
traveller who avails himself of the testamentary fourpence may easily resume his journey as far as Chatham without breaking his treasure. Is not this the
place where little Davy Copperfield slept under a
cannon on his journey from London to Dover to
join his aunt, Miss Trotwood ? The two towns are
really but one, which forms an interminable crooked
thoroughfare, lighted up in the dusk, as I measured
it up and down, with the red coats of the vesper-

tinal soldier quartered at the various barracks of Chatham.

The cathedral of Rochester is small and plain, hidden away in rather an awkward corner, without a verdant close to set it off. It is dwarfed and effaced by the great square Norman keep of the adjacent castle. But within it is very charming, especially beyond the detestable wall, the vice of almost all the English cathedrals, which shuts in the choir and breaks the sacred perspective of the aisle. Here, as at Canterbury, you ascend a high range of steps, to pass through the small door in this wall. When I speak slightingly, by the way, of the outside of Rochester cathedral, I intend my faint praise in a relative sense. If we were so happy as to possess this inferior edifice in America, we should go barefoot to see it; but here it stands in the great shadow of Canterbury, and that makes it humble. I remember, however, an old priory gateway which leads you to the church, out of the main street; I remember a kind of haunted-looking deanery, if that be the technical name, at the base of the eastern walls; I remember a fluted tower that took the afternoon light and let the rooks and the swallows come circling and clamouring around it. Better than these things, however, I remember the ivy-draped mass of the castle—a very noble and imposing ruin. The old walled precinct has been converted into a little public garden, with flowers and benches, and a pavilion for a band, and the place was not empty, as such places in England never are. The result is agreeable, but I believe the process was barbarous, involving the destruction and dispersion of many

222

interesting portions of the ruin. I sat there for a long time, however, looking in the fading light at what was left. This rugged pile of Norman masonry will be left when a great many solid things have departed; it is a sort of satire on destruction or decay. Its walls are fantastically thick; their great time-bleached expanses and all their rounded roughnesses, their strange mixture of softness and grimness, have an undefinable fascination for the eye. English ruins always come out peculiarly when the day begins to fail. Weather-bleached, as I say they are, they turn even paler in the twilight and grow consciously solemn and spectral. I have seen many a mouldering castle, but I remember in no single mass of ruin more of the helpless, amputated look.

It is not the absence of a close that damages Canterbury; the cathedral stands amid grass and trees, with a cultivated margin all round it, and is placed in such a way that, as you pass out from under the gate-house, you appreciate immediately its grand feature—its extraordinary and magnificent length. None of the English cathedrals seems more beautifully isolated, more shut up to itself. It is a long walk, beneath the walls, from the gateway of the close to the farther end of the last chapel. Of all that there is to observe in this upward-gazing stroll I can give no detailed account; I can speak only of the general impression. This is altogether delightful. None of the rivals of Canterbury has a more complicated and elaborate architecture, a more perplexing intermixture of periods, a more charming jumble of Norman arches and English points and perpendiculars. What makes the side-view superb, moreover, is the double transepts, which produce a fine agglomeration of gables and buttresses. It is as if two great churches had joined forces toward the middle—one giving its nave and the other its choir, and each keeping its own great cross-aisles. Astride of the roof, between them, sits a huge gothic tower, which is one of the latest portions of the building, though it looks like one of the earliest, so crumbled and blunted and suffused is it by time and weather. Like the rest of the structure it has a magnificent colour—a sort of rich dull yellow, a something that is neither brown nor gray. This is particularly appreciable from the cloisters on the farther side of the church—the side, I mean, away from the town and the open garden-sweep I spoke of; the side that looks toward a damp old clerical house, lurking behind a brown archway, through which you see young ladies in Gainsborough hats playing something on a patch of velvet turf; the side, in short, that is somehow intermingled with a green quadrangle—a quadrangle serving as a playground to a King's School, and adorned externally with a very precious and picturesque old fragment of Norman staircase. This cloisters is not " kept up;" it is very dusky and mouldy and dilapidated, and of course very sketchable. The old black arches and capitals are various and handsome, and in the centre are tumbled together a group of crooked gravestones, themselves almost buried in the deep soft grass. Out of the cloisters opens the chapter-house, which is not kept up either, but which is none the less a magnificent structure; a noble, lofty hall, with a beautiful wooden roof, simply arched like that of a tunnel, without columns or

brackets. The place is now given up to dust and
echoes; but it looks more like a banqueting-hall
than a council-room of priests, and as you sit on the
old wooden bench, which, raised on two or three
steps, runs round the base of the four walls, you may
gaze up and make out the faint ghostly traces of
decorative paint and gold upon the brown ceiling.
A little patch of this has been restored, " to give an
idea." From one of the angles of the cloisters you
are recommended by the verger to take a view of the
great tower, which indeed detaches itself with tremendous effect. You see it base itself upon the
roof as broadly as if it were striking roots in earth,
and then pile itself away to a height which seems to
make the very swallows dizzy, as they drop from the
topmost shelf. Within the cathedral you hear a
great deal, of course, about poor Thomas A'Becket,
and the great sensation of the place is to stand on
the particular spot where he was murdered and look
down at a small fragmentary slab which the verger
points out to you as a bit of the pavement that
caught the blood-drops of the struggle. It was late
in the afternoon when I first entered the church;
there had been a service in the choir, but that was
well over, and I had the place to myself. The
verger, who had some pushing-about of benches to
attend to, turned me into the locked gates and left
me to wander through the side-aisles of the choir
and into the great chapel beyond it. I say I had
the place to myself; but it would be more decent to
affirm that I shared it, in particular, with another
gentleman. This personage was stretched upon a
couch of stone, beneath a quaint old canopy of wood;

his hands were crossed upon his breast, and his
pointed toes rested upon a little griffin or leopard.
He was a very handsome fellow and the image of a
gallant knight. His name was Edward Plantagenet,
and his sobriquet was the Black Prince. "*De la
mort ne pensai-je mye*," he says in the beautiful
inscription embossed upon the bronze base of his
image; and I too, as I stood there, lost the sense of
death in a momentary impression of personal nearness to him. One had been farther off, after all,
from other famous knights. In this same chapel for
many a year stood the shrine of St. Thomas of Canterbury, one of the richest and most potent in Christen-
dom. The pavement which lay before it has kept
its place, but Henry VIII. swept away everything
else in his famous short cut to reform. Becket was
originally buried in the crypt of the church; his
ashes lay there for fifty years, and it was only little
by little that his martyrdom was, as the French say,
"exploited." Then he was transplanted into the
Lady Chapel; every grain of his dust became a
priceless relic, and the pavement was hollowed by
the knees of pilgrims. It was on this errand of
course that Chaucer's story-telling cavalcade came to
Canterbury. I made my way down into the crypt,
which is a magnificent maze of low, dark arches and
pillars, and groped about till I found the place where
the frightened monks had first shuffled the inanimate
victim of Moreville and Fitzurse out of the reach of
further desecration. While I stood there a violent
thunderstorm broke over the cathedral; great rumbling gusts and rain-drifts came sweeping through
the open sides of the crypt, and, mingling with the

226

darkness which seemed to deepen and flash in corners, and with the potent mouldy smell, made me feel as if I had descended into the very bowels of history. I emerged again, but the rain had settled down and spoiled the evening, and I splashed back to my inn and sat in an uncomfortable chair by the coffee-room fire, reading Dean Stanley's agreeable *Memorials of Canterbury,* and wondering over the musty appointments and meagre resources of English hostels. This establishment had entitled itself (in compliment to the Black Prince, I suppose) the " Fleur-de-Lis." The name was very pretty (I had been foolish enough to let it attract me to the inn), but the lily was sadly deflowered.

London at Midsummer

I BELIEVE it is supposed to require a good deal of courage to confess that one has spent the month of August in London; and I will therefore, taking the bull by the horns, plead guilty at the very outset to this dishonourable weakness. I might attempt some ingenious extenuation of it. I might say that my remaining in town had been the most unexpected necessity or the merest inadvertence; I might pretend I liked it—that I had done it, in fact, for the love of the thing; I might claim that you don't really know the charms of London until on one of the dog-days you have imprinted your boot-sole in the slumbering dust of Belgravia, or, gazing along the empty vista of the Drive, in Hyde Park, have beheld, for almost the first time in England, a landscape without figures. But little would remain of these specious apologies save the naked fact that I had distinctly failed to retire from the metropolis— either on the first of August with the ladies and children, or on the thirteenth with the members of Parliament, or on the twelfth when the grouse-

231

shooting began. (I am not sure that I have got my dates right to a day, but these were about the proper opportunities.) I have, in fact, survived the departure of everything genteel, and the three millions of persons who remained behind with me have been witnesses of my shame.

I cannot pretend, on the other hand, that, having lingered in town, I have found it a very odious or painful experience. Being a stranger, I have not felt it necessary to incarcerate myself during the day and steal abroad only under cover of the darkness—a line of conduct imposed by public opinion, if I am to trust the social criticism of the weekly papers (which I am far from doing), upon the native residents who allow themselves to be overtaken by the unfashionable season. I have indeed always had a theory that few things are pleasanter than during the hot weather to have a great city, and a large house within it, quite to one's self.

These majestic conditions have not been combined in my own metropolitan sojourn, and I have received an impression that in London it would be rather difficult for a person not having the command of a good deal of powerful machinery to find them united. English summer weather is rarely hot enough to make it necessary to darken one's house and disrobe. The present year has indeed in this respect been " exceptional," as any year is, for that matter, that one spends anywhere. But the manners of the people are, to American eyes, a sufficient indication that at the best (or the worst) even the highest flights of the thermometer in the British Islands betray a broken wing. People live with closed windows in August, very much as they do in January, and there is to the eye no appreciable difference in the character of their apparel. A " bath " in England, for the most part all the year round, means a little portable tin tub and a sponge. Peaches and pears, grapes and melons, are not a more obvious ornament of the market at midsummer than at Christmas. This matter of peaches and melons, by the way, offers one of the best examples of that fact to which a foreign commentator on English manners finds himself constantly recurring, and to which he grows at last almost ashamed of alluding—the fact that the beauty and luxury of the country—that elaborate system known and revered all over the world as " English comfort "— is a limited and restricted, an essentially private, affair. I am not one of those irreverent strangers who talk of English fruit as a rather audacious *plaisanterie*, though I could see very well what was meant a short time since by an anecdote related to me in a tone of contemptuous generalisation by a couple of my fellow-countrywomen. They had arrived in London in the dog-days, and, lunching at their hotel, had asked to be served with some fruit. The hotel was of the stateliest pattern, and they were waited upon by a functionary whose grandeur was proportionate. This gentleman bowed and retired, and, after a long delay reappearing, placed before them, with an inimitable gesture, a dish of gooseberries and currants. It appeared upon investigation that these acrid vegetables were the only things of succulence that the establishment could undertake to supply; and it seemed to increase the irony of the situation that the establishment was as near as possible to Buckingham Palace. I say that the heroines of my anecdote seemed disposed to generalise : this was sufficiently the case, I mean, to give me a pretext for assuring them that on a thousand charming estates the most beautiful peaches and melons were at that moment ripening under glass. My auditors tossed their heads, of course, at the beautiful estates and the glass ; and indeed at their ascetic hostelry close to Buckingham Palace such a piece of knowledge was but scantily consoling.

It is to a more public fund of entertainment that the desultory stranger in any country chiefly appeals, especially in summer weather ; and as I have implied that there is little encouragement in England to such an appeal, it may appear remarkable that I should not have found London, at this season, at least as uncongenial as orthodoxy pronounces it. But one's liking for London—a stranger's liking at least—is at the best an anomalous and illogical sentiment, of which he may feel it hardly less difficult to give a categorical account at one time than at another. I am far from meaning by this that there are not in this mighty metropolis a thousand sources of interest, entertainment, and delight : what I mean is, that for one reason and another, with all its social resources, the place lies heavy on the foreign consciousness. It seems grim and dusky, fierce and unmerciful. And yet the foreign consciousness accepts it at last with an active satisfaction, and finds something warm and comfortable, something that if removed would be greatly missed, in its tremendous pressure. It must be admitted, however, that, granting that every one is out of town, your choice of pastimes is not embarrassing. If it has been your fortune to spend a certain amount of time in foreign cities, London will seem to you but slenderly provided with innocent diversions. This, indeed, brings us back simply to that question of the absence of a "public fund" of amusement to which reference was just now made. You must give up the idea of going to sit somewhere in the open air, to eat an ice and listen to a band of music. You will find neither the seat, the ice, nor the band; but, on the other hand, faithful to your profession of observant foreigner, you may supply the place of these delights by a little private meditation upon the deep-lying causes of the English indifference to them. In such reflections nothing is idle—every grain of testimony counts; and one need therefore not be accused of jumping too suddenly from small things to great if one traces a connection between the absence of ices and music and the aristocratic constitution of English society. This aristocratic constitution of English society is the great and ever-present fact to the mind of a stranger: there is hardly a detail of English life that does not appear in some degree to point to it. It is really only in a country in which a good deal of democratic feeling prevails that people of "refinement," as we say in America, will be willing to sit at little round tables, on a pavement or a gravel-walk, at the door of a café. The upper classes are too refined, and the lower classes are too miserable. One must hasten to add too, in justice, that the upper classes are, as a general thing, quite too well furnished with entertainments of their own; they have those special resources to which I alluded a moment since. They are people of fortune, and are naturally independent of communistic pleasures. If you can sit on a terrace in a high-walled garden and have your *café noir* handed to you in Pompadour cups by servants in powder and plush, you have hardly a decent pretext for going to a public-house. In France and Italy, in Germany and Spain, the count and countess will sally forth and encamp for the evening, under a row of coloured lamps, upon the paving-stones, but it is ten to one that the count and countess live on a single floor, up several pair of stairs. They are, however, I think, not appreciably affected by considerations which operate potently in England. An Englishman who should propose to sit down at a café-door would find himself remembering that he is exposing himself to the danger of meeting his social inferiors. The danger is great, because his social inferiors are so numerous; and I suspect that if we could look straight into the English consciousness we should be interested to find how serious a danger it appears, and how good—given the texture of English life—are some of his reasons for wishing not to expose himself.

The consideration of these reasons, however, would lead us very far from the potential little tables for ices in—where shall I say?—in Oxford Street; but, after all, there is no reason why our imagination should hover about these articles of furniture. I am afraid they would not strike us as happily situated. In such matters everything hangs together, and I

236

am certain that the customs of the Boulevard des
Italiens and the Piazza Colonna would not harmonise
with the scenery of the great London thoroughfare.
A gin-palace right and left and a detachment of the
London rabble in an admiring semicircle—these, I
confess, strike me as some of the more obvious
features of the affair. Yet at the season of which
I write, one's social studies must at the least be
studies of low life, for wherever one may go for a
stroll or to spend the summer afternoon, the unfashionable side of things is uppermost. There is
no one in the parks save the rough characters who
are lying on their faces in the sheep-polluted grass.
These people are always tolerably numerous in the
Green Park, through which I frequently pass, and I
never fail to drop a wondering glance upon them.
But your wonder will go far if it begins to bestir
itself on behalf of the recumbent British tramp.
You perceive among them some rich possibilities.
Their velveteen legs and their colossal high-lows,
their purple necks and ear-tips, their knotted sticks
and little greasy hats, make them look like stage-
villains in a realistic melodrama. I may do them
great injustice, but I always assume that they have
had a taste of penal servitude—that they have paid
the penalty of stamping on some weaker human
head with those huge square heels that are turned
up to the summer sky. But, actually, they are
innocent enough, for they are sleeping as peacefully
as the most accomplished philanthropist, and it is
their look of having walked over half England, and
of being confoundedly hungry and thirsty, that constitutes their romantic attractiveness. These six

square feet of brown grass are their present suffi-
ciency; but how long will they sleep, whither will
they go next, and whence did they come last? You
permit yourself to wish that they might sleep for
ever and go nowhere else at all.

The month of August is so uncountenanced in
London that going a few days since to Greenwich,
that famous resort, I found it possible to get but
half a dinner. The celebrated hotel had put out its
stoves and locked up its pantry. But for this dis-
covery I should have mentioned the little expedition
to Greenwich as a charming relief to the monotony
of a London August. Greenwich and Richmond
are, classically, the two suburban dining-places. I
know not how it may be at this time with Richmond, but the Greenwich incident brings me back
(I hope not once too often) to the element of what
has lately been called "particularism" in English
pleasures. It was in obedience to a perfectly logical
argument that the Greenwich hotel had, as I say,
locked up its pantry. All well-bred people leave
London after the first week in August, *ergo* those
who remain behind are not well-bred, and cannot
therefore rise to the conception of a "fish dinner."
Why, then, should we have anything ready? I had
other impressions, fortunately, of this interesting
suburb, and I hasten to declare that during the period
of good-breeding the dinner at Greenwich is the most
amusing of all dinners. It begins with fish and it
continues with fish: what it ends with—except songs
and speeches and affectionate partings—I hesitate to
affirm. It is a kind of mermaid reversed; for I do
know, in a vague way, that the tail of the creature is

elaborately and interminably fleshy. If it were not grossly indiscreet, I should risk an allusion to the particular banquet which was the occasion of my becoming acquainted with the Greenwich *cuisine*. I would affirm that it is very pleasant to sit in a company of clever and distinguished men, before the large windows that look out upon the broad brown Thames. The ships swim by confidently, as if they were part of the entertainment and put down in the bill; the light of the afternoon fades ever so slowly. We eat all the fish of the sea, and wash them down with liquids that bear no resemblance to salt water. We partake of any number of those sauces with which, according to the French adage, one could swallow one's grandmother with a good conscience. To speak of the particular merits of my companions would indeed ·be indiscreet, but there is nothing indelicate in expressing a high appreciation of the frankness and robustness of English conviviality. The stranger—the American at least—who finds himself in the company of a number of Englishmen assembled for a convivial purpose becomes conscious of a certain indefinable and delectable something which, for want of a better name, he will call their superior richness of temperament. He takes note of the liberal share of the individual in the magnificent temperament of the people. This seems to him one of the finest things in the world, and his satisfaction will take a keener edge from such an incident as the single one I may permit myself to mention. It was one of those little incidents which can occur only in an old society—a society in which every one that a newly-arrived observer meets strikes him as having in some degree or other a sort of historic identity, being connected with some one or something that he has heard of. If they are not the rose, they have lived more or less near it. There is an old English song-writer whom we all know and admire—whose songs are sung wherever the language is spoken. Of course, according to the law I just hinted at, one of the gentlemen sitting opposite must needs be his great-grandson. After dinner there are songs, and the gentleman trolls out one of his ancestral ditties with the most charming voice and the most finished art.

I have still other memories of Greenwich, where there is a charming old park, on a summit of one of whose grassy undulations the famous observatory is perched. To do the thing completely, you must take passage upon one of the little grimy sixpenny steamers that ply upon the Thames, perform the journey by water, and then, disembarking, take a stroll in the park to get up an appetite for dinner. I find an irresistible charm in any sort of river-navigation, but I am rather at a loss how to speak of the little voyage from Westminster Bridge to Greenwich. It is in truth the most prosaic possible form of being afloat, and to be recommended rather to the inquiring than to the fastidious mind. It initiates you into the duskiness, the blackness, the crowdedness, the intensely commercial character of London. Few European cities have a finer river than the Thames, but none certainly has expended more ingenuity in producing an ugly river-front. For miles and miles you see nothing but the sooty backs of warehouses, or perhaps they are the sooty fronts: in buildings so very expressionless it is impossible to distinguish. They stand massed together on the banks of the wide, turbid stream, which is fortunately of too opaque a quality to reflect the dismal image. A damp-looking, dirty blackness is the universal tone. The river is almost black, and is covered with black barges; above the black housetops, from among the far-stretching docks and basins, rises a dusky wilderness of masts. The little puffing steamer is dingy and gritty—it belches a sable cloud that keeps you company as you go. In this carboniferous shower your companions, who belong chiefly, indeed, to the less brilliant classes, assume an harmonious grayness; and the whole picture, glazed over with the glutinous London mist, becomes a masterly composition. But it is very impressive in spite of its want of lightness and brightness, and though it is ugly it is not insignificant. Like so many of the aspects of English civilisation that are untouched by elegance or grace, it has the merit of expressing something very serious. Viewed in this intellectual light, the polluted river, the sprawling barges, the dead-faced warehouses, the frowsy people, the atmospheric impurities, become richly suggestive. It sounds rather absurd to say so, but all this sordid detail reminds me of nothing less than the wealth and power of the British empire at large; so that a kind of metaphysical magnificence hovers over the scene, and supplies what may be literally wanting. I don't exactly understand the association, but I know that when I look off to the left at the East India Docks, or pass under the dark, hugely-piled bridges, where the railway trains and the

human processions are for ever moving, I feel a kind
of imaginative thrill. The tremendous piers of the
bridges, in especial, seem the very pillars of the
British empire aforesaid.

It is doubtless owing to this habit of obtrusive
and unprofitable reverie that the sentimental tourist
thinks it very fine to see the Greenwich observatory
lifting its two modest little brick towers. The sight
of this useful edifice gave me an amount of pleasure
which may at first seem unreasonable. The reason
was, simply, that I used to see it as a child, in
woodcuts, in school-geographies, and in the corners
of large maps which had a glazed, sallow surface,
and which were suspended in unexpected places, in
dark halls and behind doors. The maps were hung
so high that my eyes could reach only to the lower
corners, and these corners usually contained a print
of a strange-looking house, standing among trees
upon a grassy bank that swept down before it with
the most engaging steepness. I used always to
think that it must be an immense pleasure to hurl
one's self down this curving precipice. Close at
hand was usually something printed about something
being at such and such a number of degrees " east
of Greenwich." Why east of Greenwich? The
vague wonder that the childish mind felt on this
point gave the place a mysterious importance, and
seemed to put it into relation with the difficult and
fascinating parts of geography—the countries of un-
intentional outline and the lonely-looking pages of
the atlas. Yet there it stood the other day, the
precise point from which the great globe is measured;
there was the plain little façade, with the old-

242

fashioned cupolas; there was the bank on which it would be so delightful not to be able to stop running. It made me feel terribly old to find that I was not even tempted to begin. There are indeed a great many steep banks in Greenwich Park, which tumbles up and down in the most picturesque fashion. It is a charming place, rather shabby and footworn, as befits a strictly popular resort, but with a character all its own. It is filled with magnificent foreign-looking trees, of which I know nothing but that they have a vain appearance of being chestnuts, planted in long, convergent avenues, with trunks of extraordinary girth and limbs that fling a dusky shadow far over the grass; there are plenty of benches, and there are deer as tame as sleepy children; and from the tops of the bosky hillocks there are views of the widening Thames, and the moving ships, and the two classic inns by the waterside, and the great pompous buildings, designed by Inigo Jones, of the old Hospital, which have been despoiled of their ancient pensioners and converted into a kind of naval academy.

Taking note of all this, I arrived at a far-away angle in the wall of the park, where a little postern door stood ajar. I pushed the door open, and found myself, by a picturesque transition, upon Blackheath Common. One had often heard of Blackheath: well, here it was—a great green, breezy place, where various lads in corduroys were playing cricket. I always admire an English common; it may be curtailed and cockneyfied, as this one was —which had lamp-posts stuck about on its turf and a fresh-painted banister all around—but it is sure to be one of the places that remind you vividly that you are in England. Even if the turf is too much trodden, there is, to foreign eyes, an English greenness about it, and there is something peculiarly insular in the way the high-piled, weather-bearing clouds hang over it and drizzle down their gray light. Still further to identify this spot, here was the British soldier emerging from two or three of the roads, with his cap upon his ear, his white gloves in one hand and his foppish little cane in the other. He wore the uniform of the artillery, and I asked him where he had come from. I learned that he had walked over from Woolwich, and that this feat might be accomplished in half an hour. Inspired again by vague associations, I proceeded to accomplish its equivalent. I bent my steps to Woolwich, a place which I knew, in a general way, to be a nursery of British valour. At the end of my half hour I emerged upon another common, where local colour was still more intense. The scene was very entertaining. The open grassy expanse was immense, and, the evening being beautiful, it was dotted with strolling soldiers and townsfolk. There were half a dozen cricket matches, both civil and military. At one end of this peaceful *campus martius*, which stretches over a hilltop, rises an interminable façade—one of the fronts of the artillery barracks. It has a very honourable air, and more windows and doors, I imagine, than any building in Britain. There is a great clean parade before it, and there are many sentinels pacing in front of neatly-kept places of ingress to officers' quarters. Everything it looks out upon is military

—the distinguished college (where the poor young man whom it would perhaps be premature to call the last of the Bonapartes lately studied the art of war) on one side ; a sort of model camp—a collection of the tidiest plank huts—on the other; a hospital, on a well-ventilated site, at the remoter end. And then in the town below there are a great many more military matters—barracks on an immense scale ; a dockyard that presents an interminable dead wall to the street ; an arsenal which the gatekeeper (who refused to admit me) declared to be " five miles " in circumference ; and, lastly, grogshops enough to inflame the most craven spirit. These latter institutions I glanced at on my way to the railway station at the bottom of the hill; but before departing I had spent half an hour in strolling about the common in vague consciousness of certain emotions that are called into play (I speak but for myself) by almost any glimpse of the imperial machinery of this great country. The glimpse may be of the slightest ; it stirs a peculiar sentiment. I know not what to call this sentiment unless it be simply an admiration for the greatness of England. The greatness of England ; that is a very off-hand phrase, and of course I don't pretend to use it analytically. I use it sentimentally—as it sounds in the ears of any American who finds in English history the sacred source of his own national affection. I think of the great part that England has played in human affairs, the great space she has occupied, her tremendous might, her far-stretching sway. That these clumsily-general ideas should be suggested by the sight of some infinitesimal fraction of the English adminis-

trative system may seem to indicate a cast of fancy
too hysterical; but if so, I must plead guilty to
the weakness. Why should a sentry-box more or
less set one thinking of the glory of this little island,
which has found in her bosom the means of so vast
a dominion? This is more than I can say; and all
I shall attempt to say is, that in the difficult days
that are now elapsing a sympathetic stranger finds
his meditations singularly quickened. It is the
dramatic element in English history that he has
chiefly cared for, and he finds himself wondering
whether the dramatic epoch is completely closed.
It is a moment when all the nations of Europe
seem to be doing something, and he waits to see
what England, who has done so much, will do. He
has been meeting of late a good many of his country-
people—Americans who live on the Continent and
pretend to speak with assurance of continental ways
of feeling. These people have been passing through
London, and many of them are in that irritated condition of mind which appears to be the portion of
the American sojourner in the British metropolis
when he is not given up to the delights of the historic
sentiment. They have affirmed with emphasis that
the continental nations have ceased to care a straw
for what England thinks, that her traditional prestige
is completely extinct, and that the affairs of Europe
will be settled quite independently of the power
whose capital is on the Thames. England will do
nothing, will risk nothing; there is no cause bad
enough for her not to find a selfish interest in it—
there is no cause good enough for her to fight about
it. Poor old England is exploded; it is about time

she should haul in her nets. To all this the sympathetic stranger replies that, in the first place, he doesn't believe a word of it; and, in the second place, he doesn't care a fig for it—care, that is, what the continental nations think. If the greatness of England were really waning, it would be to him as a personal grief; and as he strolls about the breezy common of Woolwich, with all those mementoes of British dominion around him, he is quite too keenly exhilarated to be distracted by such vapours.

He wishes, nevertheless, as I said before, that England would do something—something striking and powerful, which should be at once characteristic and unexpected. He asks himself what she can do, and he remembers that this greatness of England which he so much admires was formerly much exemplified in her " taking " something. Can't she " take " something now ? There is the *Spectator*, who wants her to occupy Egypt: can't she occupy Egypt ? The *Spectator* considers this her moral duty—inquires even whether she has a right *not* to bestow the blessings of her beneficent rule upon the down-trodden Fellaheen. I found myself in company with an acute young Frenchman a day or two after this eloquent plea for a partial annexation of the Nile had appeared in the most ingenious of journals. Some allusion was made to it, and my companion proceeded to pronounce it a finished example of British hypocrisy. I don't know how powerful a defence I made of it, but while I read it I certainly had been carried away by it. I recalled it while I pursued my contemplations, but I recalled at the same time that sadly prosaic speech of Mr. Gladstone's to which it had been a reply. Mr. Gladstone had said that England had much more urgent duties than the occupation of Egypt: she had to attend to the great questions of—— What were the great questions? Those of local taxation and the liquor-laws! Local taxation and the liquor-laws! The phrase, to my ears, just then made a painful discord. These were not the things I had been thinking of; it was not as she should bend anxiously over these doubtless interesting subjects that the sympathetic stranger would seem to see England in his favourite posture—that, as Macaulay says, of hurling defiance at her foes. Of course, Mr. Gladstone was probably right, but Mr. Gladstone was not a sympathetic stranger.

Two Excursions

THEY differed greatly from each other, but each had an interest of its own. There seemed (as regards the first) a general consensus of opinion as to its being a great pity that a stranger in England should miss the Derby day. Every one assured me that this was the great festival of the English people, and the most characteristic of national holidays. So much, since it had to do with horse-flesh, I could readily believe. Had not the newspapers been filled for weeks with recurrent dissertations upon the animals concerned in the ceremony? and was not the event, to the nation at large, only imperceptibly less momentous than the other great question of the day—the fate of empires and the reapportionment of the East? The space allotted to sporting intelligence in a compact, eclectic, " intellectual" journal like the *Pall Mall Gazette*, had seemed to me for some time past a measure of the hold of such questions upon the British mind.

These things, however, are very natural in a country in which in "society" you are liable to make the acquaintance of some such syllogism as the following. You are seated at dinner next a foreign lady, who has on her other hand a native gentleman, by whom she is being instructed in the art of getting the right point-of-view for looking at English life. I profit by their conversation, and I learn that this point-of-view is apparently the saddle. "You see, English life," says the gentleman, "is really English country life. It's the country that is the basis of English society. And you see, country life is— well, it's the *hunting*. It's the hunting that is at the bottom of it all." In other words, "the hunting" is the basis of English society. Duly initiated into this interpretation of things, the American observer is prepared for the colossal proportions of the annual pilgrimage to Epsom. This pilgrimage, however, I was assured, though still well worth taking part in, is by no means so characteristic as in former days. It is now performed in a large measure by rail, and the spectacle on the road has lost its ancient brilliancy. The road has been given up more and more to the populace and the strangers, and has ceased to be graced by the presence of ladies. Nevertheless, as a man and a stranger, I was strongly recommended to take it; for the return from the Derby is still, with all its abatements, a classic spectacle.

I mounted upon a four-horse coach, a charming coach, with a yellow body, and handsome, clean-flanked leaders; placing myself beside the coachman, as I had been told this was the point of vantage.

The coach was one of the vehicles of the new fashion—the fashion of public conveyances driven, for the entertainment of themselves and of the public, by gentlemen of leisure. On the Derby day all the coaches that start from the classic headquarters—the "White Horse," in Piccadilly—and stretch away from London toward a dozen different and well-selected goals, had been dedicated to the Epsom road. The body of the vehicle is empty, as no one thinks of occupying any but one of the thirteen places on the top. On the Derby day, however, a properly laden coach carries a company of hampers and champagne-baskets in its inside places. I must add that on this occasion my companion was by exception a professional whip, who proved an entertaining cicerone. Other companions there were, perched in the twelve places behind me, whose social quality I made less of a point of testing—though in the course of the expedition their various characteristics, under the influence of champagne, expanded so freely as greatly to facilitate the operation. We were a society of exotics—Spaniards, Frenchmen, Germans. There were only two Britons, and these, according to my theory, were Australians—an antipodal bride and groom, on a centripetal wedding-tour.

The drive to Epsom, when you get well out of London, is sufficiently pretty; but the part of it which most took my fancy was a suburban district —the classic neighbourhood of Clapham. The vision of Clapham had been a part of the furniture of my imagination—the vision of its respectable common, its evangelical society, and its goodly brick

253

mansions of the Georgian era. I now beheld these objects for the first time, and I thought them very charming. This epithet, indeed, scarcely applies to the evangelical society, which naturally, on the morning of the Derby day, and during the desecrating progress of the Epsom revellers, was not much in the foreground. But all around the verdant, if cockneyfied common, are ranged commodious houses of a sober red complexion, from under whose neoclassic pediments you expect to see a mild-faced lady emerge—a lady in a cottage-bonnet and mittens, distributing tracts from a little satchel. It would take an energetic piety, however, to stem the current of heterogeneous vehicles which at about this point takes up its metropolitan affluents and bears them in its rumbling, rattling tide. The concourse of wheeled conveyances of every possible order here becomes dense, and the spectacle from the top of the coach proportionately absorbing. You begin to perceive that the brilliancy of the road has in truth departed, and that well-appointed elegance is not the prevailing characteristic. But when once you have grasped this fact your entertainment is continuous. You perceive that you are "in," as the phrase is, for something vulgar, something colossally, unimaginably, heroically vulgar; all that is necessary is to accept this situation and look out for illustrations. Beside you, before you, behind you, is the mighty London populace, taking its *ébats*. You get for the first time a notion of the London population at large. It has piled itself into carts, into omnibuses, into every possible and impossible species of "trap." A large proportion of it is of course on foot, trudging

along the perilous margin of the middle way, in such
comfort as may be gathered from fifteen miles' dodging of broken shins. The smaller the vehicle, the
more rat-like the animal that drags it, the more
numerous and ponderous its human freight; and as
every one is nursing in his lap a parcel of provender
as big as himself, wrapped in ragged newspapers, it
is not surprising that roadside halts are frequent,
and that the taverns all the way to Epsom (it is
wonderful how many there are) are encompassed by
dense groups of dusty pilgrims, indulging liberally
in refreshment for man and beast. And when I say
man I must by no means be understood to exclude
woman. The female contingent on the Derby day
is not the least remarkable part of the London multitude. Every one is prepared for an " outing," but
the women are even more brilliantly and resolutely
prepared than the men ; it is the best possible chance
to observe the various types of the British female of
the lower orders. The lady in question is usually
not ornamental. She is useful, robust, prolific, excellently fitted to play the somewhat arduous part
allotted to her in the great scheme of English civilisation. But she has not those graces which enable
her to become easily and harmoniously festal. On
smaller holidays—or on simple working-days—in
London crowds, I have often thought her handsome ;
thought, that is, that she has handsome points,
and that it was not impossible to see how it is that
she helps to make the English race, on the whole,
the comeliest in the world. But at Epsom she is
too stout, too hot, too red, too thirsty, too boisterous,
too strangely accoutred. And yet I wish to do her

255

justice; so I must add that if there is something to which an American cannot refuse a tribute of admiration in the gross plebeian jollity of the Derby day, it is not evident why these lusty she-revellers should not get part of the credit of it. The striking thing, the interesting thing, both on the outward drive and on the return, was that the holiday was so frankly, heartily, good-humouredly taken. The people that of all peoples is habitually the most governed by decencies, proprieties, rigidities of conduct, was, for one happy day, unbuttoning its respectable straight-jacket and letting its powerful, carnal, healthy temperament take the air. In such a spectacle there was inevitably much that was unlucky and unprofitable; these things came uppermost chiefly on the return, when demoralisation was supreme, when the temperament in question had quite taken what the French call the key of the fields, and seemed in no mood to come back and give an account of itself. For the rest, to be dressed with a kind of brutal gaudiness, to be very thirsty and violently flushed, to laugh perpetually at everything and at nothing, thoroughly to enjoy, in short, a momentous occasion—all this is not, in simple persons of the more susceptible sex, an unpardonable crime.

The course at Epsom is in itself very pretty, and disposed by nature herself in sympathetic prevision of the sporting passion. It is something like the crater of a volcano, without the mountain. The outer rim is the course proper; the space within it is a vast, shallow, grassy concavity in which vehicles are drawn up and beasts tethered, and in which the greater part of the multitude—the mountebanks, the betting-men, and the myriad hangers-on of the scene—are congregated. The outer margin of the uplifted rim in question is occupied by the grand stand, the small stands, the paddock. The day was exceptionally beautiful; the charming sky was spotted over with little idle-looking, loafing, irresponsible clouds; the Epsom Downs went swelling away as greenly as in a coloured sporting-print, and the wooded uplands, in the middle distance, looked as innocent and pastoral as if they had never seen a policeman or a rowdy. The crowd that spread itself over this immense expanse was the richest representation of human life that I have ever looked upon. One's first fate after arriving, if one is perched upon a coach, is to see the coach guided, by means best known to the coachman himself, through the tremendous press of vehicles and pedestrians, introduced into a precinct roped off and guarded from intrusion save under payment of a fee, and then drawn up alongside of the course, as nearly as possible opposite the grand stand and the winning post. Here you have only to stand up in your place—on tiptoe, it is true, and with a good deal of stretching—to see the race fairly well. But I hasten to add that seeing the race is indifferent entertainment. If I might be Irish on the occasion of a frolic, I would say that in the first place you do not see it at all, and in the second place you perceive it to be not much worth the seeing. It may be very fine in quality, but in quantity it is inappreciable. The horses and their jockeys first go dandling and cantering along the course to the starting-point, looking as insubstantial as sifted sunbeams. Then there is a long wait, during which, of the sixty thousand people present (my figures are imaginary) thirty thousand affirm positively that they have started, and thirty thousand as positively deny it. Then the whole sixty thousand are suddenly resolved into unanimity by the sight of a dozen small jockey-heads whizzing along a very distant sky-line. In a shorter space of time than it takes me to write it, the whole thing is before you, and for the instant it is anything but beautiful. A dozen furiously revolving arms— pink, green, orange, scarlet, white—whacking the flanks of as many straining steeds; a glimpse of this, and the spectacle is over. The spectacle, how- ever, is of course an infinitesimally small part of the purpose of Epsom and the interest of the Derby. The interest is in having money in the affair, and doubtless those most interested do not trouble them- selves particularly to watch the race. They learn soon enough whether they are, in the English phrase, to the good or to the bad.

When the Derby stakes had been carried off by a horse of which I confess I am barbarous enough to have forgotten the name, I turned my back to the running, for all the world as if I too were largely "interested," and sought entertainment in looking at the crowd. The crowd was very animated; that is the most succinct description I can give of it. The horses of course had been removed from the vehicles, so that the pedestrians were free to surge against the wheels and even to a certain extent to scale and overrun the carriages. This tendency

258

became most pronounced when, as the mid-period of the day was reached, the process of lunching began to unfold itself and every coach-top to become the scene of a picnic. From this moment, at the Derby, demoralisation begins. I was in a position to observe it, all around me, in the most characteristic forms. The whole affair, as regards the conventional rigidities I spoke of a while since, becomes a real *dégringolade*. The shabbier pedestrians bustle about the vehicles, staring up at the lucky mortals who are perched in a kind of tormentingly near empyrean—a region in which dishes of lobster-salad are passed about and champagne-corks cleave the air like celestial meteors. There are nigger-minstrels and beggars and mountebanks and spangled persons on stilts, and gipsy matrons, as genuine as possible, with glowing Oriental eyes and dropping their *h*'s; these last offer you for sixpence the promise of everything genteel in life except the aspirate. On a coach drawn up beside the one on which I had a place, a party of opulent young men were passing from one stage of exhilaration to another with a punctuality which excited my admiration. They were accompanied by two or three young ladies of the kind that usually shares the choicest pleasures of youthful British opulence—young ladies in whom nothing has been neglected that can make a complexion Titianesque. The whole party had been drinking deep, and one of the young men, a pretty lad of twenty, had in an indiscreet moment staggered down as best he could to the ground. Here his cups proved too many for him, and he collapsed and rolled over. In plain English, he was beastly

drunk. It was the scene that followed that arrested
my observation. His companions on the top of the
coach called down to the people herding under the
wheels to pick him up and put him away inside.
These people were the grimiest of the rabble, and a
couple of men who looked like coal-heavers out of
work undertook to handle this hapless youth. But
their task was difficult; it was impossible to imagine
a young man more drunk. He was a mere bag of
liquor—at once too ponderous and too flaccid to be
lifted. He lay in a helpless heap under the feet of
the crowd—the best intoxicated young man in
England. His extemporised chamberlains took him
first in one way and then in another; but he was
like water in a sieve. The crowd hustled over
him; every one wanted to see; he was pulled and
shoved and fumbled. The spectacle had a grotesque
side, and this it was that seemed to strike the
fancy of the young man's comrades. They had not
done lunching, so they were unable to bestow upon
the incident the whole of that consideration which
its high comicality deserved. But they did what
they could. They looked down very often, glass in
hand, during the half-hour that it went on, and they
stinted neither their generous, joyous laughter, nor
their appreciative comments. Women are said to
have no sense of humour; but the Titianesque
young ladies did liberal justice to the pleasantry of
the scene. Toward the last, indeed, their attention
rather flagged; for even the best joke suffers by
reiteration, and when you have seen a stupefied
young man, infinitely bedusted, slip out of the
embrace of a couple of clumsy paupers for the

twentieth time, you may very properly suppose
that you have arrived at the farthest limits of the
ludicrous.

After the great race had been run I quitted my
perch and spent the rest of the afternoon in wandering about that grassy concave I have mentioned. It
was amusing and picturesque; it was like a huge
Bohemian encampment. Here also a great number
of carriages were stationed, freighted in like manner
with free-handed youths and young ladies with
gilded tresses. These young ladies were almost the
only representatives of their sex with pretensions
to elegance; they were often pretty and always exhilarated. Gentlemen in pairs, mounted on stools,
habited in fantastic sporting garments, and offering
bets to whomsoever listed, were a conspicuous
feature of the scene. It was equally striking that
they were not preaching in the desert and that they
found plenty of patrons among the baser sort. I
returned to my place in time to assist at the rather
complicated operation of starting for the drive back
to London. Putting in horses and getting vehicles
into line seemed in the midst of the general crush
and entanglement a process not to be facilitated
even by the most liberal swearing on the part of
those engaged in it. But little by little we came
to the end of it; and as by this time a kind of
mellow cheerfulness pervaded the upper atmosphere
—the region of the perpendicular whip—even those
interruptions most trying to patience were somehow
made to minister to jollity. It was for people
below to not get trampled to death or crunched
between opposing wheel-hubs, if they could manage

261

it.   Above, the carnival of "chaff" had set in, and
it deepened as the lock of vehicles grew denser.
As they were all locked together (with a comfortable padding of pedestrians at points of acutest
contact), they contrived somehow to move together;
so that we gradually got away and into the road.
The four or five hours consumed on the road were
simply as I say, a carnival of "chaff," the profusely
good-humoured savour of which, on the whole, was
certainly striking.   The chaff was not brilliant nor
subtle nor especially graceful; and here and there
it was quite too tipsy to be even articulate.   But
as an expression of that unbuttoning of the popular
straight-jacket of which I spoke awhile since, it
had its wholesome and even innocent side.   It
took, indeed, frequently an importunate physical
form; it sought emphasis in the use of pea-shooters
and water-squirts.   At its best, too, it was extremely
low and rowdyish.   But a stranger even of the most
refined tastes might be glad to have a glimpse of this
popular revel, for it would make him feel that he was
learning something more about the English people.
It would give a meaning to the old words "merry
England."   It would remind him that the natives
of that country are subject to some of the most
frolicsome of the human passions, and that the
decent, dusky vistas of the London residential streets
—those discreet creations of which Thackeray's
"Baker Street" is the type—are not a complete
symbol of the complicated race that erected them.

II.

It seemed to me such a piece of good fortune to have been asked down to Oxford at Commemoration by a gentleman implicated in the remarkable ceremony which goes on under that name, who kindly offered me the hospitality of his college, that I scarcely waited even to thank him—I simply took the first train. I had had a glimpse of Oxford in former years, but I had never slept in a low-browed room looking out on a grassy quadrangle, opposite a mediæval clock-tower. This satisfaction was vouchsafed me on the night of my arrival; I was inducted into the rooms of an absent undergraduate. I sat in his deep arm-chairs; I burned his candles and read his books. I hereby thank him as tenderly as possible. Before going to bed I took a turn through the streets and renewed in the silent darkness that impression of the charm imparted to them by the quiet college-fronts, which I had gathered in former years. The college-fronts were now quieter than ever, the streets were empty, and the old scholastic city was sleeping in the warm starlight. The undergraduates had retired in large numbers, encouraged in this impulse by the collegiate authorities, who deprecate their presence at Commemoration. However many young gownsmen may be sent away, there always remain enough to make a noise. There can be no better indication of the resources of Oxford in a spectacular way than this fact that the first step toward preparing an impressive ceremony is to get rid of the undergraduates.

In the morning I breakfasted with a young American who, in common with a number of his countrymen, had come hither to seek stimulus for a finer quality of study. I know not whether he would have reckoned as such stimulus the conversation of a couple of those ingenuous youths of Britain whose society I always find charming; but it added, from my own point of view, to the local colour of the entertainment. After this was over I repaired, in company with a crowd of ladies and elderly people, interspersed with gownsmen, to the hoary rotunda of the Sheldonian theatre, which every visitor to Oxford will remember, with its curious cincture of clumsily-carven heads of warriors and sages perched upon stone posts. The interior of this edifice is the scene of the classic hooting, stamping, and cat-calling by which the undergraduates confer the last consecration upon the distinguished gentlemen who come up for the honorary degree of D.C.L. It is with the design of attenuating as much as possible this incongruous chorus, that the heads of colleges, on the close of the term, a few days before Commemoration, speed their too demonstrative disciples upon the homeward way. As I have already hinted, however, the contingent of irreverent lads was on this occasion quite large enough to produce a very handsome specimen of the traditional rumpus. This made the scene a very singular one. An American of course, with his fondness for antiquity, his relish for picturesqueness, his " emotional " attitude at historic shrines, takes Oxford much more

seriously than its customary denizens can be expected
to do. These people are not always upon the high
horse; they are not always in an acutely sentient
condition. Nevertheless, there is a certain maximum of disaccord with their beautiful circumstances
which the ecstatic Occidental vaguely expects them
not to transcend. No effort of the intellect beforehand would enable him to imagine one of those
silver-gray temples of learning converted into a semblance of the Bowery Theatre when the Bowery
Theatre is being trifled with.

The Sheldonian edifice, like everything at Oxford, is more or less monumental. There is a double
tier of galleries, with sculptured pulpits protruding
from them; there are full-length portraits of kings
and worthies; there is a general air of antiquity and
dignity, which, on the occasion of which I speak,
was enhanced by the presence of certain ancient
scholars, seated in crimson robes in high-backed
chairs. Formerly, I believe, the undergraduates
were placed apart—packed together in a corner of
one of the galleries. But now they are scattered
among the general spectators, a large number of
whom are ladies. They muster in especial force,
however, on the floor of the theatre, which has been
cleared of its benches. Here the dense mass is at
last severed in twain by the entrance of the prospective D.C.L.'s walking in single file, clad in crimson
gowns, preceded by mace-bearers and accompanied
by the Regius professor of Civil Law, who presents
them individually to the Vice-Chancellor of the
university, in a Latin speech which is of course a
glowing eulogy. The five gentlemen to whom this

265

distinction had been offered in 1877 were not among
those whom fame has trumpeted most loudly; but
there was something very pretty in their standing in
their honourable robes, with heads modestly bent,
while the orator, equally brilliant in aspect, recited
their titles sonorously to the venerable dignitary in
the high-backed chair. Each of them, when the
little speech is ended, ascends the steps leading to
the chair; the Vice-Chancellor bends forward and
shakes his hand, and the new D.C.L. goes and sits
in the blushing row of his fellow-doctors. The impressiveness of all this is much diminished by the
boisterous conduct of the collegians, who super-
abound in extravagant applause, in impertinent in-
terrogation, and in lively disparagement of the
orator's Latinity. Of the scene that precedes the
episode I have just described I have given no account; vivid portrayal of it is not easy. Like the
return from the Derby, it is a carnival of "chaff";
and it is a singular fact that the scholastic festival
should have forcibly reminded me of the great
popular "lark." In each case it is the same race
enjoying a certain definitely chartered license; in
the young votaries of a liberal education and the
London rabble on the Epsom road it is the same
perfect good-humour, the same muscular jocosity.

After the presentation of the doctors came a
series of those collegiate exercises which have a
generic resemblance all the world over: a reading of
Latin verses and English essays, a spouting of prize
poems and Greek paraphrases. The prize poem
alone was somewhat attentively listened to; the other
things were received with an infinite variety of

266

critical ejaculation. But after all, I reflected, as the ceremony drew to a close, this discordant racket is more characteristic than it seems; it is at bottom only another expression of the venerable and historic side of Oxford. It is tolerated because it is traditional; it is possible because it is classical. Looking at it in this light, one might manage at last to find it impressive and romantic.

I was not obliged to find ingenious pretexts for thinking well of another ceremony of which I was witness after we adjourned from the Sheldonian theatre. This was a lunch-party at the particular college in which I should find it the highest privilege to reside. I may not further specify it. Perhaps, indeed, I may go so far as to say that the reason for my dreaming of this privilege is that it is deemed by persons of a reforming turn the best-appointed abuse in a nest of abuses. A commission for the expurgation of the universities has lately been appointed by Parliament to look into it—a commission armed with a gigantic broom, which is to sweep away all the fine old ivied and cobwebbed improprieties. Pending these righteous changes, one would like while one is about it—about, that is, this business of admiring Oxford—to attach one's self to the abuse, to bury one's nostrils in the rose before it is plucked. At the college in question there are no undergraduates. I found it agreeable to reflect that those gray-green cloisters had sent no delegates to the slangy congregation I had just quitted. This delightful spot exists for the satisfaction of a small society of Fellows who, having no dreary instruction to administer, no noisy hobbledehoys to govern, no

267

obligations but toward their own culture, no care save for learning as learning and truth as truth, are presumably the happiest and most charming people in the world. The party invited to lunch assembled first in the library of the college, a cool, gray hall, of very great length and height, with vast wall-spaces of rich - looking book - titles and statues of noble scholars set in the midst. Had the charming Fellows ever anything more disagreeable to do than to finger these precious volumes and then to stroll about together in the grassy courts, in learned comradeship, discussing their precious contents ? Nothing, apparently, unless it were to give a lunch at Commemoration in the dining-hall of the college. When lunch was ready there was a very pretty procession to go to it. Learned gentlemen in crimson gowns, ladies in brilliant toilets, paired slowly off and marched in a stately diagonal across the fine, smooth lawn of the quadrangle, in a corner of which they passed through a hospitable door. But here we cross the threshold of privacy; I remained on the farther side of it during the rest of the day. But I brought back with me certain memories of which, if I were not at the end of my space, I should attempt a discreet adumbration: memories of a fête champêtre in the beautiful gardens of one of the other colleges—charming lawns and spreading trees, music of Grenadier Guards, ices in striped marquees, mild flirtation of youthful gownsmen and bemuslined maidens; memories, too, of quiet dinner in common-room, a decorous, excellent repast; old portraits on the walls and great windows open upon the ancient court, where the afternoon light was fading in the stillness;

superior talk upon current topics, and over all the peculiar air of Oxford——the air of liberty to care for intellectual things, assured and secured by machinery which is in itself a satisfaction to sense.

In Warwickshire

THERE is no better way for the stranger who wishes to know something of England, to plunge in *medias res*, than to spend a fortnight in Warwickshire. It is the core and centre of the English world; mid-most England, unmitigated England. The place has taught me a great many English secrets; I have interviewed the genius of pastoral Britain. From a charming lawn—a lawn delicious to one's sentient boot-sole—I looked without obstruction at a sombre, soft, romantic mass, whose outline was blurred by mantling ivy. It made a perfect picture; and in the foreground the great trees overarched their boughs from right and left, so as to give it a majestic frame. This interesting object was the castle of Kenilworth. It was within distance of an easy walk, but one hardly thought of walking to it, any more than one would have thought of walking to a purple-shadowed tower in the background of a Berghem or a Claude. Here there were purple shadows, and slowly-shifting lights, and a soft-hued, bosky country in the middle distance.

Of course, however, I did walk over to the castle; and of course the walk led me through leafy lanes, and beside the hedgerows that make a tangled screen for lawn-like meadows. Of course too, I am bound to add, there was a row of ancient pedlars outside the castle-wall, hawking twopenny pamphlets and photographs. Of course, equally, at the foot of the grassy mound on which the ruin stands, there were half a dozen public houses; and, always of course, there were half a dozen beery vagrants sprawling on the grass in the moist sunshine. There was the usual respectable young woman to open the castle-gate and to receive the usual sixpenny fee. And there were the usual squares of printed cardboard, suspended upon venerable surfaces, with further enumeration of twopence, threepence, fourpence. I do not allude to these things querulously, for Kenilworth is a very tame lion—a lion that, in former years, I had stroked more than once. I remember perfectly my first visit to this romantic spot; how I chanced upon a picnic; how I stumbled over beer-bottles; how the very echoes of the beautiful ruin seemed to have dropped all their h's. That was a sultry afternoon; I allowed my spirits to sink, and I came away hanging my head. This was a beautiful fresh morning, and in the interval I had grown philosophic. I had learned that, with regard to most romantic sites in England, there is a sort of average cockneyfication with which you must make your account. There are always people on the field before you, and there is generally something being drunk on the premises.

I hoped, on the occasion of which I am now

speaking, that the average would be low; and indeed, for the first five minutes I flattered myself that this was the case. In the beautiful grassy court of the castle, on my entrance, there were not more than eight or ten fellow-intruders. There were a couple of old ladies on a bench, eating something out of a newspaper; there was a dissenting minister, also on a bench, reading the guide-book aloud to his wife and sister-in-law; there were three or four children pushing each other up and down the turfy hillocks. This was sweet seclusion indeed; and I got a capital start with the various noble square-windowed fragments of the stately pile. They are extremely majestic, with their even, pale-red colour, their deep-green drapery, their princely vastness of scale. But presently the tranquil ruin began to swarm like a startled hive. There were plenty of people, if they chose to show themselves. They emerged from crumbling doorways and gaping chambers, with the best conscience in the world; but I know not, after all, why I should bear them a grudge, for they gave me a pretext for wandering about in search of a quiet point of view. I cannot say that I found my point of view, but in looking for it I saw the castle, which is certainly an admirable ruin. And when the respectable young woman had let me out of the gate again, and I had shaken my head at the civil-spoken pedlars who form a little avenue for the arriving and departing visitor, I found it in my good-nature to linger a moment on the trodden, grassy slope, and to think that in spite of the hawkers, the paupers, and the beer-shops, there was still a good deal of old England in the scene. I say in spite of these things, but it may have been, in some degree, because of them. Who shall resolve into its component parts any impression of this richly complex English world, where the present is always seen, as it were, in profile, and the past presents a full face ? At all events the solid red castle rose behind me, towering above its small old ladies and its investigating parsons ; before me, across the patch of common, was a row of ancient cottages, black-timbered, red-gabled, pictorial, which evidently had a memory of the castle in its better days. A quaintish village straggled away on the right, and on the left the dark, fat meadows were lighted up with misty sun-spots and browsing sheep. I looked about for the village stocks ; I was ready to take the modern vagrants for Shakespearean clowns ; and I was on the point of going into one of the ale-houses to ask Mrs. Quickly for a cup of sack.

I began these remarks, however, with no intention of talking about the celebrated curiosities in which this region abounds, but with a design, rather, of noting a few impressions of some of the shyer and more elusive ornaments of the show. Stratford, of course, is a very sacred place, but I prefer to say a word, for instance, about a charming old rectory, a good many miles distant, and to mention the pleasant picture it made of a summer afternoon, during a domestic festival. These are the happiest of a stranger's memories of English life, and he feels that he need make no apology for lifting the corner of the curtain. I drove through the leafy lanes I spoke of just now, and peeped over the hedges into

fields where the yellow harvest stood waiting. In
some places they were already shorn, and while the
light began to redden in the west and to make a
horizontal glow behind the dense wayside foliage,
the gleaners, here and there, came brushing through
gaps in the hedges with enormous sheaves upon
their shoulders. The rectory was an ancient, gabled
building, of pale red brick, with facings of white
stone and creepers that wrapped it up. It dates, I
imagine, from the early Hanoverian time; and as it
stood there upon its cushiony lawn, among its
ordered gardens, cheek to cheek with its little Norman church, it seemed to me the model of a quiet,
spacious, easy English home. The cushiony lawn,
as I have called it, stretched away to the edge of
a brook, and afforded to a number of very amiable
people an opportunity of playing lawn-tennis. There
were half a dozen games going forward at once, and
at each of them a great many "nice girls," as they
say in England, were distinguishing themselves.
These young ladies kept the ball going with an
agility worthy of the sisters and sweethearts of a
race of cricketers, and gave me a chance to admire
their flexibility of figure and their freedom of action.
When they came back to the house, after the
games, flushed a little and a little dishevelled, they
might have passed for the attendant nymphs of
Diana, flocking in from the chase. There had,
indeed, been a chance for them to wear the quiver,
a target for archery being erected on the lawn. I
remembered George Eliot's Gwendolen, and waited to
see her step out of the muslin groups; but she was
not forthcoming, and it was plain that if lawn-

tennis had been invented in Gwendolen's day, this young lady would have captivated Mr. Grandcourt by her exploits with the racket. She certainly would have been a mistress of the game; and, if the suggestion is not too gross, the alertness that she would have learned from it might have proved an inducement to her boxing the ears of the insupportable Deronda.

After a while it grew too dark for lawn-tennis; but while the twilight was still mildly brilliant I wandered away, out of the grounds of the charming parsonage, and turned into the little churchyard beside it. The small weather-worn, rust-coloured church had an appearance of high antiquity; there were some curious Norman windows in the apse. Unfortunately I could not get inside; I could only glance into the open door across the interval of an old-timbered, heavy-hooded, padlocked porch. But the sweetest evening stillness hung over the place, and the sunset was red behind a dark row of rook-haunted elms. The stillness seemed the greater because three or four rustic children were playing, with little soft cries, among the crooked, deep-buried grave-stones. One poor little girl, who seemed deformed, had climbed some steps that served as a pedestal for a tall, mediæval-looking cross. She sat perched there, staring at me through the gloaming. This was the heart of England, unmistakably; it might have been the very pivot of the wheel on which her fortune revolves. One need not be a rabid Anglican to be extremely sensible of the charm of an English country church—and indeed of some of the features of an English rural Sunday. In London there is a certain flatness in the observance of this festival; but in the country some of the ceremonies that accompany it have an indefinable harmony with an ancient, pastoral landscape. I made this reflection on an occasion that is still very fresh in my memory. I said to myself that the walk to church from a beautiful country-house, of a lovely summer afternoon, may be the prettiest possible adventure. The house stands perched upon a pedestal of rock, and looks down from its windows and terraces upon a shadier spot in the wooded meadows, of which the blunted tip of a spire explains the character. A little company of people, whose costume denotes the highest pitch of civilisation, winds down through the blooming gardens, passes out of a couple of small gates, and reaches the footpath in the fields. This is especially what takes the fancy of the sympathetic stranger; the level, deep-green meadows, studded here and there with a sturdy oak; the denser grassiness of the footpath, the lily-sheeted pool beside which it passes, the rustic stiles, where he stops and looks back at the great house and its wooded background. It is in the highest degree probable that he has the privilege of walking with a very pretty girl, and it is morally certain that he thinks a pretty English girl the prettiest creature in the world. He knows that she doesn't know how lovely is this walk of theirs; she has been taking it—or taking another quite as good—any time these twenty years. But her quiet-eyed unsuspectingness only makes her the more a part of his delicate entertainment. The latter continues unbroken while they reach the little churchyard, and pass up to the ancient porch, round which the rosy rustics are standing decently and deferentially, to watch the arrival of the smarter contingent. This party takes its place in a great square pew, as large as a small room, and with seats all round, and while he listens to the respectable intonings the sympathetic stranger reads over the inscriptions on the mural tablets before him, all to the honour of the earlier bearers of a name which is, for himself, a symbol of hospitality.

When I came back to the parsonage the entertainment had been transferred to the interior, and I had occasion to admire the maidenly vigour of those charming young girls who, after playing lawn-tennis all the afternoon, were modestly expecting to dance all the evening. And in regard to this it is not impertinent to say that from almost any group of English maidens—though preferably from such as have passed their lives in quiet country homes—an American observer receives a delightful impression of something that he can best describe as an intimate salubrity. He notices face after face in which this rosy absence of a morbid strain—this simple, natural, affectionate development—amounts to positive beauty. If the young lady have no other beauty, the look I speak of is a sufficient charm ; but when it is united, as it so often is, to real perfection of feature and colour, the result is the most delightful thing in nature. It makes the highest type of English beauty, and to my sense there is nothing so high as that. Not long since I heard a clever foreigner indulge, in conversation with an English lady—a very wise and liberal woman—in a little lightly restrictive criticism of her countrywomen. "It is possible," she answered, in regard to one of his objections; "but such as they are, they are inexpressibly dear to their husbands." This is doubtless true of good wives all over the world; but I felt, as I listened to these words of my friend, that there is often something in an English girl-face which gives it an extra touch of *justesse*. Such as the woman is, she has here, more than elsewhere, the look of being completely and profoundly at the service of the man she loves. This look, after one has been a while in England, comes to seem so much a proper and indispensable part of a "nice" face, that the absence of it appears a sign of irritability or of shallowness. Depth of tenderness as regards a masculine counterpart—that is what it means; and I confess that seems to me a very agreeable meaning.

As for the prettiness, I cannot forbear, in the face of a fresh reminiscence, to give it another word. And yet in regard to prettiness, what do words avail? This was what I asked myself the other day as I looked at a young girl who stood in an old oaken parlour, the rugged panels of which made a background for her lovely head, in simple conversation with a handsome lad. I said to myself that the faces of English young people had often a singular charm, but that this same charm is too soft and shy a thing to talk about. The face of this fair creature had a pure oval, and her clear brown eyes a quiet warmth. Her complexion was as bright as a sunbeam after rain, and she smiled in a way that made any other way of smiling than that seem a shallow grimace—a mere creaking of the facial muscles. The young man stood facing her, slowly scratching his thigh and shifting from one foot to the other. He was tall and very well made, and so sun-burned that his fair hair was lighter than his complexion. He had honest, stupid blue eyes, and a simple smile that showed his handsome teeth. He was very well dressed. Presently I heard what they were saying. "I suppose it's pretty big," said the beautiful young girl. "Yes; it's pretty big," said the handsome young man. "It's nicer when they are big," said his interlocutress. The young man looked at her, and at everything in general, with his slowly-apprehending blue eye, and for some time no further remark was made. "It draws ten feet of water," he at last went on. "How much water is there?" said the young girl. She spoke in a charming voice. "There are thirty feet of water," said the young man. "Oh, that's enough," rejoined the damsel. I had had an idea they were flirting, and perhaps indeed that is the way it is done. It was an ancient room and extremely delightful; everything was polished over with the brownness of centuries. The chimney-piece was carved a foot thick, and the windows bore, in coloured glass, the quarterings of ancestral couples. These had stopped two hundred years before; there was nothing newer than that date. Outside the windows was a deep, broad moat, which washed the base of gray walls—gray walls spotted over with the most delicate yellow lichens.

In such a region as this mellow, conservative War-

wickshire an appreciative American finds the small
things quite as suggestive as the great. Everything,
indeed, is suggestive, and impressions are constantly
melting into each other and doing their work before
he has had time to ask them whence they came
He cannot go into a cottage muffled in plants, to see
a genial gentlewoman and a "nice girl," without
being reminded forsooth of "The Small House at
Allington." Why of "The Small House at Allington?" There is a larger house at which the ladies
come up to dine; but that is surely an insufficient
reason. That the ladies are charming—even that
is not reason enough; for there have been other nice
girls in the world than Lily Dale, and other mellow
matrons than her mamma. Reminded, however, he
is—especially when he goes out upon the lawn. Of
course there is lawn-tennis, and it seems all ready
for Mr. Crosbie to come and play. This is a small
example of the way in which in the presence of
English life the imagination must be constantly at
play, on the part of members of a race in whom it
has necessarily been trained to do extra service. In
driving and walking, in looking and listening, everything seemed to me in some degree or other characteristic of a rich, powerful, old-fashioned society.
One had no need of being told that this is a conservative county; the fact seemed written in the
hedgerows and in the verdant acres behind them.
Of course the owners of these things were conservative; of course they were stubbornly unwilling to
see the harmonious edifice of Church and State the
least bit shaken. I had a feeling, as I went about,
that I should find some very ancient and curious

opinions still comfortably domiciled in the fine old houses whose clustered gables and chimneys appeared here and there, at a distance, above their ornamental woods. Self-complacent British Toryism, viewed in this vague and conjectural fashion—across the fields and behind the oaks and beeches—is by no means a thing the irresponsible stranger would wish away; it deepens the local colour; it may be said to enhance the landscape. I got a sort of constructive sense of its presence in the picturesque old towns of Coventry and Warwick, which appear to be filled with those institutions—chiefly of an eleemosynary order—that Toryism takes a genial comfort in. There are ancient charities in these places—hospitals, almshouses, asylums, infant-schools—so quaint and venerable that they almost make the existence of poverty a delectable and satisfying thought. In Coventry in especial, I believe, these pious foundations are so numerous as almost to place a premium upon misery. Invidious reflections apart, however, there are few things that speak more quaintly and suggestively of the old England that an American loves than these clumsy little monuments of ancient benevolence. Such an institution as Leicester's Hospital at Warwick seems indeed to exist primarily for the sake of its spectacular effect upon the American tourists, who, with the dozen rheumatic old soldiers maintained in affluence there, constitute its principal *clientèle*.

The American tourist usually comes straight to this quarter of England—chiefly for the purpose of paying his respects to the birthplace of Shakespeare. Being here, he comes to Warwick to see the castle;

and being at Warwick, he comes to see the odd little theatrical-looking refuge for superannuated warriors which lurks in the shadow of one of the old gate-towers. Every one will remember Hawthorne's account of the place, which has left no touch of charming taste to be added to any reference to it. The hospital struck me as a little museum kept up for the amusement and confusion of those inquiring Occidentals who are used to seeing charity more dryly and practically administered. The old hospitallers —I am not sure, after all, whether they are necessarily soldiers, but some of them happen to be—are at once the curiosities and the keepers. They sit on benches outside of their door, at the receipt of custom, all neatly brushed and darned, and ready, like Mr. Cook, to conduct you personally. They are only twelve in number, but their picturesque dwelling, perched upon the old city rampart, and full of dusky little courts, cross-timbered gable-ends and deeply sunken lattices, seems a wonderfully elaborate piece of machinery for its humble purpose. Each of the old gentlemen must be provided with a wife or " housekeeper ; " each of them has a dusky parlour of his own ; and they pass their latter days in their scoured and polished little refuge as softly and honourably as a company of retired lawgivers or pensioned soothsayers.

At Coventry I went to see a couple of old charities of a similar pattern—places with black-timbered fronts, little clean-swept courts and Elizabethan windows. One of them was a romantic residence for a handful of old women, who sat, each of them, in a cosy little bower, in a sort of mediæval darkness ;

the other was a school for little boys of humble origin, and this last establishment was charming. I found the little boys playing at " top " in a gravelled court, in front of the prettiest old building of tender-coloured stucco and painted timber, ornamented with two delicate little galleries and a fantastic porch. They were dressed in small blue tunics and odd caps, like those worn by sailors, but, if I remember rightly, with little yellow tags affixed to them. I was free, apparently, to wander all over the establishment; there was no sign of pastor or master anywhere; nothing but the little yellow-headed boys playing before the ancient house, and practising most correctly the Warwickshire accent. I went indoors and looked at a fine old oaken staircase; I even ascended it, and walked along a gallery and peeped into a dormitory at a row of very short beds; and then I came down and sat for five minutes on a bench hardly wider than the top rail of a fence, in a little, cold, dim refectory, where there was not a crumb to be seen, nor any lingering odour of bygone repasts to be perceived. And yet I wondered how it was that the sense of many generations of boyish feeders seemed to abide there. It came, I suppose from the very bareness and, if I may be allowed the expression, the clean-licked aspect of the place, which wore the appearance of the famous platter of Jack Sprat and his wife.

Inevitably, of course, the sentimental tourist has a great deal to say to himself about this being Shakespeare's county—about these densely verdant meadows and parks having been, to his musing eyes, the normal landscape. In Shakespeare's day, doubtless, the coat of nature was far from being so prettily trimmed as it is now ; but there is one place, nevertheless, which, as he passes it in the summer twilight, the traveller does his best to believe unaltered. I allude, of course, to Charlecote park, whose venerable verdure seems a survival from an earlier England, and whose innumerable acres, stretching away, in the early evening, to vaguely seen Tudor walls, lie there like the backward years receding to the age of Elizabeth. It was, however, no part of my design in these remarks to pause before so thickly besieged a shrine as this ; and if I were to allude to Stratford, it would not be in connection with the fact that Shakespeare came into the world there. It would be rather to speak of a delightful old house near the Avon which struck me as the ideal home for a Shakespearean scholar, or indeed for any passionate lover of the poet. Here, with books, and memories, and the recurring reflection that he had taken his daily walk across the bridge, at which you look from your windows straight down an avenue of fine old trees, with an ever-closed gate at the end of them and a carpet of turf stretched over the decent drive—here, I say, with old brown wainscotted chambers to live in, old polished doorsteps to lead you from one to the other, deep window-seats to sit in, with a play in your lap —here a person for whom the cares of life should have resolved themselves into a care for the greatest genius who has represented and ornamented life, might find a very congruous asylum. Or, speaking a little wider of the mark, the charming, rambling, low-gabled, many-staired, much-panelled mansion would be a very agreeable home for any person of taste who should prefer an old house to a new. I find I am talking about it quite like an auctioneer; but what I chiefly had at heart was to commemorate the fact that I had lunched there, and while I lunched kept saying to myself that there is nothing in the world so delightful as the happy accidents of old English houses.

And yet that same day, on the edge of the Avon, I found it in me to say that a new house too may be a very charming affair. But I must add that the new house I speak of had really such exceptional advantages that it could not fairly be placed in the scale. Besides, was it new after all? I suppose that it was, and yet one's impression there was all of a kind of silvery antiquity. The place stood upon a decent Stratford street, from which it looked usual enough; but when, after sitting a while in a charming modern drawing-room, one stepped thoughtlessly through an open window upon a verandah, one found that the horizon of the morning-call had been wonderfully widened. I will not pretend to relate all that I saw after I stepped off the verandah; suffice it that the spire and chancel of the beautiful old church in which Shakespeare is buried, with the Avon sweeping its base, were one of the elements of the vision. Then there were the smoothest lawns in the world stretching down to the edge of this lovely stream, and making, where the water touched them, a line as even as the rim of a champagne-glass—a verge near which you inevitably lingered to see the spire and the chancel—the church was close at hand—among the well-grouped trees, and look for their reflection in the river. The place was

a garden of delight; it was a stage set for one of
Shakespeare's comedies—for *Twelfth Night* or *Much
Ado*. Just across the river was a level meadow,
which rivalled the lawn on which I stood, and this
meadow seemed only the more essentially a part of
the scene by reason of the voluminous sheep that
were grazing on it. These sheep were by no means
mere edible mutton; they were poetic, historic,
romantic sheep; they were there to be picturesque,
and they knew it. And yet, knowing as they were,
I doubt whether the wisest old ram of the flock
could have told me how to explain why it was that
this happy mixture of lawn and river and mirrored
spire and blooming garden seemed to me for a quarter
of an hour the prettiest corner of England.

If Warwickshire is Shakespeare's country, I found
myself remembering that it is also George Eliot's.
The author of *Adam Bede* and *Middlemarch* has
called the rural background of those admirable fic-
tions by another name, but I believe it long ago
ceased to be a secret that her native Warwickshire
had been in her intention. The stranger who wanders over its velvety surface recognises at every turn
the elements of George Eliot's novels—especially
when he carries himself back in imagination to the
Warwickshire of forty years ago. He says to himself that it would be impossible to conceive anything
more conservatively bucolic, more respectably pastoral. It was in one of the old nestling farmhouses,
beyond a hundred hedgerows, that Hetty Sorrel
smiled into her milk-pans, as if she were looking for
a reflection of her pretty face; it was at the end of
one of the leafy-pillared avenues that poor Mrs.

Casaubon paced up and down in fervid disappointment. The country suggests, in especial, both the social and the natural scenery of *Middlemarch.* There must be many a genially perverse old Mr. Brooke there yet, and whether there are many Dorotheas or not, there must be many a well-featured and well-acred young country gentleman, of the pattern of Sir James Chettam, who, as he rides along the leafy lanes, softly cudgels his brain to know why a clever girl shouldn't wish to marry him. But I doubt whether there are many Dorotheas, and I suspect that the Sir James Chettams of the county are not often pushed to that intensity of meditation. You feel, however, that George Eliot could not have placed her heroine in a local medium better fitted to throw her fine impatience into relief—a community more likely to be startled and perplexed by a questioning attitude on the part of a well-housed and well-fed young gentlewoman.

Among the edifying days that I spent in these neighbourhoods there is one in especial of which I should like to give a detailed account. But I find on consulting my memory that the details have melted away into the single deep impression of a perfect ripeness of civilisation. It was a long excursion, by rail and by carriage, for the purpose of seeing three extremely interesting old country-houses. Our errand led us, in the first place, into Oxfordshire, through the ancient market-town of Banbury, where of course we made a point of looking out for the Cross referred to in the famous nursery-rhyme. It stood there in the most natural manner —though I am afraid it has been "done up"—with various antique gables around it, from one of whose exiguous windows the young person appealed to in the rhyme may have looked at the old woman as she rode and heard the music of her bells. The houses we went to see have not a national reputation; they are simply interwoven figures in the rich pattern of the Midlands. They have, indeed, a local renown, but they are not thought to be very exceptionally curious or beautiful, and the stranger has a feeling that his surprises and ecstasies are held to betray a meagre bringing-up. Such places, to a Warwickshire mind of good habits, must appear to be the pillars and props of a heaven-appointed order of things; and accordingly, in a land on which heaven smiles, they are as natural as the geology of the county or the supply of mutton. But nothing could well give a stranger a stronger impression of the wealth of England in such matters — of the interminable list of her territorial homes — than this fact that the enchanting old mansions I speak of should have but a limited fame — should not be lions of the first magnitude. Of one of them, the finest in the group, one of my companions, who lived but twenty miles away, had never even heard. Such a place was not thought a matter to boast about. Its peers and its mates are scattered all over the country; half of them are not even mentioned in the county guide-books. You stumble upon them in a drive or a walk. You catch a glimpse of an ivied front at the midmost point of a great estate, and taking your way, by leave of a serious old woman at a lodge-gate, along an overarching avenue, you find yourself introduced to an edifice so human-looking in its beauty, that it seems for the occasion to reconcile art and morality.

To Broughton Castle, the first seen in this beautiful group, I must do no more than allude; but this is not because I failed to think it, as I think every house I see, the most delightful residence in England. It lies rather low, and its woods and pastures slope down to it; it has a deep, clear moat all around it, spanned by a bridge that passes under a charming old gate-tower, and nothing can be prettier than to see its clustered walls of yellow-brown stone so sharply islanded, while its gardens bloom on the other side of the water. Like several other houses in this part of the country, Broughton Castle played a part (on the Parliamentary side) in the civil wars, and not the least interesting features of its beautiful interior are the several mementoes of Cromwell's station there. It was within a moderate drive of this place that in 1642 the battle of Edgehill was fought—the first great battle of the war—and gained by neither party. We went to see the battlefield, where an ancient tower and an artificial ruin (of all things in the world) have been erected for the entertainment of convivial visitors. These ornaments are perched upon the edge of a slope which commands a view of the exact scene of the contest, upwards of a mile away. I looked in the direction indicated, and saw misty meadows, a little greener perhaps than usual, and colonnades of elms, a trifle denser. After this we paid our respects to another old house which is full of memories and suggestions of that most dramatic period of English history. But of Compton Wyniates (the name of this enchanting domicile), I despair of giving any coherent or adequate account. It belongs to the Marquis of Northampton, and it stands empty all the year round. It sits on the grass at the bottom of a wooded hollow, and the glades of a superb old park go wandering upward, away from it. When I came out in front of the house from a short and steep but stately avenue, I said to myself that here surely we had arrived at the farthest limits of what ivy-smothered brick-work and weather-beaten gables, conscious old windows and clustered mossy roofs, can accomplish for the eye. It is impossible to imagine a more perfect picture. And its air of solitude and delicate decay — of having been dropped into its grassy hollow as an ancient jewel is deposited upon a cushion, and being shut in from the world and back into the past by its circling woods—all this highly increased its impressiveness. The house is not large, as great houses go, and it sits, as I have said, upon the grass, without even a flagging or a footpath to conduct you from the point where the avenue stops to the beautiful sculptured doorway which admits you into the small, quaint, inner court. From this court you are at liberty to pass through the crookedest series of oaken halls and chambers, adorned with treasures of old wainscotting and elaborate doors and chimney-pieces. Outside, you may walk all round the house on a grassy bank, which is raised above the level on which it stands, and find it from every point of view a more charming composition. I should not omit to men-

293

tion that Compton Wyniates is supposed to have
been in Scott's eye when he described the dwelling
of the old royalist knight in *Woodstock*. In this
case he simply transferred the house to the other
side of the county. He has indeed given several
of the features of the place, but he has not given
what one may call its colour. I must add that if
Sir Walter could not give the colour of Compton
Wyniates, it is useless for any other writer to
attempt it. It is a matter for the brush and not
for the pen.

And what shall I say of the colour of Wroxton
Abbey, which we visited last in order, and which in
the thickening twilight, as we approached its great
ivy-muffled face, made an ineffaceable impression on
my fancy ? Wroxton Abbey, as it stands, is a
house of about the same period as Compton Wyniates
—the latter years, I suppose, of the sixteenth century. But it is quite another affair. The place is
inhabited, " kept up," and full of the most interesting
and most splendid detail. Its happy occupants,
however, were fortunately not actually staying there
(happy occupants, in England, are almost always
absent), and the house was exhibited with a civility
worthy of its merit. Everything that in the material
line can render life noble and charming has been
gathered into it with a profusion which makes the
whole place a monument to past opportunity. As
I wandered from one rich room to another, looking
at these things, that ineffaceable impression upon
my fancy which I just mentioned was delightfully
deepened. But who can tell the pleasures of fancy

when fancy takes her ease in an old English country-house, while the twilight darkens the corners of expressive rooms, and the appreciative intruder, pausing at the window, turns his glance from the observing portrait of a handsome ancestral face and sees the great soft billows of the lawn melt away into the park ?

Abbeys and Castles

Iт is a frequent reflection with the stranger in England that the beauty and interest of the country are private property, and that to get access to them a key is always needed. The key may be large or it may be small, but it must be something that will turn a lock. Of the things that contribute to the happiness of an American observer in the country of parks and castles, I can think of very few that do not come under this definition of private property. When I have mentioned the hedgerows and the churches I have almost exhausted the list. You can enjoy a hedgerow from the public road, and I suppose that even if you are a Dissenter you may enjoy a Norman abbey from the street. If, therefore, one talk of anything beautiful in England, the presumption will be that it is private; and indeed such is my admiration of this delightful country that I feel inclined to say that if one talk of anything private the presumption will be that it is beautiful. This is something of a dilemma. If the observer permit himself to commemorate charming

impressions, he is in danger of giving to the world
the fruits of friendship and hospitality. If, on the
other hand, he withhold his impression, he lets
something admirable slip away without having
marked its passage, without having done it proper
honour. He ends by mingling discretion with
enthusiasm, and he says to himself that it is not
treating a country ill to talk of its treasures when
the mention of each has tacit reference to an act of
private courtesy.

The impressions I have in mind in writing these
lines were gathered in a part of England of which I
had not before had even a traveller's glimpse; but
as to which, after a day or two, I found myself quite
ready to agree with a friend who lived there, and
who knew and loved it well, when he said very
frankly, "I do believe it is the loveliest corner of
the world!" This was not a dictum to quarrel
about, and while I was in the neighbourhood I was
quite of his opinion. I felt that it would not take
a great deal to make me care for it very much as
he cared for it; I had a glimpse of the peculiar
tenderness with which such a country may be loved.
It is a capital example of the great characteristic of
English scenery—of what I should call density of
feature. There are no waste details; everything in
the landscape is something particular—has a history,
has played a part, has a value to the imagination.
It is a region of hills and blue undulations, and,
though none of the hills are high, all of them are
interesting—interesting as such things are interesting in an old, small country, by a kind of exquisite
modulation, something suggesting that outline and

colouring have been retouched and refined by the hand of time. Independently of its castles and abbeys, the definite relics of the ages, such a landscape seems historic. It has human relations, and it is intimately conscious of them. That little speech about the loveliness of his county, or of his own part of his county, was made to me by my companion as we walked up the grassy slope of a hill, or "edge," as it is called there, from the crest of which we seemed in an instant to look away over most of the remainder of England. Certainly I should have grown affectionate with regard to such a view as that. The "edge" plunged down suddenly, as if the corresponding slope on the other side had been excavated, and one might follow the long ridge for the space of an afternoon's walk with this vast, charming prospect before one's eyes. Looking across an English county into the next but one is a very pretty entertainment, the county seeming by no means so small as might be supposed. How can a county seem small in which, from such a vantage-point as the one I speak of, you see, as a darker patch across the lighter green, the great estate of one of their lordships? Beyond these are blue undulations of varying tone, and then another bosky-looking spot, which constitutes, as you are told, the residential umbrage of another peer. And to right and left of these, in wooded expanses, lie other domains of equal consequence. It was therefore not the smallness but the vastness of the country that struck me, and I was not at all in the mood of a certain American who once, in my hearing, burst out laughing at an English answer to my inquiry as to whether my interlocutor often saw Mr. B——. "Oh no," the answer had been, "we never see him: he lives away off in the West." It was the western part of his county our friend meant, and my American humorist found matter for infinite jest in his meaning. "I should as soon think of saying my western hand and my eastern," he declared.

I do not think, even, that my disposition to form a sentimental attachment for this delightful region— for its hillside prospect of old red farmhouses lighting up the dark-green bottoms, of gables and chimney-tops of great houses peeping above miles of woodland, and, in the vague places of the horizon, of far away towns and sites that one had always heard of—was conditioned upon having "property" in the neighbourhood, so that the little girls in the town should suddenly drop curtsies to me in the street; though that too would certainly have been pleasant. At the same time, having a little property would without doubt have made the sentiment stronger. People who wander about the world without money in their pockets indulge in dreams—dreams of the things they would buy if their pockets were complete. These dreams are very apt to have relation to a good estate in any neighbourhood in which the wanderer may happen to find himself. For myself, I have never been in a country so unattractive that it did not seem a peculiar felicity to be able to purchase the most considerable house it contained. In New England and other portions of the United States I have coveted the large mansion with Doric columns and a pediment of white-painted timber;

in Italy I have made imaginary proposals for the
yellow-walled villa with statues on the roof. In
England I have rarely gone so far as to fancy myself in treaty for the best house, but, failing this, I
have rarely failed to feel that ideal comfort for the
time would be to call one's self owner of what is
denominated here a "good" place. Is it that
English country life seems to possess such irresistible
charms? I have not always thought so; I have
sometimes suspected that it is dull; I have remembered that there is a whole literature devoted to
exposing it (that of the English novel "of manners");
and that its recorded occupations and conversations
occasionally strike one as lacking a certain indispensable salt. But, for all that, when, in the region
to which I allude, my companion spoke of this and
that place being likely sooner or later to come to the
hammer, it seemed as if nothing could be more
delightful than to see the hammer hanging upon
one's own liberality. And this in spite of the fact
that the owners of the places in question would
part with them because they could no longer afford
to keep them up. I found it interesting to learn,
in so far as was possible, what sort of income was
implied by the possession of country-seats such as
are not in America a concomitant of even the largest
fortunes; and if in these revelations I sometimes
heard of a very long rent-roll, on the other hand I
was frequently surprised at the shortness of purse
attributed to people living in the depths of an oak-
studded park. Then, certainly, English country-life
seemed to me the most advantageous thing in the
world; on conditions such as these one would gladly

be dull; surrounded by luxury of so moderate a cost one would joyfully stagnate.

There was one place in particular of which I said to myself that if I had the money to buy it, I would "move in" on the morrow. I saw this place, unfortunately, to small advantage; I saw it in the rain. But I am rather glad that fine weather did not meddle with the affair, for I think that in this case the irritation of envy might have made me ill. It was a long, wet Sunday, and the waters were deep. I had been in the house all day, for the weather can best be described by my saying that it had been deemed to exonerate me from church-going. But in the afternoon, the prospective interval between lunch and tea assuming formidable proportions, my host took me out to walk, and in the course of our walk he led me into a park which he described as "the paradise of a small English country-gentleman." It was indeed a modern Eden, and the trees might have been trees of knowledge. They were of high antiquity and magnificent girth and stature; they were strewn over the grassy levels in extraordinary profusion, and scattered upon and down the slopes in a fashion than which I have seen nothing more charming since I last looked at the chestnuts on the Lake of Como. It appears that the place was not very large, but I was unable to perceive its limits. Shortly before we turned into the park the rain had renewed itself, so that we were awkwardly wet and muddy; but, being near the house, my companion proposed to leave his card in a neighbourly way The house was most agreeable; it stood on a kind of terrace, in the middle of a lawn and garden, and

the terrace overlooked one of the most copious
rivers in England, and across to those blue undulations of which I have already spoken. On the
terrace also was a piece of ornamental water, and
there was a small iron paling to divide the lawn
from the park. All this I beheld in the rain.
My companion gave his card to the butler, with the
remark that we were too much bespattered to come
in, and we turned away to complete our circuit.
As we turned away I became acutely conscious of
what I should have been tempted to call the cruelty
of this proceeding. My imagination gauged the
whole position. It was a Sunday afternoon, and it
was raining. The house was charming, the terrace
delightful, the oaks magnificent, the view most interesting. But the whole thing was—not to repeat the
invidious epithet of which just now I made too gross
a use—the whole thing was quiet. In the house
was a drawing-room, and in the drawing-room was
—by which I meant *must be*—a lady, a charming
English lady. It seemed to me that there was
nothing fatuous in believing that on this rainy Sunday afternoon it would not please her to be told that
two gentlemen had walked across the country to her
door only to go through the ceremony of leaving a
card. Therefore, when, before we had gone many
yards, I heard the butler hurrying after us, I felt
how just my sentiment of the situation had been.
Of course we went back, and I carried my muddy
boots into the drawing-room—just the drawing-room
I had imagined—where I found—I will not say just
the lady I had imagined, but a lady even more
charming. Indeed, there were two ladies, one of

whom was staying in the house. In whatever com
pany you find yourself in England, you may always
be sure that some one present is "staying." I
seldom hear this participle nowadays without remembering an observation made to me in France
by a lady who had seen much of English manners.
"Ah, that dreadful word *staying!* I think we are
so happy in France not to be able to translate it—
not to have any word that answers to it." The large
windows of the drawing-room I speak of looked
away over the river to the blurred and blotted hills,
where the rain was drizzling and drifting. It was
very quiet, as I say; there was an air of large
leisure. If one wanted to do something here, there
was evidently plenty of time—and indeed of every
other appliance—to do it. The two ladies talked
about "town:" that is what people talk about in
the country. If I were disposed I might represent
them as talking about it with a certain air of yearn-
ing. At all events, I asked myself how it was
possible that one should live in this charming place
and trouble one's head about what was going on in
London in July. Then we had excellent tea.

I returned to the habitation of my companion—
for I too was guilty of "staying"—through an old
Norman portal, massively arched and quaintly
sculptured, across whose hollow threshold the eye of
fancy might see the ghosts of monks and the shadows
of abbots pass noiselessly to and fro. This aperture
admits you to a beautiful ambulatory of the thirteenth century—a long stone gallery or cloister,
repeated in two stories, with the interstices of
its traceries now glazed, but with its long, low,

narrow, charming vista still perfect and picturesque
—with its flags worn away by monkish sandals, and
with huge round-arched doorways opening from its
inner side into great rooms roofed like cathedrals.
These rooms are furnished with narrow windows, of
almost defensive aspect, set in embrasures three feet
deep, and ornamented with little grotesque mediæval
faces. To see one of the small monkish masks
grinning at you while you dress and undress, or
while you look up in the intervals of inspiration
from your letter writing, is a mere detail in the
entertainment of living in a *ci-devant* priory. This
entertainment is inexhaustible ; for every step you
take in such a house confronts you in one way or
another with the remote past. You feast upon the
pictorial, you inhale the historic. Adjoining the
house is a beautiful ruin, part of the walls and
windows and bases of the piers of the magnificent
church administered by the predecessor of your host,
the abbot. These relics are very desultory, but they
are still abundant, and they testify to the great
scale and the stately beauty of the abbey. You may
lie upon the grass at the base of an ivied fragment,
measure the girth of the great stumps of the central
columns, half smothered in soft creepers, and think
how strange it is that in this quiet hollow, in the
midst of lonely hills, so exquisite and elaborate a
work of art should have arisen. It is but an hour's
walk to another great ruin, which has held together
more completely. There the central tower stands
erect to half its altitude, and the round arches and
massive pillars of the nave make a perfect vista on
the unencumbered turf. You get an impression

that when catholic England was in her prime, great
abbeys were as thick as milestones. By native
amateurs, even now, the region is called "wild,"
though to American eyes it seems almost suburban
in its smoothness and finish. There is a noiseless
little railway running through the valley, and there
is an ancient little town at the abbey-gates—a town,
indeed, with no great din of vehicles, but with goodly
brick houses, with a dozen "publics," with tidy,
whitewashed cottages, and with little girls, as I have
said, bobbing curtsies in the street. But even now,
if one had wound one's way into the valley by the
railroad, it would be rather a surprise to find a
small ornamental cathedral in a spot on the whole so
natural and pastoral. How impressive then must
the beautiful church have been in the days of its
prosperity, when the pilgrim came down to it from
the grassy hillside and its bells made the stillness
sensible! The abbey was in those days a great
affair; as my companion said, it sprawled all over
the place. As you walk away from it you think
you have got to the end of its geography, but you
encounter it still in the shape of a rugged out-
house enriched with an early-English arch, or an
ancient well, hidden in a kind of sculptured cavern.
It is noticeable that even if you are a traveller from
a land where there are no early-English—and indeed
few late-English—arches, and where the well-covers
are, at their hoariest, of fresh-looking shingles, you
grow used with little delay to all this antiquity.
Anything very old seems extremely natural; there
is nothing we accept so implicitly as transmitted
associations. It is not too much to say that after

308

spending twenty-four hours in a house that is six
hundred years old, you seem yourself to have lived
in it for six hundred years. You seem yourself to
have hollowed the flags with your tread, and to have
polished the oak with your touch. You walk along
the little stone gallery where the monks used to
pace, looking out of the gothic window-places at
their beautiful church, and you pause at the big
round, rugged doorway that admits you to what is
now the drawing-room. The massive step by which
you ascend to the threshold is a trifle crooked, as it
should be; the lintels are cracked and worn by
the myriad-fingered years. This strikes your casual
glance. You look up and down the miniature
cloister before you pass in; it seems wonderfully
old and queer. Then you turn into the drawing-
room, where you find modern conversation and late
publications and the prospect of dinner. The new
life and the old have melted together; there is no
dividing-line. In the drawing-room wall is a queer
funnel-shaped hole, with the broad end inward, like
a small casemate. You ask what it is, but people
have forgotten. It is something of the monks;
it is a mere detail. After dinner you are told that
there is of course a ghost—a gray friar who is seen
in the dusky hours at the end of passages. Sometimes the servants see him; they afterwards go sur-
reptitiously to sleep in the village. Then, when you
take your chamber-candle and go wandering bedward
by a short cut through empty rooms, you are conscious of a peculiar sentiment toward the gray friar
which you hardly know whether to interpret as a
hope or a reluctance.

A friend of mine, an American, who knew this country, had told me not to fail, while I was in the neighbourhood, to go to S—— and two or three other places. "Edward IV. and Elizabeth," he said, "are still hanging about there." So admonished, I made a point of going at least to S——, and I saw quite what my friend meant. Edward IV. and Elizabeth, indeed, are still to be met almost anywhere in the county; as regards domestic architecture, few parts of England are still more vividly old-English. I have rarely had, for a couple of hours, the sensation of dropping back personally into the past in a higher degree than while I lay on the grass beside the well in the little sunny court of this small castle, and lazily appreciated the still definite details of mediæval life. The place is a capital example of what the French call a small *gentilhommière* of the thirteenth century. It has a good deep moat, now filled with wild verdure, and a curious gatehouse of a much later period—the period when the defensive attitude had been wellnigh abandoned. This gatehouse, which is not in the least in the style of the habitation, but gabled and heavily timbered, with quaint cross-beams protruding from surfaces of coarse white plaster, is a very effective anomaly in regard to the little gray fortress on the other side of the court. I call this a fortress, but it is a fortress which might easily have been taken, and it must have assumed its present shape at a time when people had ceased to peer through narrow slits at possible besiegers. There are slits in the outer walls for such peering, but they are noticeably broad and not particularly oblique, and might easily have been

310

applied to the uses of a peaceful parley. This is
part of the charm of the place; human life there
must have lost an earlier grimness; it was lived in
by people who were beginning to believe in good
intentions. They must have lived very much together; that is one of the most obvious reflections
in the court of a mediæval dwelling. The court was
not always grassy and empty, as it is now, with only
a couple of gentlemen in search of impressions lying
at their length, one of whom has taken a wine-flask
out of his pocket and has coloured the clear water
drawn for them out of the well in a couple of tum-
blers by a decent, rosy, smiling, talking old woman,
who has come bustling out of the gatehouse, and
who has a large, dropsical, innocent husband standing
about on crutches in the sun, and making no sign
when you ask after his health. This poor man has
reached that ultimate depth of human simplicity at
which even a chance to talk about one's ailments is
not appreciated. But the civil old woman talks for
every one, even for an artist who has come out of
one of the rooms, where I see him afterward repro-
ducing its mouldering repose. The rooms are all
unoccupied and in a state of extreme decay, though
the castle is, as yet, far from being a ruin. From
one of the windows I see a young lady sitting under
a tree, across a meadow, with her knees up, dipping
something into her mouth. It is a camel's hair
paint-brush; the young lady is sketching. These
are the only besiegers to which the place is exposed
now, and they can do no great harm, as I doubt
whether the young lady's aim is very good. We
wandered about the empty interior, thinking it a

pity such things should fall to pieces. There is a beautiful great hall—great, that is, for a small castle (it would be extremely handsome in a modern house) —with tall, ecclesiastical-looking windows, and a long staircase at one end, climbing against the wall into a spacious bedroom. You may still apprehend very well the main lines of that simpler life; and it must be said that, simpler though it was, it was apparently by no means destitute of many of our own conveniences. The chamber at the top of the staircase ascending from the hall is charming still, with its irregular shape, its low-browed ceiling, its cupboards in the walls, and its deep bay window formed of a series of small lattices. You can fancy people stepping out from it upon the platform of the staircase, whose rugged wooden logs, by way of steps, and solid, deeply-guttered hand-rail, still remain. They looked down into the hall, where, I take it, there was always a congregation of retainers, much lounging and waiting and passing to and fro, with a door open into the court. The court, as I said just now, was not the grassy, æsthetic spot which you may find it at present of a summer's day; there were beasts tethered in it, and hustling men-at-arms, and the earth was trampled into puddles. But my lord or my lady, looking down from the chamber-door, commanded the position and, no doubt, issued their orders accordingly. The sight of the groups on the floor beneath, the calling up and down, the oaken tables spread, and the brazier in the middle—all this seemed present again; and it was not difficult to pursue the historic vision through the rest of the building—through the portion which connected the

great hall with the tower (here the confederate of the
sketching young lady without had set up the peaceful
three-legged engine of his craft); through the dusky,
roughly circular rooms of the tower itself, and up
the corkscrew staircase of the same to that most
charming part of every old castle, where visions must
leap away off the battlements to elude you—the
bright, dizzy platform at the tower-top, the place
where the castle-standard hung and the vigilant
inmates surveyed the approaches.   Here, always,
you really overtake the impression of the place—
here, in the sunny stillness, it seems to pause, pant-
ing a little, and give itself up.

It was not only at Stokesay—I have written the
name at last, and I will not efface it—that I lingered
a while on the summit of the keep to enjoy the complete impression so overtaken.   I spent such another
half hour at Ludlow, which is a much grander and
more famous monument.   Ludlow, however, is a
ruin—the most impressive and magnificent of ruins.
The charming old town and the admirable castle
form a capital object of pilgrimage.   Ludlow is an
excellent example of a small English provincial town
that has not been soiled and disfigured by industry ;
it exhibits no tall chimneys and smoke-streamers,
with their attendant purlieus and slums.   The little
city is perched upon a hill near which the goodly
Severn wanders, and it has a remarkable air of civic
dignity.   Its streets are wide and clean, empty and
a little grass-grown, and bordered with spacious,
mildly-ornamental brick houses, which look as if
there had been more going on in them in the first
decade of the century than there is in the present,

but which can still, nevertheless, hold up their heads and keep their window-panes clear, their knockers brilliant and their door steps whitened. The place seems to say that a hundred years, and less, ago it was the centre of a large provincial society, and that this society was very "good" of its kind. It must have transported itself to Ludlow for the season— in rumbling coaches and heavy curricles—and there entertained itself in decent emulation of that metropolis which a choice of railway lines had not as yet placed within its immediate reach. It had balls at the assembly rooms ; it had Mrs. Siddons to play ; it had Catalani to sing. Miss Burney's and Miss Austen's heroines might perfectly well have had their first love-affair there ; a journey to Ludlow would certainly have been a great event to Fanny Price or Emma Woodhouse, or even to those more exalted young ladies, Evelina and Cecilia. It is a place on which a provincial "gentry" has left a sensible stamp. I have seldom seen so good a collection of houses of the period between the elder picturesqueness and the modern baldness. Such places, such houses, such relics and intimations, always carry me back to the near antiquity of that pre-Victorian England which it is still easy for a stranger to picture with a certain vividness, thanks to the partial survival of many of its characteristics. It is still easier for a stranger who has stayed a while in England to form an idea of the tone, the habits, the aspect of English social life before its classic insularity had begun to wane, as all observers agree that it did, about thirty years ago. It is true that the mental operation in this matter reduces

314

itself to fancying some of the things which form
what Mr. Matthew Arnold would call the peculiar
"notes" of England infinitely exaggerated—the rigidly
aristocratic constitution of society, for instance ; the
unæsthetic temper of the people ; the private character of most kinds of comfort and entertainment.
Let an old gentleman of conservative tastes, who
can remember the century's youth, talk to you at a
club *temporis acti*—tell you wherein it is that from
his own point of view London, as a residence for a
gentleman, has done nothing but fall off for the last
forty years. You will listen, of course, with an air
of decent sympathy, but privately you will say to
yourself how difficult a place of sojourn London
must have been in those days for a stranger—how
little cosmopolitan, how bound in a thousand ways,
with narrowness of custom. What is true of the
metropolis at that time is of course doubly true of
the provinces ; and a genteel little city like the one
I am speaking of must have been a kind of focus
of insular propriety. Even then, however, the
irritated alien would have had the magnificent ruins
of the castle to dream himself back into good
humour in. They would effectually have transported him beyond all waning or waxing Phil-
istinisms.

An English New Year

IT will hardly be pretended this year that the English Christmas has been a merry one, or that the New Year has the promise of being particularly happy. The winter is proving very cold and vicious —as if nature herself were loath to be left out of the general conspiracy against the comfort and self-complacency of man. The country at large has a sense of embarrassment and depression, which is brought home more or less to every class in the closely-graduated social hierarchy, and the light of Christmas firesides has by no means dispelled the gloom. Not that I mean to overstate the gloom. It is difficult to imagine any combination of adverse circumstances powerful enough to infringe very sensibly upon the appearance of activity and prosperity, social stability and luxury, which English life must always present to a stranger. Nevertheless, the times are distinctly hard—there is plenty of evidence of it—and the spirits of the public are not high. The depression of business is extreme and universal; I am ignorant whether it has reached

319

so calamitous a point as that almost hopeless pros-
tration of every industry which you have lately
witnessed in America, and I believe things are by
no means so bad as they have been on two or three
occasions within the present century. The possibility of distress among the lower classes has been
minimised by the gigantic poor-relief system, which
is so characteristic a feature of English civilisation,
and which on particular occasions is supplemented
(as is the case at present) by private charity proportionately huge. I notice, too, that in some parts
of the country discriminating groups of work-people
have selected these dismal days as a happy time for
striking. When the labouring classes are able to
indulge in the luxury of a strike I suppose the
situation may be said to have its cheerful side.
There is, however, great distress in the North, and
there is a general feeling of impecuniosity throughout the country. The *Daily News* has sent a correspondent to the great industrial regions, and almost
every morning for the last three weeks a very
cleverly-executed picture of the misery of certain
parts of Yorkshire and Lancashire has been served
up with the matutinal tea and toast. The work is
a good one and, I take it, eminently worth doing,
as it appears to have had a visible effect upon the
purse-strings of the well-to-do. There is nothing
more striking in England than the success with
which an " appeal " is always made. Whatever the
season or whatever the cause, there always appears
to be enough money and enough benevolence in the
country to respond to it in sufficient measure—a
remarkable fact when one remembers that there is

never a moment of the year when the custom of
"appealing" intermits. Equally striking, perhaps,
is the perfection to which the science of distributing charity has been raised — the way it has
been analysed and explored and made one of the
exact sciences. One perceives that it has occupied for a long time a foremost place among
administrative questions, and has received all the
light that experience and practice can throw upon
it. The journal I quoted just now may perhaps, without reproach, be credited with a political
arrière-pensée. It would obviously like its readers
to supply in this matter of the stagnation of trade
the missing link between effect and cause—or the
link which, if not absolutely missing, is at any rate
difficult to lay one's hand upon. The majority
in Parliament were not apparently of the opinion
that the disorganisation of business is the fault of
Lord Beaconsfield ; but there is no doubt that it is
a misfortune for the Conservative party that this
bad state of things coincides very much with its
tenure of office. When an Administration may be
invidiously described as " restless," " reckless," and
" adventurous," and when at the same time business
is very bad and distress increasing, it requires no
great ingenuity to represent the former fact as
responsible for the latter.

I have spoken of the rigour of the time in the
lower walks of English life ; and it is not out of
place to say that among those happier people who
stand above the reach of material incommodity, the
Christmas season has been overshadowed sentimentally—or at least conventionally—by the death of

Princess Alice. If I had written to you at the
moment this event occurred I should have been
tempted to make some general reflections upon it,
and it is even now perhaps not too late to say that
there was, to an observer, something very interesting and characteristic in the manner in which the
news was received. Broadly speaking, it produced
much more commotion than I should have expected;
the papers overflowed with articles on the subject,
the virtues of the deceased lady and the grief of
the Queen were elaborately commemorated; many
shops, on the day of the Princess's funeral, were
partially closed, and the whole nation, it may be
said—or the whole of what professes, in any degree
whatever, to be "society"—went into mourning.
There was enough in all this to make a stranger
consider and interrogate; and the result of his
reflections would, I think, have been that, after all
abatements are made, the monarchy has still a great
hold upon the affections of the people. The people
takes great comfort in its royal family. The love
of social greatness is extraordinarily strong in
England, and the royal family appeals very con-
veniently to this sentiment. People in the immense
obscurity of that middle class which constitutes the
bulk of the English world like to feel that they are
related in some degree to something that is socially
great. They cannot pretend that they are related
to dukes and earls and people of that sort; but
they are able to cultivate a certain sense of being
related to the royal family. They may talk of
"our" princes and princesses—and the most exalted
members of the peerage may do no more than that;

322

they may possess photographs of the Queen's children, and read of their daily comings and goings with an agreeable sense of property, and without incurring that reproach of snobbishness which sometimes attaches to too eager an interest in the doings of the great nobility. There is no reason to suppose that the Queen takes the humorous view of this situation; her Majesty is indeed credited with a comfortable, motherly confidence in the salutary effect of the court-circle upon the mind of the middle class; and there is a kind of general feeling that, socially speaking, the Queen and the middle class understand each other. There was something natural, therefore, in the great impression made by the death of a princess who was personally known but to an incalculably small proportion of the people who mourned for her, and on whose behalf propriety would have resented the idea that she could personally be missed. It is nevertheless true that Lord Beaconsfield is felt rather to have overdone his part in announcing the event to the House of Lords in language in which he might have proclaimed some great national catastrophe. I was told by a person who was present that the House felt itself to be at the mercy of his bad taste—that men looked at each other with a blush and a kind of shudder, and asked each other what was coming next. He remarked, among other things, that the manner in which the Princess Alice had contracted her fatal illness (her tender imprudence in kissing her sick children) was an act worthy to be commemorated in art—"in painting, in sculpture, and in gems." I have heard these last two words wittily quoted in illustration of his Semitic origin. An ordinarily florid speaker would have contented himself with saying "in painting and in sculpture." The addition "in gems" betrays the genius of the race which supplies the world with pawnbrokers.

I left town a short time before Christmas and went to spend the festive season in the North, in a part of the country with which I was unacquainted. It was quite possible to absent one's self from London without a sense of sacrifice, for the charms of the metropolis during the last several weeks have been obscured by peculiarly atrocious weather. It is, of course, a very old story that London is foggy, and this simple statement is not of necessity alarming. But there are fogs and fogs, and these murky visitations, during the present winter, have been of the least tolerable sort. The fog that draws down and absorbs the smoke of the housetops, causes it to hang about the streets in impenetrable density, forces it into one's eyes and down one's throat, so that one is half-blinded and quite sickened—this atmospheric abomination has been much more frequent than usual. Just before Christmas, too, there was a heavy snow-storm, and even a tolerably light fall of snow has London quite at its mercy. The emblem of purity is almost immediately converted into a sticky, lead-coloured mush, the cabs skulk out of sight or take up their stations before the lurid windows of a public-house, which glares through the sleety darkness at the desperate wayfarer with an air of vulgar bravado. This state of things in the London streets made a rather sorry Christmas, though I believe the Christmas hearth is supposed to burn the more brightly in proportion as the outer world is less attractive. The wonderful London shops were, of course, duly transfigured, but they seemed to me, for the most part, to have an aspect of vain expectation, and I hear that their proprietors give a melancholy account of the profits of the season. It was only at a certain charming little French establishment in Bond Street that I observed any great activity—a little chocolate-shop where light-fingered young women from Paris dispense the most wonderful bonbonnières.

To keep one's self in good humour with English civilisation, however, one must do what I alluded to just now—one must go into the country; one must limit one's horizon, for the time, to the spacious walls of one of those admirable homes which at this season overflow with hospitality and good cheer. By this means the result is triumphantly attained —these are conditions that you cordially appreciate. Of all the great things that the English have invented and made a part of the glory of the national character, the most perfect, the most characteristic, the one they have mastered most completely in all its details, so that it has become a compendious illustration of their social genius and their manners, is the well-appointed, well-administered, well-filled country-house. The grateful stranger makes these reflections—and others besides—as he wanders about in the beautiful library of such a dwelling of an inclement winter afternoon just at the hour when six o'clock tea is impending. Such a place and such a time abound in agreeable episodes; but I suspect that the episode from which, a fortnight ago, I received the most ineffaceable impression was but indirectly connected with the charms of a luxurious fireside. The country I speak of was a populous manufacturing region, full of tall chimneys and of an air that is gray and gritty. A lady had made a present of a Christmas-tree to the children of a workhouse, and she invited me to go with her and assist at the distribution of the toys. There was a drive through the early dusk of a very cold Christmas eve, followed by the drawing-up of a lamp-lit brougham in the snowy quadrangle of a grim-looking charitable institution. I had never been in an English workhouse before, and this one transported me, with the aid of memory, to the early pages of *Oliver Twist*. We passed through certain cold, bleak passages, to which an odour of suet-pudding, the aroma of Christmas cheer, failed to impart an air of hospitality; and then, after waiting a while in a little parlour appertaining to the superintendent, where the remainder of a dinner of by no means eleemosynary simplicity and the attitude of a gentleman asleep with a flushed face on the sofa seemed to effect a tacit exchange of references, we were ushered into a large frigid refectory, chiefly illumined by the twinkling tapers of the Christmas-tree. Here entered to us some hundred and fifty little children of charity, who had been making a copious dinner, and who brought with them an atmosphere of hunger memorably satisfied—together with other traces of the occasion upon their pinafores and their small red faces. I have said that the place reminded me of *Oliver Twist*, and I glanced through this little herd for an infant figure that should look as if it

326

were cut out for romantic adventures. But they were all very prosaic little mortals. They were made of very common clay indeed, and a certain number of them were idiotic. They filed up and received their little offerings, and then they compressed themselves into a tight infantine bunch, and lifting up their small hoarse voices, directed a melancholy hymn toward their benefactress. The scene was a picture I shall not forget, with its curious mixture of poetry and sordid prose—the dying wintry light in the big, bare, stale room; the beautiful Lady Bountiful, standing in the twinkling glory of the Christmas-tree; the little multitude of staring and wondering, yet perfectly expressionless, faces.

English Vignettes

TOWARD the last of April, in Monmouthshire, the primroses were as big as your fist. I say " in Monmouthshire," because I believe that a certain grassy mountain which I gave myself the pleasure of climbing, and to which I took my way across the charming country, through lanes where the hedges were perched upon blooming banks, lay within the borders of this ancient province. It was the festive Eastertide, and a pretext for leaving London had not been wanting. Of course it rained,—it rained a good deal,—for man and the weather are usually at cross-purposes. But there were intervals of light and warmth, and in England a couple of hours of fine weather, islanded in moisture, assert their independence and leave an uncompromised memory. These bright episodes were even of longer duration; that whole morning, for instance, on which, with a companion, I scrambled up the little Skirrid. One had a feeling that one was very far from London;

331

as, in fact, one was, after six or seven hours in a
smooth, swift English train. In England this is a
great remoteness; it seemed to justify the half-re-
luctant confession which I heard constantly made,
that the country was extremely "wild." There is
wildness and wildness, I thought; and though I had
not been a great explorer, I compared this rough
district with several neighbourhoods in another part
of the world that passed for tame. I went even
so far as to wish that some of its ruder features
might be transplanted to that relatively unregulated
landscape and commingled with its suburban sava-
gery. I went over the elements of this English prospect and of human life in the midst of it, and
wondered whether, if I were to enumerate them
and leave them to be added up by the dwellers
beyond the sea, the total would be set down as a
wilderness. We were close to the Welsh border,
and a dozen little mountains in the distance were
peeping over each other's shoulders. But nature
was open to the charge of no worse disorder than this.
The Skirrid (I like to repeat the name) wore, it is
true, at a distance, the aspect of a magnified ex-
tinguisher; but when, after a bright, breezy walk
through lane and meadow, we had scrambled over
the last of the thickly-flowering hedges which lay
around its shoulders like loosened strings of coral
and began to ascend the grassy cone (very much in
the attitude of Nebuchadnezzar), it proved as
smooth-faced as a garden-mound. Hard by, on the
flanks of other hills, were troops of browsing sheep,
and the only thing in which there was any harshness
of suggestion was the strong, damp wind. But even

332

this had a good deal of softness in it, and ministered to my sense of the agreeable in scenery by the way it blew about the pearly morning mists that were airing themselves upon neighbouring ridges, and kept shaking the vaporous veil that fluttered down in the valley over the picturesque little town of Abergavenny. A breezy, grassy English hill-top, looking down on a country full of suggestive names and ancient memories, belongs (especially if you are exhilarated by a beautiful walk, and you have a flask in your pocket) decidedly to the category of smooth scenery. And so with all the rest of it.

On Sunday I stayed away from church, because I learned that the sacred edifice had a mediæval chill, and that if I should sit there for a couple of hours I might inherit a lumbago three hundred years old. The fact was formidable, but the idea was, in a certain way, attractive; there was nothing crude in a rheumatism which descended from the Norman times. Practical considerations, however, determined me not to expose myself to this venerable pain ; so in the still hours, when the roads and lanes were empty, I simply walked to the church-yard and sat upon one of the sun-warmed grave-stones. I say the roads were empty, but they were peopled with the big primroses I just now spoke of —primroses of the size of ripe apples, and yet, in spite of their rank growth, of as pale and tender a yellow as if their gold had been diluted with silver. It was indeed a mixture of gold and silver, for there was a wealth of the white wood-anemone as well, and these delicate flowers, each of so perfect a coinage, were tumbled along the green wayside as if a prince had been scattering largesse. The outside of an old English country-church in service-time is a very pleasant place; and this is as near as I often care to approach to the celebration of the Anglican mysteries. A just sufficient sense of their august character may be gathered from that vague sound of village-music which makes its way out into the stillness, and from the perusal of those portions of the Prayer-Book which are inscribed upon mouldering slabs and dislocated headstones. The church I speak of was a beautiful specimen of its kind—intensely aged, variously patched, but still solid and useful, and with no touch of restoration. It was very big and massive, and, hidden away in the fields, it had a kind of lonely grandeur; there was nothing in particular near it but its out-of-the-world little parsonage. It was only one of ten thousand; I had seen a hundred such before. But I watched the watery sunshine upon the rugosities of its ancient masonry; I stood a while in the shade of two or three spreading yews which stretched their black arms over graves decorated for Easter, according to the custom of that country, with garlands of primrose and dog-violet; and I reflected that in a wild region it was a blessing to have so quiet a place of refuge as that.

Later, I chanced upon a couple of other asylums which were more spacious and no less tranquil. Both of them were old country-houses, and each in its way was charming. One was a half-modernised feudal dwelling, lying in a wooded hollow—a large concavity filled with a delightful old park. The house had a long gray façade and half a dozen towers, and the usual supply of ivy and of clustered chimneys relieved against a background of rook-haunted elms. But the windows were all closed and the avenue was untrodden; the house was the property of a lady who could not afford to live in it in becoming state, and who had let it, furnished, to a rich young man "for the shooting." The rich young man occupied it but for three weeks in the year, and for the rest of the time left it a prey to the hungry gaze of the passing stranger, the would-be redresser of æsthetic wrongs. It seemed a great æsthetic wrong that so charming a place should not be a conscious, sentient home. But in England all this is very common. It takes a great many plain people to keep a gentleman going; it takes a great deal of wasted sweetness to make up a property. It is true that, in the other case I speak of, the sweet-ness, which here was even greater, was less sensibly squandered. If there was no one else in the house, at least there were ghosts. It had a dark red front and grim-looking gables; it was perched upon a sort of terrace, quite high in the air, which was reached by steep, crooked, mossy steps. Beneath these steps was an ancient bit of garden, and from the hither side of the garden stretched a great expanse of turf. Out of the midst of the turf sprang a magnificent avenue of Scotch firs — a perfect imitation of the Italian stone-pine. It looked like the Villa Bor-ghese transplanted to the Welsh hills. The huge, smooth stems, in their double row, were crowned with dark parasols. In the Scotch fir or the Italian pine there is always an element of grotesqueness; the open umbrella in a rainy country is not a poetical analogy, and the case is ˚not better if you compare the tree to a colossal mushroom. But, without analogies, there was something very striking in the effect of this enormous, rigid vista, and in the grassy carpet of the avenue, with the dusky, lonely, high-featured house looking down upon it. There was something solemn and tragical; the place was made to the hand of a romancer, and he might have found his characters within; the leaden lattices were open.

II.

The Isle of Wight is disappointing at first. I wondered why it should be, and then I found the reason in the influence of the detestable little railway. There can be no doubt that a railway in the Isle of Wight is a gross impertinence; it is in evident contravention to the natural style of the place. The place is minutely, delicately picturesque, or it is nothing at all. It is purely ornamental; it exists for the entertainment of tourists. It is separated by nature from the dense railway-system of the less diminutive island, and it is the corner of the world where a good carriage-road is most in keeping. Never was there a better place for sacrificing to prettiness; never was there a better chance for not making a railway. But now there are twenty trains a day, and the prettiness is twenty times less. The island is so small that the hideous embankments and tunnels are obtrusive; the sight of them is as painful as it would be to see a pedlar's pack on the shoulders of a pretty woman. This is your first impression as you travel (naturally by the objec-

tionable conveyance) from Ryde to Ventnor; and
the fact that the train rumbles along very smoothly,
and stops at half a dozen little stations, where the
groups on the platform enable you to perceive that
the population consists almost exclusively of gentlemen in costumes suggestive of unlimited leisure for
attention to cravats and trousers (an immensely large
class in England), of old ladies of the species denominated in France *rentières*, of young ladies of the
highly-educated and sketching variety, this circumstance fails to reconcile you to the chartered cicatrix
which forms your course. At Ventnor, however,
face to face with the sea, and with the blooming
shoulder of the Undercliff close behind you, you lose
sight to a certain extent of the superfluities of civilisation. Not, indeed, that Ventnor has not been
diligently civilised. It is a well-regulated little
watering-place, and it has been subjected to a due
measure of cockneyfication. But the glittering
ocean remains, shimmering at moments with blue
and silver, and the large gorse-covered downs rise
superbly above it. Ventnor hangs upon the side of
a steep hill, and here and there it clings and scram-
bles, it is propped and terraced, like one of the
bright-faced little towns that look down upon the
Mediterranean. To add to the Italian effect, the
houses are all denominated villas, though it must be
added that nothing is less like an Italian villa than
an English one. Those which ornament the successive ledges at Ventnor are for the most part small
semi-detached boxes, predestined, even before they
had fairly come into the world, to the entertainment
of lodgers. They stand in serried rows all over the

place, with the finest names in the British *Peerage* painted upon their gate-posts. Their severe similarity of aspect, however, is such that even the difference between Plantagenet and Percival, between Montgomery and Montmorency, is hardly sufficient to enlighten the puzzled visitor. An English watering-place is much more comfortable than an American; in a Plantagenet villa the art of receiving "summer guests" has usually been brought to a higher perfection than in an American rural hotel. But what strikes an American, with regard to even so charmingly-nestled a little town as Ventnor, is that it is far less natural, less pastoral and bosky, than his own fond image of a summer-retreat. There is too much brick and mortar; there are too many smoking chimneys and shops and public-houses; there are no woods nor brooks, nor lonely headlands; there is none of the virginal stillness of Nature. Instead of these things, there is an esplanade, mostly paved with asphalt, bordered with benches and little shops, and provided with a German band. To be just to Ventnor, however, I must hasten to add that once you get away from the asphalt there is a great deal of vegetation. The little village of Bonchurch, which closely adjoins it, is buried in the most elaborate verdure, muffled in the smoothest lawns and the densest shrubbery. Bonchurch is simply delicious, and indeed in a manner quite absurd. It is like a model village in imitative substances, kept in a big glass case; the turf might be of green velvet and the foliage of cut paper. The villagers are all happy gentlefolk, the cottages have plate-glass windows, and the rose-trees on their walls are tended by an under-gardener. Passing from Ventnor through the elegant umbrage of Bonchurch, and keeping along the coast toward Shanklin, you come to the prettiest part of the Undercliff, or, in other words, to the prettiest place in the world. The immense grassy cliffs which form the coast of the island make what the French would call a " false descent" to the sea. At a certain point the descent is broken, and a wide natural terrace, all overtangled with wild shrubs and flowers, hangs there in mid-air, half-way above the ocean. It is impossible to imagine anything more charming than this long, blooming platform, protected from the north by huge green bluffs and plunging on the other side into the murmuring tides. This delightful arrangement constitutes for a distance of some fifteen miles the south shore of the Isle of Wight; but the best of it, as I have said, is to be found in the four or five miles that separate Ventnor from Shanklin. Of a lovely afternoon in April these four or five miles are an enchanting walk.

Of course you must first catch your lovely afternoon. I caught one; in fact, I caught two. On the second I climbed up the downs, and perceived that it was possible to put their gorse-covered stretches to still other than pedestrian uses—to devote them to sedentary pleasures. A long lounge in the lee of a stone wall, the lingering, fading afternoon light, the reddening sky, the band of blue sea above the level-topped bunches of gorse—these things, enjoyed as an undertone to the conversation of an amiable compatriot, seemed indeed a very sufficient substitute for that primitive stillness of the absence of which I ventured just now to complain.

III.

It was probably a mistake to stop at Portsmouth. I had done so, however, in obedience to a familiar theory that seaport-towns abound in local colour, in curious types, in the quaint and the strange. But these charms, it must be confessed, were signally wanting to Portsmouth, along whose sordid streets I strolled for an hour, vainly glancing about me for an overhanging façade or a group of Maltese sailors. I was distressed to perceive that a famous seaport could be at once untidy and prosaic. Portsmouth is dirty, but it is also dull. It may be roughly divided into the dock-yard and the public-houses. The dock-yard, into which I was unable to penetrate, is a colossal enclosure, signalised externally by a grim brick wall, as featureless as an empty blackboard. The dockyard eats up the town, as it were, and there is nothing left over but the gin-shops, which the town drinks up. There is not even a crooked old quay of any consequence, with brightly patched houses looking out upon a forest of masts. To begin with, there are no masts; and then there are no polyglot sign-boards, no overhanging upper stories, no outlandish parrots and macaws perched in open lattices. I had another hour or so before my train departed, and it would have gone hard with me if I had not bethought myself of hiring a boat and being pulled about in the harbour. Here a certain amount of entertainment was to be found. There were great iron-clads, and white troopships that looked vague

340

and spectral, like the floating home of the Flying
Dutchman, and small, devilish vessels whose mission
was to project the infernal torpedo.   I coasted about
these metallic islets; and then, to eke out my entertainment, I boarded the *Victory*.   The *Victory* is
an ancient frigate of enormous size, which in the
days of her glory carried I know not how many
hundred guns, but whose only function now is to
stand year after year in Portsmouth waters and ex-
hibit herself to the festive cockney.   Bank-holiday
is now her great date; once upon a time it was
Trafalgar.   The *Victory*, in short, was Nelson's ship;
it was on her huge deck that he was struck and in
her deep bowels he breathed his last.   The venerable vessel is provided with a company of ushers,
like the Tower of London or Westminster Abbey,
and it is hardly less solid and spacious than either
of those edifices.   A good man in uniform did me
the honours of the ship with a terrible displacement
of *h*'s, and there seemed something strange in the
way it had lapsed from its heroic part.   It had carried two hundred guns and a mighty warrior, and
boomed against the enemies of England; it had been
the scene of one of the most thrilling and touching
events in English history.   Now, it was hardly more
than a mere source of income to the Portsmouth
watermen—an objective point for Whitsuntide ex-
cursionists—a thing that a foreign observer must
allude to very casually, for fear of seeming vulgar,
or even serious.

IV.

But I recouped myself, as they say in England, by stopping afterwards at Chichester. In this dense and various old England two places may be very near together and yet strike a very different note. I knew in a general way that there was a cathedral at Chichester; indeed, I had seen its beautiful spire from the window of the train. I had always regarded an afternoon in a little cathedral-town as a high order of entertainment, and a morning at Portsmouth had left me in the mood for not missing such an exhibition. The spire of Chichester at a little distance greatly resembles that of Salisbury. It is on a smaller scale, but it tapers upward with a delicate slimness which, like that of its famous rival, makes a picture of the level landscape in which it stands. Unlike the spire of Salisbury, however, it has not at present the charm of antiquity. A few years ago the old steeple collapsed and tumbled into the church, and the present structure is but a modern facsimile. The cathedral is not of the highest interest; it is rather plain and bare, and, except a curious old detached bell-tower which stands beside it, has no particular element of unexpectedness. But an English cathedral of restricted grandeur may yet be a very charming affair; and I spent an hour or so lounging around this highly respectable edifice, without the spell of contemplation being broken by satiety. I approached it, from the station, by the usual quiet red-brick street of the usual cathedral town—a street of small, excellent shops, before which, here and there,

one of the vehicles of the neighbouring gentry was
drawn up beside the curbstone, while the grocer or
the bookseller, who had hurried out obsequiously,
was waiting upon the comfortable occupant. I went
into a bookseller's to buy a Chichester guide, which
I perceived in the window; I found the shopkeeper
talking to a young curate in a soft hat. The guide
seemed very desirable, though it appeared to have
been but scantily desired; it had been published in
the year 1841, and a very large remnant of the
edition, with a muslin back and a little white label
and paper-covered boards, was piled up on the counter.
It was dedicated, with terrible humility, to the Duke
of Richmond, and ornamented with primitive woodcuts and steel plates; the ink had turned brown and
the page musty; and the style itself—that of a
provincial antiquary of upwards of forty years ago
penetrated with the grandeur of the aristocracy—
had grown rather sallow and stale. Nothing could
have been more mellifluous and urbane than the
young curate : he was arranging to have the *Times*
newspaper sent him every morning for perusal. " So
it will be a penny if it is fetched away at noon ? "
he said, smiling very sweetly and with the most
gentlemanly voice possible; "and it will be three
halfpence if it is fetched away at four o'clock ? " At
the top of the street, into which, with my guide-book,
I relapsed, was an old market-cross, of the fifteenth
century—a florid, romantic little structure. It consists of a stone pavilion, with open sides and a number
of pinnacles and crockets and buttresses, besides a
goodly medallion of the high-nosed visage of Charles
I., which was placed above one of the arches, at the

Restoration, in compensation for the violent havoc wrought upon the little town by the Parliamentary soldiers, who had wrested the place from the Royalists, and who amused themselves, in their grim fashion, with infinite hacking and hewing in the cathedral. Here, to the left, the cathedral discloses itself, lifting its smart gray steeple out of a pleasant garden. Opposite to the garden was the Dolphin or the Dragon —in fine, the most eligible inn. I must confess that for a time it divided my attention with the cathedral, in virtue of an ancient, musty parlour on the second floor, with hunting-pictures hung above haircloth sofas; of a red-faced waiter, in evening dress; of a big round of cold beef and a tankard of ale. The prettiest thing at Chichester is a charming little three-sided cloister, attached to the cathedral, where, as is usual in such places, you may sit upon a gravestone amid the deep grass in the middle, and measure the great central mass of the church—the large gray sides, the high foundations of the spire, the parting of the nave and transept. From this point the greatness of a cathedral seems more complex and impressive. You watch the big shadows slowly change their relations; you listen to the cawing of rooks and the twittering of swallows; you hear a slow footstep echoing in the cloisters.

V.

If Oxford were not the finest thing in England, Cambridge would certainly be. Cambridge was so, for that matter, to my imagination, for thirty-six hours. To the barbaric mind, ambitious of culture,

Oxford is the usual image of the happy reconcilia-
tion between research and acceptance. It typifies,
to an American, the union of science and sense—of
aspiration and ease. A German university gives a
greater impression of science, and an English country-
house or an Italian villa a greater impression of idle
enjoyment; but in these cases, on one side, knowledge is too rugged, and, on the other, satisfaction is
too trivial. Oxford lends sweetness to labour and
dignity to leisure. When I say Oxford, I mean
Cambridge, for a barbarian is not in the least obliged
to know the difference, and it suddenly strikes me
as being both very pedantic and very good-natured
in him to pretend to know it. What institution is
more majestic than Trinity College? what can be
more touching to an American than the hospitality
of such an institution? The first quadrangle is of
immense extent, and the buildings that surround it,
with their long, rich fronts of time-deepened gray,
are the stateliest in the world. In the centre of the
court are two or three acres of close-shaven lawn, in
the midst of which rises a splendid gothic fountain,
where the serving-men fill up their buckets. There
are towers and battlements and statues, and besides
these things there are cloisters and gardens and
bridges. There are charming rooms in a kind of
stately gate-tower, and the rooms, occupying the
thickness of the building, have windows looking out
on one side over the magnificent quadrangle, with half
a mile or so of Decorated architecture, and on the
other into deep-bosomed trees. And in the rooms
is the best company conceivable—distinguished men
who are remarkably good fellows. I spent a beauti-

ful Sunday morning walking about Cambridge, with
one of these gentlemen, and attempting, as the
French say, to *débrouiller* its charms. These are a
very complicated affair, and I do not pretend, in
memory, to keep the colleges apart. There are,
however, half a dozen points that make ineffaceable
pictures. Six or eight of the colleges stand in a
row, turning their backs to the river; and hereupon
ensues the loveliest confusion of gothic windows and
ancient trees, of grassy banks and mossy balustrades,
of sun-chequered avenues and groves, of lawns and
gardens and terraces, of single-arched bridges span-
ning the little stream, which is small and shallow,
and looks as if it had been "turned on" for ornamental purposes. The scantily-flowing Cam appears
to exist simply as an occasion for these enchanting
little bridges—the beautiful covered gallery of
John's or the slightly-collapsing arch of Clare. In
the way of college-courts and quiet scholastic porticoes, of gray-walled gardens and ivied nooks of study,
in all the pictorial accidents of a great English university, Cambridge is delightfully and inexhaustibly
rich. I looked at these one by one, and said to
myself always that the last was the best. If I
were called upon, however, to mention the prettiest
corner of the world, I should heave a tender sigh
and point the way to the garden of Trinity Hall.
My companion, who was very competent to judge
(but who spoke, indeed, with the partiality of a son
of the house), declared, as he ushered me into it,
that it was, to his mind, the most beautiful *small*
garden in Europe. I freely accepted, and I promptly
repeat, an affirmation so ingeniously conditioned.

The little garden at Trinity Hall is narrow and crooked; it leans upon the river, from which a low parapet, all muffled in ivy, divides it; it has an ancient wall, adorned with a thousand matted creepers on one side, and on the other a group of extraordinary horse-chestnuts. These trees are of prodigious size; they occupy half the garden, and they are remarkable for the fact that their giant limbs strike down into the earth, take root again, and emulate, as they rise, the majesty of the parent tree. The manner in which this magnificent group of horse-chestnuts sprawls about over the grass, out into the middle of the lawn, is one of the most picturesque features of the garden of Trinity Hall. Of course the single object at Cambridge that makes the most abiding impression is the famous chapel of King's College— the most beautiful chapel in England. The effect it attempts to produce within belongs to the order of sublimity. The attempt succeeds, and the success is attained by means so light and elegant that at first it almost defeats itself. The sublime usually has more of a frown and straddle, and it is not until after you have looked about you for ten minutes that you perceive that the chapel is saved from being the prettiest church in England by the accident of its being one of the noblest. It is a cathedral without aisles or columns or transepts, but (as a compensation) with such a beautiful slimness of clustered tracery soaring along the walls, and spreading, bending and commingling in the roof, that its simplicity seems only a richness the more. I stood there for a quarter of an hour on a Sunday morning; there was no service, but in the choir behind the great screen which divides the chapel in half, the young choristers were rehearsing for the afternoon. The beautiful boy-voices rose together and touched the splendid vault; they hung there, expanding and resounding, and then, like a rocket that spends itself, they faded and melted toward the end of the building. The sound was angelic.

VI.

Cambridgeshire is one of the so-called ugly counties; which means that it is observably flat. It is for this reason that Newmarket is, in its own peculiar fashion, so thriving a locality. The country is like a board of green cloth; the turf presents itself as a friendly provision of nature. Nature offers her gentle bosom as a gaming-table; card-tables, billiard-tables are but a humble imitation of Newmarket Heath. It was odd to think that amid this gentle, pastoral scenery, there is more betting than anywhere else in the world. The large, neat English meadows roll away to a humid-looking sky, the young partridges jump about in the hedges, and nature does not look in the least as if she were offering you odds. The gentlemen do, though—the gentlemen whom you meet on the roads and in the railway carriage; they have that indefinable look— it pervades a man from the cut of his whisker to the shape of his boot-toe — which denotes a familiarity with the turf. It is brought home to you that to an immense number of people in England the events in the *Racing Calendar* constitute the most important portion of contemporary history. The very air about Newmarket appears to contain a vague echo of stable-talk, and you perceive that this is the landscape depicted in those large coloured prints of the " sporting " genus which you have admired in inn-parlours.

The destruction of partridges is, if an equally classical, a less licentious pursuit, for which, I believe, Cambridgeshire offers peculiar facilities. Among these is a certain shooting-box, which is a triumph of accidental picturesqueness (the highest order) and a temple of delicate hospitality. The shooting belongs to the autumn, not to this vernal period; but as I have spoken of echoes, I suppose that if I had listened attentively I might have heard the ghostly crack of some of the famous shots that have been discharged there. The air, I believe, had vibrated to several august rifles, but all that I happened to hear by listening was some excellent talk.

In England, I said just now, a couple of places may be very near together, and yet have what the philosophers call a connotation strangely different. Only a few miles beyond Newmarket lies Bury St. Edmunds, a town whose tranquil antiquity makes horse-racing, and even partridge-shooting, appear a restless and fidgety mode of passing the time. I confess that I went to Bury St. Edmunds simply on the strength of its name, which I had often encountered, and which had always seemed to me to have a high value for the tourist I knew that St. Edmund had been an Anglo-Saxon worthy, but my conviction that the little town that bore his name would afford entertainment between trains had nothing definite to rest upon. The event, however, rewarded my faith—rewarded it with the sight of a magnificent old gatehouse of the thirteenth century, the most substantial of many relics of the great abbey which once flourished there. There are many others; they are scattered about the old precinct of the abbey, a large portion of which has been converted into a rambling botanic garden, the resort at Whitsuntide of a thousand very modern merry-makers. The monument I speak of has the proportions of a triumphal arch; it is at once a gateway and a fortress; it is covered with beautiful ornament, and is altogether the lion of Bury.